Fostering Empathy through Museums

Elif M. Gokcigdem

ROWMAN & LITTLEFIELD
Lanham • Boulder • New York • London

Published by Rowman & Littlefield
A wholly owned subsidiary of The Rowman & Littlefield Publishing Group, Inc.
4501 Forbes Boulevard, Suite 200, Lanham, Maryland 20706
www.rowman.com

Unit A, Whitacre Mews, 26-34 Stannary Street, London SE11 4AB, United Kingdom

British Library Cataloguing in Publication Information Available

Library of Congress Cataloguing-in-Publication Data
Names: Gokcigdem, Elif M.
Title: Fostering empathy through museums/edited by Elif M. Gokcigdem.
Description: Lanham : Rowman & Littlefield, [2016] | Includes bibliographical
  references and index.
Identifiers: LCCN 2016015189| ISBN 9781442263567 (cloth : alk. paper) |
  ISBN 9781442263574 (pbk. : alk. paper) | ISBN 9781442263581 (Electronic)
Subjects: LCSH: Museums—Social aspects. | Museums—Psychological aspects. |
  Museums—Educational aspects. | Empathy—Social aspects.
Classification: LCC AM7 .F675 2016 | DDC 069/.1—dc23
LC record available at https://lccn.loc.gov/2016015189

♾™ The paper used in this publication meets the minimum requirements of
American National Standard for Information Sciences—Permanence of Paper for
Printed Library Materials, ANSI/NISO Z39.48-1992.

Printed in the United States of America

Contents

Foreword

Emlyn Koster

> Evolution has produced a mind that evolves towards an appreciation of the vastness of our collective design, and emotions that enable us to enact these loftier notions. We are wired for good.[1]

One afternoon in late September 2001, I joined a ferry taking several hundred next-of-kin of New Jersey victims from the World Trade Center across the Hudson River to Lower Manhattan's North Cove Marina, the closest dock to Ground Zero. Grieving family members clutched teddy bears given to them as we boarded.[2] Arranged by the New Jersey Family Assistance Center at Liberty State Park (where Liberty Science Center was involved; see chapter 14), this trip was their first opportunity to visit the remains of the fallen World Trade Center twin towers. Anxiously huddled together, we slowly walked past ash-laden trees and walls covered with frantic messages about missing loved ones, past emergency officials and site workers with bowed heads, across empty roads, and onto a makeshift platform overlooking the smoldering mountain of jagged debris. Weeping and whispering were the only sounds as we solemnly reflected on the riveting scene before us. Indivisible were the gravity and uncertainty of the entire Ground Zero situation and the overwhelming, deeply personal sadness of everyone there. Personal tension was exponentially compounded by the indescribable sorrow of the next-of-kin all around me.

Fostering Empathy through Museums is an unusual but timely contribution to the body of literature serving the entire museum field. More than ever, museums need to maximize their value in this troubled world[3] and blur their boundaries.[4] Yet museums of various types rarely discuss any commonality of intent, including empathy.[5] Psychology—the scientific study of the human mind and its functions, especially those affecting behavior in a given context—has rarely been a focus. A pioneering exception was the centennial vision of the American Psychological Association in 1992, when it partnered with the Ontario Science Centre for an interactive exhibition titled *Understanding Ourselves, Understanding Each Other.*[6] Then in 2008 and 2013, the Exploratorium partnered with the Association for Psychological Science and the American Psychological Association for new exhibitions.[7]

In the twenty-first century, with the news filled with stories of indifference, suspicion, and aggression, the whole museum field would be wise to remember its roots in Greek mythology: the Muses stood for the values of reflection and inspiration. Coupling this definition with Aristotle's view that leadership is ideally about the harmonious pursuit of positive consequences in the world,[8] the museum field would serve its most beneficial role if it would maximize opportunities to illuminate positive human qualities. This book does so for empathy, generally defined as the ability to recognize, understand, and share another's feelings in their situation, up to and including distress.[9]

For most practitioners, viewing the museum field through a lens of empathy is likely to be a rather jolting journey, given the paucity of empathy-focused thinking and evaluation tools, and, where it has existed, the range of perspectives across our profession. One outlook might be that experiences are rarely designed with this emotion as an intended result. Another might be that to achieve an outcome of empathy, whether or not anticipated, would be the mark of a successful design. Yet another, more comprehensive one might be a sense that an impact of empathy arises from a case-specific conjunction of three independent variables—the museum's specific content, an atmosphere conducive to contemplation, and the visitor's related frame of mind.

Collected in this book are accounts of forging empathy by art, history, science, civil rights, and children's museums, by consultancies and government agencies, and by some other types of nonprofit organizations. Although the United States is predominant in these cases, they all contribute to a palette for "glocal" (that is, local and global) introspection. The toolkit of a progressive museum contains, at least in theory, several prime content candidates for deep emotional engagement that may rise to the level of fostering empathy. The most probable ones are personal stories and personal objects about both tragedies and successes in societal and environmental circumstances, past and present.

Readers of *Fostering Empathy through Museums* may also wish to become familiar with the philosophy and practice of the International Coalition of Sites of Conscience,[10] a New York City–based "global network of historic sites, museums, and memory initiatives connecting past struggles to today's movements for human rights and social justice." It is in the designed experiences about memory at member sites that I have found the most success in engaging visitors from around the world with reactions of empathy to locally specific circumstances. Here are several examples: in Cape Town, South Africa, the District Six Museum[11] memorializes the ejection of some sixty thousand inhabitants during the Apartheid regime; in Berlin, the Jewish Museum[12] weaves architecture and content to make German Jewish history tangible and leaves visitors with reflective questions; in Washington, DC, the US Holocaust Memorial Museum[13] leverages the power of concentration camp artifacts to raise awareness of crimes against humanity; and in New York, the Lower East Side Tenement Museum[14] (the subject of chapter 7) is a time capsule of the unanticipated squalor facing early immigrants from Europe. Visitors leave museums with a vast array of feelings that range from the fleeting to the lasting. Experiences at the just-cited museums left me consumed with empathy for tragic individual circumstances, as well as with memories that are as vivid today as they were when I left each place. Sometimes a place that relives distressing stories can also convey great joy when remarkable perseverance and courage triumphs over seemingly insurmountable adversity. Empathy, after all, exists across a wide spectrum of deeply absorbed feelings.

It takes a rare and determined mind to bring an unusual book to fruition. With her PhD in the history of Islamic arts from Istanbul Technical University and a Museum Studies graduate certificate from George Washington University, for almost a decade Elif Gokcigdem has advised on a major cultural center project in the Middle East in the areas of content development and integration, local capacity building, culture in sustainable economic development, and strategic international partnerships.[15] Her research interests include the promotion of creative thinking, perspective taking, and empathy building through museums[16] toward positive behavior change and societal progress. Spanning the past decade, Elif and I have frequently conversed at museum conferences. In October 2015, she described her vision for this book. Wishing to contribute, I found a way to be involved through a joint contribution with Donna Gaffney, DNSc, a trauma psychologist with whom I had closely worked after 9/11.

As an advocate and practitioner for the pursuit of relevance in museums,[17] it is an honor for me to also provide this invited foreword. Elif Gokcigdem is a distinctive asset to the museum field at large. Welcome to her thoughtful compilation!

NOTES

1. Dacher Keltner, *Born to be Good: The Science of a Meaningful Life* (New York: W. W. Norton, 2009).

2. "What We Do," *Hugs Across America*, www.hugsacrossamerica.net (accessed February 15, 2016).

3. Robert Janes, *Museums in a Troubled World: Renewal, Irrelevance or Collapse?* (New York: Routledge, 2009).

4. Robert Janes, *Museums without Borders* (New York: Routledge, 2015).

5. Gretchen Jennings, "The Empathetic Museum: Institutional Body Language," *Museum Commons Blog*, http://www.museumcommons.com/2013/06/the-empathetic-museum-institutional.html (accessed February 15, 2016); Edwin Rutsch, "Creating the Empathetic Museum with Gretchen Jennings," *Center for Building a Culture of Empathy Blog*, http://cultureofempathy.com/References/Experts/others/Gretchen-Jennings.htm (accessed February 15, 2016).

6. "Psychology: Understanding Ourselves, Understanding Each Other," *American Psychological Association*, http://www.apa.org/pubs/videos/4316320.aspx (accessed February 15, 2016).

7. Jesse Erwin, "Exploring the Mind," *Observer*, Association for Psychological Science, 21, no. 3 (March 2008), http://www.psychologicalscience.org/index.php/publications/observer/2008/march-08/exploring-the-mind.html (accessed February 15, 2016); Lea Winerman, "Psychology Takes Center Stage at San Francisco's Exploratorium," *American Psychological Association*, Upfront 44, no. 4 (April 2013): 14, http://www.apa.org/monitor/2013/04/san-francisco.aspx (accessed February 15, 2016).

8. Richard Barker, *On the Nature of Leadership* (Lanham, MD: University Press of America, 2002).

9. "Empathy vs. Sympathy," *Grammarist*, http://grammarist.com/usage/empathy-sympathy/ (accessed February 15, 2016); "Hide and Seek," *Psychology Today*, https://www.pschologytoday.com/blog/hide-and-seek/201505/empathy-vs-sympathy (accessed February 15, 2016).

10. *International Coalition of Sites of Conscience*, http://www.sitesofconscience.org/ (accessed February 15, 2016).

11. *District Six Museum*, http://www.districtsix.co.za/ (accessed February 15, 2016).

12. *Jewish Museum Berlin*, https://www.berlin.de/en/museums/3108776-3104050-juedisches-museum-berlin.en.html (accessed February 15, 2016).

13. *United States Holocaust Memorial Museum*, http://www.ushmm.org/ (accessed February 15, 2016).

14. *Tenement Museum*, https://tenement.org/ (accessed February 15, 2016).

15. Elif M. Gokcigdem and Michelle Seaters, "One *Zellij* at a Time: Building Local and Global Cultural Connections and Creative Thinking Skills through an Exhibit of Islamic Arts for Children in Saudi Arabia," in *Museums in a Global Context: National Identity, International Understanding*, ed. Jennifer W. Dickey, Samir El Azhar, and Catherine M. Lewis (Washington, DC: The AAM Press, 2013), 162–85.

16. Elif Gokcigdem, *Empathy-building through Museums Blog*, https://greatolivetree.wordpress.com/ (accessed February 15, 2016); Gokcigdem, "Empathy, Museums, and Design-Thinking Societal Progress," *Academia.edu*, April 21,

2014, http://www.academia.edu/9159221/Empathy_Museums_and_Design-Thinking_Societal_Progress (accessed February 15, 2015).

17. Emlyn Koster, "The Evolution of Purpose in Science Museums and Science Centers," in *Hot Topics, Public Culture, Museums*, ed. Fiona Cameron and Lynda Kelly (Newcastle-upon-Tyne: Cambridge Scholars Publishing, 2010); Koster, "The Relevant Museum: A Reflection on Sustainability," in *Reinventing the Museum: The Evolving Conversation on the Paradigm Shift*, 2nd edition, ed. Gail Anderson (Lanham, MD: Altamira Press, 2012); Koster, "From Apollo to the Anthropocene, the Odyssey of Nature and Science Museums in Externally Responsible Contexts," in *Museums, Ethics and Cultural Heritage*, ed. Bernice Murphy (Paris: International Council of Museums, in press).

Acknowledgments

I would like to extend my deep gratitude to all contributors who believed in the concept behind this book and brought it to life with their essays that collectively illustrate the immense potential of empathy toward personal, institutional, and societal progress. Their dedication and diligent work make our museums sanctuaries for the cultivation of empathy—a vital ingredient that our world direly needs. I am grateful to Dr. Emlyn Koster for sharing his deep knowledge and wisdom on the relevance and the social value of museums through the thoughtful, informative, and inspiring foreword he generously contributed. I would also like to thank Dean Phelus from the American Alliance of Museums, Dr. Deborah Mack from the National Museum of African American History and Culture, and Ruth Shelly from the Portland Children's Museum for their recommendations of case studies for inclusion in this volume. I am grateful to Fatih M. Durmus for creating the original and meaningful illustrations that depict empathy, its layers, and its potential in the introduction, as well as the empathy spiral designs that accompany each chapter throughout the book. My special thanks go to my peer review counterparts Dr. Emlyn Koster, Donna Gaffney, DNSc, and Dr. Zorana Ivcevic for generously spending their time and attention to review and comment on my draft introduction and its accompanying visuals. I am indebted to Charles Harmon of Rowman and Littlefield for believing in the importance and the timeliness of this topic, and for taking a chance on an unknown independent scholar such as myself to compile *Fostering Empathy through Museums*.

My journey in empathy-building through museums has been a series of creative explorations driven by a simple belief that our world can be a better place if we could all exercise empathy toward the "Whole"—our unified humanity and the planet, inclusive of all living beings as well as its life-supporting natural resources. Because we cannot simply wait for this type of worldview to materialize, we must strategically invest in its shaping now, utilizing all resources and platforms available to us while perfecting our tools along the way.

I would like to thank Marcia Feola, who encouraged me back in 2014 to put my thoughts on empathy-building through museums first on paper, and then into action. Once in a story format, I found the courage to share my aspirations with four individuals whom I only knew from their inspirational work on human behavior, creativity, and social transformation. From my kitchen table and over a quiet Christmas break, I emailed my short story titled "A Recipe for Empathy-building through Museums" to Mr. David M. Kelley, founder of Stanford University's d.school and IDEO; Mr. Kabir Helminski, founder of the Threshold Society and an expert on Sufism and Rumi's poetry; Dr. Robert Root-Bernstein, an expert on creative thinking and a professor of physiology at Michigan State Universityl; and Dr. Dacher Keltner, founding director of the University of California–Berkeley's Greater Good Science Center. The fact that they all gracefully responded to my email inquiry and indicated that my idea resonated with them gave me the confidence to move forward and follow my intuition.

My friends, associates, and colleagues all contributed to the evolution of the idea behind this book: Sena Mutlu, Michelle Seaters, Fuad Al-Therman, Fatimah Al-Rashid, Ramona Sakiestewa, Andrew Merriell, Vincent Beggs, Joseph Katona, Hugh McDonald, Susan Norton, Carol Bossert, Canan Abayhan, Kelly Swain, Laura Willumsen, Jaap Otte, Kathleen Pasley, Amy Landau, Melissa Forstrom Al Kadhi, Richard Doughty, Arthur Clark, Leena Nasser, Mohamed and Sally Zakariya, Kabir Helminski, Elena Son, Gunseli Baygan-Robinett, Marcia Feola, Kendall Haven, and Zeynep Simavi. Thank you for your encouragement and for spending your precious time with me for wonderful, enriching conversations, and for sharing your knowledge, recommendations, and wisdom.

I have had the privilege of studying with Professor Dr. Semra Ogel at Istanbul Technical University and Dr. Esin Atil at the Smithsonian Institution's Freer and Sackler Galleries. Veterans of the history of Turkish and Islamic arts and architecture, Professor Ogel in Istanbul and Dr. Atil in Washington, DC, were my co-mentors and advisors throughout my master's and doctorate studies. I am deeply grateful to both for sharing their wisdom, knowledge, and passion for the arts with me, and for supporting me in my international quest for education. Professor Marie C. Malaro, the former head of George Washington University's museum studies program, was equally an important figure in my academic studies and my journey into the museum world. She welcomed me wholeheartedly when I first arrived in the United States and provided guidance and encouragement throughout my studies at GWU. I could not have accomplished any of the above without the financial support of the Turkish Education Foundation (TEV). After a highly competitive selection process, they provided me with a scholarship to conduct my graduate studies in museum studies in the United States, allowing me to connect my two passions, art history and museums, while widening my horizon toward new possibilities.

My understanding of empathy would have remained a lofty ideal if I had not been exposed to the sincere actions of my parents who effortlessly modeled empathy, compassion, and altruism all their lives. My father, M. Necati Durmus, was the kind of person who could see the universe in a grain of sand. He could tell a story about three random objects on the coffee table, but the moral of the story would be about the meaning of our existence, how everything in this universe is connected to each other, and what it means to be a human being in this complex, interconnected world—and he would do this with great ease, humor, and wit, all the while drinking many cups of Turkish coffee. I am honored to humbly claim that his values and worldview somehow permeated through his stories and found their way into my everyday choices as an adult. I cannot describe my deep gratitude for my loving and wise mother, Ayten Durmus, and my dear friend and aunt, Nurten Erbey, for always being there for me. Thank you for continuously and selflessly supporting my education and development and for nourishing my well-being and my soul with your wisdom and love. I am deeply grateful for my brother Fatih M. Durmus for believing in my quest for an empathy-driven world and for sharing his wisdom and talents with me. I would also like to thank my brother M. Yavuz Durmus for gently forcing my hand into choosing art history for my undergraduate studies many years ago—in a way, he is responsible for all of this and for introducing me to the world of learning organizations and experiential learning. I am grateful to my mother-in-law, Turkan Gokcidem, and my sister-in-law Ayse McCarthy, who continue to be my wonderful, supportive confidantes, always encouraging me in my various empathy-building endeavors. I am also grateful to my husband, Murat Gokcigdem, for his unwavering support and encouragement throughout. My beautiful children, Ela and Ali—you are such a blessing! Thank you for the joy and meaning you bring to my life and for your unconditional love. I wish you could have spent more time with Necati *Dede* to hear his stories, but perhaps museums will be your sanctuaries that will empower you with a pair of lenses through which you can also view our amazing interconnected universe, and discover your special roles in it.

Any errors and shortcomings in this volume belong to me, and all appreciation and gratitude are due those who contributed their years of hard work, knowledge, inspiration, and determination in the form of fifteen case studies that collectively brought this book to life.

Prologue

Elif M. Gokcigdem

Out beyond ideas of wrongdoing and rightdoing,
there is a field.
I will meet you there.
When the soul lies down in that grass, the world is too full to talk about.
Ideas, language, even the phrase *each other* doesn't make any sense.

—Rumi[1]

My father had a story for every occasion, but my favorite childhood story was "watch our garden grow," where on long summer days he would take me on a contemplative journey through the eyes of simple seeds. No matter which plant I became, the story always ended with a mysterious tone in his voice as he delivered the punch line: "How come you were one of the many tiny seeds that looked alike and was nurtured by the very same earth, the sun, the air, and the rain, yet you became a tomato, while the others became sweet grapes, hot peppers, sour cherries, or cucumbers?" This was my father's way of sharing his wisdom with me to help me see that the variety around us is actually a manifestation of a greater Whole that we are all a part of, gently reminding me of my individual responsibility to learn to look at it through others' eyes to appreciate and sustain its complex beauty. I still remember this, not only because my father was a great storyteller, but also because while he was telling me his stories we would be observing a variety of plants in our garden, contemplating, and sometimes making a salad out of them for lunch. These experiences of awe, wonder, and contemplation allowed me to empathize with these creatures going through various life cycles right before my eyes, and even as nourishment in my body. Little did I know then that they were the very seeds of nourishment for my soul.

Museums and empathy are a powerful combination that can provide transformative experiences of dialogue, discovery, understanding, and contemplation to all regardless of age or background. Together they can plant the seeds that nourish generations of souls.

NOTE

1. Coleman Barks, *Open Secret* (Putney, VT: Threshold Books, 1982).

Introduction

Elif M. Gokcigdem

Sixteen years into the millennium, this is not a particularly proud moment for humanity. Having visibly altered our planet's outermost layers, scientists are debating whether our footprint is worthy of naming an entire geological epoch on Earth's billions-of-years-old timescale after ourselves: Anthropocene, the Age of Humans.[1] Poverty, injustice, famine, radicalism, war, and a lack of human rights thrive in countries around the world.

A steady proliferation of new and ever more powerful technological tools seems unable to correct these ills. One must wonder why they have not succeeded. I believe it is because the tools that are at our disposal are most beneficial when filtered through a worldview that values the collective well-being of the "Whole"—our unified humanity and the planet, inclusive of all living beings as well as of its life-supporting natural resources.

Such a unifying worldview cannot be attained and sustained without empathy, our inherent ability to perceive and share the feelings of another.[2] Empathy enables us to connect with ourselves and with others while awakening us to our connectedness as parts of a greater Whole. An awareness of our connectedness calibrates and harmonizes our values, attitudes, and behavior. Awe of and appreciation for this interdependent Whole inspires us to meaningfully engage with it through acts of compassion and altruism that recent scientific findings reveal are like "chocolate" to us.[3] Not only are we wired to connect, but also to find ways to serve the greater good. This phenomenon is a self-sustaining cycle: powered by empathy, leading to compassion, altruism, and a rewarding sense of fulfillment of our humanity (see figure I.1).

Our ancestors relied on empathy as a survival skill long before writing was invented to transfer critical knowledge and wisdom through stories.

Figure I.1.   The seed of empathy can grow into altruism. Illustration by: Fatih M. Durmus.

However, we seem to have taken it for granted for so long that we left calibrating it toward the greater good to chance. Despite empathy's immense
potential for personal and societal progress, we often constrict it by extending it only to those who are like us. Perhaps this is because we are rarely
presented with an alternative and unifying worldview as a possibility.
As empathy cannot be learned from linear instructions but only through
lived experiences, it is our responsibility to design and create those contemplative experiences and venues that allow all to explore, discover, and foster
it toward our collective well-being.

The cultivation of both empathy and of the corresponding unifying
worldview are not like an on-off switch. It is a journey—individually,
institutionally, and culturally. Yet the dedication of space, time, focus, and
resources cannot wait until an empathetic worldview exists. We must now
"front load" the journey with the tools one needs to successfully progress
along its path. *Now* is the time to spark a paradigm shift toward an empathy-driven unifying worldview, and museums have a unique position and a
responsibility on this important journey.

Museums hold a mirror to our collective behavior, knowledge, conscience,
complex histories, and values. Through their educational mission, they can
provide safe and critical context to fostering empathy through experiential

learning, storytelling, artistic expression, dialogue, and contemplation. The multitude of examples and approaches presented in this volume are an indication of the tremendous potential that empathy presents as a "choice" toward positive personal, institutional, and societal change, and of the timely and critical role museums can undertake within this context.

THE SCOPE OF EMPATHY

Although I have chosen to use the dictionary meaning of empathy as a starting point in this volume, it is important to be mindful that the definition and the applications of empathy vary depending on the discipline and the context of its use. Such is the case in this book. Empathy's multifaceted nature is reflected and explored through the variety of its fluid layers, interpretations, and implications within each context presented in the chapters. A visual thread that was introduced in this volume next to each chapter title is intended to illustrate at a glance the contributing authors' inference of "empathy" within the context of their specific case study: as a point of departure, a part of the process, or as an intentional outcome.[4] The empathy definition visual (figure I.2) humbly reflects my understanding of empathy and the driving intention behind this book: an exploration of

Empathy: The feeling that you understand and share another person's experiences and emotions; the ability to share someone else's feelings.*
*Merriam-Webster dictionary definition of empathy

Types		Attributes & Levels	Skills	Outcomes	Pitfalls
Emotional		**Reactive:** Connecting with the other automatically; feeling another's emotions, experiencing their feelings.	**Instinctive:** Takes place instantaneously.	• Social awareness • Communication • Collaboration	• Research suggests some people are unable to make such connections due to brain structure • Manipulation • In-group bias
Cognitive		**Reflective:** Connecting with the other through emotional literacy, awe, wonder, and contemplation.	**Requires effortful thinking:** Perspective taking, introspection, and reflection.	• Emotional literacy • Management of emotions • Positive behavior change: Opting for kindness, compassion, tolerance, and equality; responsible decision making	• Sanitization • Fatigue
Compassionate		**Pragmatic perspective shift:** Connecting with the other as parts of a greater Whole.	**Deep contemplation:** A cultivated respect and appreciation for the Whole and all of its parts.	• Cross-disciplinary, multi-dimensional thinking • A strong sense of justice and equality for all • Humbleness, selflessness, inner peace • Social entrepreneurship • Compassionate action & altruism	

Figure I.2.   **The layers and the potential of empathy.** Illustration by: Fatih M. Durmus.

museums for their use of empathy and the potential this might present in sparking a paradigm shift toward a unifying worldview and societal progress through museums.

Much has been written on empathy in the last few decades, exploring its multifaceted nature and its implications for personal, societal, or economic development and innovation. Empathy can be many things. The domains where it can be applied vary accordingly. At one moment we use it to feel understanding and compassion for others and to care for our newborn and our elderly. At another we rely on empathy to tell compelling and effective stories as we share our knowledge and wisdom.[5]

Empathy is now recognized for its applicability as a professional problem-solving skill as part of the popular design-thinking or human-centric design method.[6] This method meshes well with our millennial generation's aspirations toward a purpose-driven society with socially and environmentally responsible institutions mindful of the big picture and toward jobs that contribute to this worldview.

The need is growing rapidly for empathy to serve as a lens through which we find our purpose and connection in a complex world. We need empathy to effectively utilize and create new problem-solving methods and to design better products and systems. Even more, we need empathy to inspire a next generation of global citizens who are mindful of our shared humanity and home no matter which career choices they make. Empathy is essential for creative thinking, collaboration across disciplines, and wise decision making.[7]

ON THE VERGE

What is essential is invisible to the eyes.

—Antoine de Saint-Exupery[8]

Environmental and societal conflicts in our communities and around the world are not new. However, we see and hear more of them thanks to technology. Even from the comfort of our homes, we increasingly find ourselves in a position in which we are urged to deeply care for and take action toward a number of local or global issues. As we greeted the turn of the millennium, the United Nations expressed determination to collectively solve many of our global development problems such as poverty, hunger, health care, inequality, and environmental sustainability.[9] Although such global goals are identified with the betterment of the people and the planet in mind, unfortunately they often leave the most important factor out of the equation: the role of the social and emotional well-being and the worldview of the problem solver, us.

The fact that we face persisting global problems indicates that we are in a continuous struggle to solve them. This chronic struggle does not stem from our lack of knowledge, know-how, or technologies, but from our lack of caring actions toward the well-being of the Whole. As we identify a checklist of problems that need solving, it is also equally crucial to carefully explore:

- How we make meaning of our existence;
- How we connect to one another and appreciate the diversity of which we are a part;
- What drives our values, perspectives, and decision making within the big picture—the Whole, the Unity, or the Universe—and
- What inspires us to take action toward our collective well-being.

From this exploration, it is vital that we come to deeply understand the forces that can make us act toward our collective well-being, instead of toward our individual, group, or tribe well-being. Empathy lies at the heart of those forces.

Empathy is not only how we instinctively connect with others through our mirror neurons, but also how we make sense of the complex, connected, and interdependent nature of our existence. In its essence, empathy enables us to understand the perspective of another. A personal awakening of empathy brings with it a realization that, at any given time and place in our universe, there are multiple ways of looking at and seeing any particular object, issue, or problem, and that there are many ways for the variety of beings to coexist and to simultaneously experience, interact, and make sense of the universe in their own ways.

It is essential that we acknowledge the current state of our civilization that tends to value "I, me, or us," easily disregarding the "other." Individuals are constantly competing over power, profit, technologies, and information, yet largely remain disconnected from the inherent empathetic capacities with which every human being is born. Empathy is an essential lynchpin of our human potential and the primary catalyst for its fulfillment through altruism and service. When we are aware and reflect on the needs of those around us, the others, and of our environment, we try to harmonize our emotions, feelings, and behavior accordingly. Through our ability to experience what it is like to be another, we gain a perspective-altering lens that awakens our sense of connectedness, respect, compassion, presence, and purpose. This valuable lens presents us with a multitude of opportunities to meaningfully engage with the Whole and to view our actions as service for its sustainability, without bias and with compassion. A unifying worldview not only sustains the fragile balance of our interconnected existence, but also meets our archetypal needs to find purpose and a sense of belonging. Ultimately, fulfilling our human potential becomes the norm, not a duty or a reward.

When our view of this interconnectedness becomes blurred, it is difficult to appreciate the big picture and our unique position and responsibility within it. Unfortunately, there is little that arms us with the inner tools to prevent such blurring. Our educational systems largely avoid teaching approaches and paradigms that reflect a holistic worldview and that facilitate and encourage our discovery of our innate social and emotional abilities.[10] Critical skills such as empathizing are often left to circumstance, and thus easily fall prey to the dangers of bias and manipulation. With this in mind, can we truly expect individuals to care, connect, and act in a positive way toward our *collective* well-being?

A THEORY OF CHANGE

The fantasy that somehow organizations can change without personal change, and especially without change on the part of people in leadership positions, underlies many change efforts doomed from the start.

—Peter Senge[11]

How might one change his or her habitual and entrenched perspective and behavior toward a unifying vision of existence? This usually requires a paradigm shift, often caused by a transformative life event, which informs a newly defined set of priorities, roles and responsibilities, standards, and rewards. Empathy, if anchored in the cultivation of a worldview that encourages an appreciation of the Whole, could be a vital portal into our connected universe and a critical tool to calibrate and harmonize our behavior within.

Astronauts are the lucky few in this case. The "overview effect," a pragmatic perspective shift experienced by astronauts seeing our planet from outer space for the first time, is known to bring with it a strong sense of peace and tranquility, a sense of uniqueness yet connectedness within an eternal landscape, and a sincere care and compassion for the Whole. Yet a single transformative life event is not itself enough. Even then, how and if one chooses to use this newly found knowledge is what matters.

For the rest of us Earthlings, unfortunately, it is getting more and more difficult to become profoundly aware of our connectedness, interdependence, and unity, let alone find ways to translate such wisdom into positive actions. Although a vital element of our nature and a catalyst for our survival, empathy has been taken for granted for so long that our civilization has not created the essential spaces, practices, and supporting ecosystems where it can be intentionally nurtured and unleashed toward the greater good.

A lack of empathy brings with it linear nondimensional thinking, an avoidance of multiple perspectives and diversity, and a disregard for the fragile balance that surrounds us. Individuals with such a mindset have decreased appreciation for common denominators such as "our shared humanity" and "our shared home." They might claim to subscribe to these ideas as long as they are somehow aligned with their self-interest. Yet rarely will such claims be backed by conscious and sincere changes of behavior at an individual level. Over time, the artificial priorities, expectations, barriers, and borders that we create for ourselves become calcified as the norm, obscuring our view of our connected existence, of our roles and responsibilities within this framework, and of how our unique abilities and individual actions matter for and to the Whole. At that point, it is easy to become numb to basic everyday wisdom such as: "What goes around comes around"—a piece of universal folksy advice with a sense of warning that invites us to reflect upon our connectedness and act accordingly . . . or else. Such common wisdom seeks to impart a strong sense of unity, balance, and justice; even if we cannot fully comprehend them, even if they take time to manifest, and even when this happens when no one is watching.

Although scientists have identified that empathy has its roots in our brain, somehow it results in a profound and transformative education of the heart. In alignment with our core humanity, a sense of unity and balance through empathy is also the essence of many spiritual traditions that value diversity and compassion toward the Whole:

- *Ubuntu*: A traditional African philosophy that promotes service to others, as "I am who I am, because of who we are."
- *Hishuk Ish Tsawalk*: "Everything is One" is how Native American wisdom describes the orderly and integrated Whole that we are a part of.
- *Yin and Yang*: Represents how in Chinese philosophy the universe is considered a harmonized entity where opposites are dynamically balanced.
- *Tikkun Olam*: A Jewish concept that promotes the repairing of the world through acts of kindness and social justice.
- *Vahdet-i Vücud*: "Oneness of Being," a concept in Islamic thought that promotes respect and compassion toward All in the body of creation, as All is a reflection of the One.

To some, these concepts might seem like utopian ideals. To others, these worldviews are just a way of seeing the universe within and around us and a way of being.[12] Through these worldviews the empathetic acts of compassion and altruism are neither a burden nor deserving of conscious merit. They become the norm of life and that elevated norm is its own reward.

In addition to our existing capabilities, such as our knowledge, know-how, and technologies, we need to rekindle the natural empathy within individuals. Increasingly complex problems of our world cannot be solved by linear thinking, segregation, or divisiveness. They require systems think-ing, deep listening skills, contemplation, dialogue, collaboration, and cross-disciplinary creative partnerships led by individuals who have the inspiration and the courage to take action to implement them.[13] None of this can be realized without an intentional and strategic cultivation of empathy toward the Whole. As long as we continue to ignore this intangible but fundamental facet of our human reality—our archetypal longing to connect with the Whole—and as long as we refuse to invest our transdisci-plinary knowledge, attention, time, and energy toward a better education that balances development of the mind with an equal emphasis on educa-tion of the heart through a journey from "I" to "Whole"—to reach a field, as Rumi suggests, where the word *other* doesn't make any sense—then we will be investing our limited time and resources on temporary solutions that ultimately jeopardize our survival.

Museums have a unique capability to bring together arts, sciences, dia-logue, experiential learning, and contemplation. In doing so, they can promote the concept of a connected worldview as an option worthy of significant exploration. As more and more individuals from various walks of life join a global community of social innovators and business entre-preneurs where design thinking and systems thinking are expected to be second nature, an increased awareness and demand for empathy as a per-sonal, professional, and/or institutional skill will be inevitable—as well as an appetite to cultivate it through neutral and safe platforms.

THE SPACE

No society can remain civil without providing places where strangers can safely associate together.

—Elaine Heuman Gurian[14]

Museums, as safe and informal learning platforms, are uniquely equipped to encourage visitors to imagine, explore, and experience empathy first-hand. Calibrating the scope of empathy toward an appreciation of the Whole would present museums with new opportunities to engage both existing and potential patrons. To avoid falling into the trap of bias by evoking or utilizing empathy only toward a part of the Whole, it is critical for museums to develop a community of practice around this concept that could help form a "shared vision," cross-disciplinary partnerships, termi-nology, standards, best practices, and evaluation mechanisms. Fostering empathy as a shared vision for museums would not be a compromise, as is evident in the increasing amount of social work they undertake.[15] Rather, they would strengthen the social status and relevancy of the museums as institutions that "empower."

The case studies in this volume provide a snapshot of how empathy is currently being utilized in a variety of museums:

- As an educational, storytelling tool—to increase knowledge, spark curiosity and dialogue regarding a specific content by making the content most accessible and relevant to visitors through audience research, experiential learning, exhibition design, creative community partnerships, educational and public programs, or through the choice of curatorial voice;
- As an integral element of a museum's institutional values and behavior[16]—by valuing diversity in workforce and designing inclusive operating systems and mechanisms, and by becoming thoughtful platforms for outreach beyond the walls of the museum to apply the museum's resources toward the well-being of its neighboring communities, not only in response to emerging societal or environmental issues, but also during times of disaster and crisis; and
- As a phenomenon that is worthy of exploration on its own, and as an intentional outcome—with the goal of better understanding, building and fostering empathy toward creativity, perspective taking, dialogue and collaboration, and the cultivation of social and emotional skills toward positive personal, environmental, and societal progress.

Museums serve society in numerous and important ways through their awe-inspiring objects, authentic stories, and by being safe and trusted places of learning, dialogue, healing, exploration, and contemplation—all essential prerequisites to the cultivation of empathy, and the very reason why museums can intentionally and strategically empower generations with their immense potential.

This volume explores a variety of examples written by museum professionals, psychologists, designers, scientists, art historians, social entrepreneurs, and educators whose work is already grounded in empathy. The following brief overview can only offer a glimpse of the variety of institutions, professional perspectives, and ideas included in the chapters ahead:

- A creative partnership between the Yale Center for Emotional Intelligence and the Botín Center in Spain explores a cultivation of emotional literacy and creativity through arts toward personal, societal, and economic development.
- Insightful observations of a museum educator from the Portland Children's Museum and the Museum School inspire us to create safe spaces to learn from and nourish children's innate abilities such as empathy, curiosity, and imagination.

- Transformative experiences at the Exploratorium's *Science of Sharing* exhibition invites us to "share," making us—our emotions, reactions, and choices—the subject of the exhibition, which allows us to reflect upon how our personal behaviors affect the society and the environment.
- An invitation to *Dialogue Exhibitions* in Germany, and its many affiliates around the world, allows us to personally step into a world as experienced by the blind, the deaf, and the aging, altering our biases and habitual perspectives on what it might be like to live with disability.
- The healing potential of response art in mental health is explored by an art therapist from The George Washington University, who conducts research in museums and exhibitions, including the US Holocaust Memorial Museum.
- Discovery Place and the Carolina Raptor Center collectively highlight how science museums and outdoor animal sanctuaries can create and facilitate experiences of awe and wonder, and what might be some innovative tools to measure success.
- An educator from the Lower East Side Tenement Museum teams up with a colleague from the Phoebe A. Hearst Museum of Anthropology at the University of California, Berkeley, to discuss how historic house museums can be transformative places by allowing the visitors to step back in time, and how psychology research can inform engaging museum experiences.
- A Center for Civil and Human Rights educator walks us through the shaping of the institution and how its inspiring exhibitions educate the public about a difficult phase in history while inspiring them with the tools toward positive change.
- An exhibition designer shares his perspective on how complexities around a sensitive exhibition topic about Arapaho chief Niwot shaped the curatorial and design decisions made by the Boulder History Museum, while also shaping a stronger community around it.
- A creative partnership between the Freer and Sackler Galleries of the Smithsonian Institution and the Turquoise Mountain—an arts revitalization and social entrepreneurship project based in Afghanistan—illustrates the importance of cross-cultural storytelling, as well as audience research and evaluation in concept development and design as recommended by the IPOP methodology developed by the Smithsonian Institution.
- A historian of Islamic arts explores the unconventional approach of giving voice to the personalities who owned and used the objects on display at the Walters Art Museum's *Pearls on a String* exhibition with the intention of creating personal connections that transcend time and cultural boundaries.

- The necessity of empathy as a core institutional value is explored through transdisciplinary examples and perspectives by two audience engagement experts at the Grand Rapids Art Museum and the Worchester Art Museum.
- A veteran museum president and CEO, along with her colleagues, reflect upon the Levine Museum of the New South's decades-long experiences in cultivating strong community connections through sincere dialogue, observation, reflection, and action.
- The director of the North Carolina Museum of Natural Sciences (former director of Liberty Science Center) collaborates with a veteran psychotherapist and an expert on trauma, loss, and violence to bring to life the role of the Liberty Science Center as a platform for healing in the immediate aftermath of 9/11.
- The Birmingham Civil Rights Institute invites us to *walk* with those who struggled for equality and justice, a struggle that continues today, so that we may discover our own paths in shaping our future.

Collectively, the chapters in this book reveal a variety of transdisciplinary ideas, tools, processes, criteria, inspiration, and lessons learned that might be useful to those who are willing to discover the potential of empathy toward personal, institutional, and societal progress. The multitude of approaches and the contexts presented in this volume are an indication of the tremendous potential that empathy presents as a "strategic, intentional choice" toward positive personal and societal change, and the timely and critical role museums can undertake within this context.

CONCLUSION

We stand at an exciting moment. The need for an empathy-driven unifying worldview has never been greater. It is at this same moment in time that a vast opportunity presents itself to us. The potential of an empathy-driven worldview is enormous. It only requires us to collectively embark on the journey and to commit ourselves to the exploration and cultivation of our individual and collective senses of empathy.

Fostering empathy and the corresponding unifying worldview is not an on-off switch—it is a journey that awaits our participation individually, institutionally, and culturally. Museums are readily available but underutilized platforms that hold the key elements for fostering empathy—more than any other institution our civilization has created. Therefore we must now utilize all the tools that are at our disposal: our knowledge, know-how, and technologies to embark on a journey toward building an empathy-driven worldview through museums while also designing, building, and perfecting our vehicles and tools to progress along its path.

I hope that this book will excite your imagination to the potential of museums as one powerful and readily adaptable platform to serve as a launching point for a strategic, intentional exploration of empathy and of its impact on our world. The power of empathy glows deep within each of our hearts and minds. I believe that the time is at hand to make it a driving force in our lives and our societies. I hope you embrace the wonder and potential of the ideas and examples in this book and use them to unlock your excitement, vision, and committed action.

NOTES

1. Elizabeth Kolbert, "Enter the Anthropocene—Age of Man," *National Geographic*, March 2011, http://ngm.nationalgeographic.com/2011/03/age-0f-man/kolbert-text/2 (accessed January 30, 2016); Joseph Stromberg, "What Is the Anthropocene and Are We in It?" *Smithsonian Magazine*, January 2013, http://www.smithsonianmag.com/science-nature/what-is-the-anthropocene-and-are-we-in-it-164801414/ (accessed January 30, 2016).

2. Merriam-Webster, online edition, s.v. "empathy," http://www.merriam-webster.com/dictionary/empathy (accessed January 30, 2016).

3. Summer Allen and Jill Suttie, "How Our Brains Make Us Generous," *Greater Good Science Center—Big Ideas Stories*, December 21, 2015, http://greatergood.berkeley.edu/article/item/how_our_brains_make_us_generous (accessed January 30, 2016); "Choosing Empathy: A Conversation with Jamil Zaki," *Edge*, October 20, 2015, http://edge.org/conversation/jamil_zaki-choosing-empathy (accessed January 30, 2016); Richard Davidson, "Cultivating Compassion: Neuroscientific and Behavioral Approaches," paper presented at the Center for Compassion and Altruism Research and Education, Stanford University, March 4, 2009, http://ccare.stanford.edu/tag/richard-davidson/ (accessed January 30, 2016); Matthieu Ricard, *Altruism* (New York: Little, Brown, 2015), 39–64.

4. I would like to extend my deepest gratitude to my brother Fatih M. Durmuş who designed the "empathy spiral" visuals for each chapter in this volume. My gratitude also goes out to all authors for providing me with their choice of words in support of this idea, summarizing their inference of empathy in only a few words within the context of their case studies. It is my wish that these visuals will serve as inspirational "collectibles" by the reader.

5. Frans De Waal, *The Age of Empathy: Nature's Lessons for a Kinder Society* (London: Souvenir Press, 2010); Dacher Keltner, *Born to be Good: The Science of a Meaningful Life* (New York: W. W. Norton, 2009); Mihaly Csikszentmihalyi, *Creativity: Flow and the Psychology of Discovery and Invention* (New York: Harper Perennial, 1997), 316–42; Robert Root-Bernstein and Michele M. Root-Bernstein, *Sparks of a Genius: The Thirteen Thinking Tools of the World's Most Creative People*

(New York: Mariner Books, 2011), 182–201; R. Root-Bernstein, "ArtSmarts: Arts and Crafts Participation Correlates with Entrepreneurial Innovation among Scientists and Engineers," paper presented at the Brookings Institution's The Arts, New Growth Theory, and Economic Development, Washington, DC, May 9, 2012; Dev Patnaik, *Wired to Care: How Companies Prosper When They Crate Widespread Empathy* (New Jersey: FT Press, 2009).

6. Tim Brown, *Change by Design* (New York: Harper Collins, 2009); Tom Kelley and David Kelley, *Creative Confidence: Unleashing the Creative Potential Within Us All* (New York: Crown Business, 2013); Katja Battarbee, Jane Fulton Suri, and Suzanne Gibbs Howard, "Empathy on the Edge: Scaling and Sustaining a Human-Centered Approach in the Evolving Practice of Design," *IDEO*, https://www.ideo.com/images/uploads/news/pdfs/Empathy_on_the_Edge.pdf (accessed January 30, 2016); "Innovators for the Public," *Ashoka*, https://www.ashoka.org/about (accessed April 18, 2014); Ashoka, "User Driven Design, Appropriate Tech, Invention for Social Good . . . It's All About Empathy in Action," *Forbes*, April 24, 2014, http://www.forbes.com/sites/ashoka/2014/04/24/ux-design-appropriate-tech-invention-for-social-good-whatever-you-call-it-its-all-about-empathy-in-action/#1111812f4b11 (accessed January 30, 2016); Elif Gokcigdem, "Empathy, Museums, and Design-Thinking Societal Progress," *Empathy-Building Through Museums Blog*, April 21, 2014, https://greatolivetree.wordpress.com/2015/02/14/empathy-museums-and-design-thinking-societal-progress/ (accessed January 30, 2016).

7. Sara Konrath, "Empathy: Across Time and Across the World," Roots of Empathy Research Symposium 2013 Proceedings, Toronto, Canada, May 8–10, 2013, 7; Diane Swanbrow, "Empathy: College Students Don't Have As Much As They Used To," *University of Michigan News Service*, May 27, 2010, http://ns.umich.edu/new/releases/7724 (accessed January 30, 2016); AshokaU Changemaker Campus, *Trends in Social Innovation Education 2014* (Arlington, VA: Ashoka Global Headquarters, 2014), 121; Csikszentmihalyi, *Creativity*, 12; Alexandra Van der Ploeg and Deirdre White, "Social Sabbaticals and the New Face of Leadership," *Stanford Social Review*, March 31, 2014; John Zogby and Joan Snyder Kuhl, First Globals: *Understanding, Managing, and Unleashing the Potential of Our Millennial Generation* (Washington, DC: John Zogby and Joan Snyder Kuhl, 2013).

8. Antoine De Saint-Exupery, *The Little Prince* (Orlando: Harcourt, Inc., 2010), 64.

9. "Launch of the UN Sustainable Development Goals," *We Can End Poverty—Millennium Development Goals and Beyond 2015*, http://www.un.org/millenniumgoals/ (accessed November 16, 2015); "Sustainable Development Goals," *Sustainable Development Goals: 17 Goals To Transform Our World*, http://www.un.org/sustainabledevelopment/sustainable-development-goals/ (accessed November 16, 2015).

10. Marc A. Brackett and Susan E. Rivers, "Transforming Students' Lives with Social and Emotional Learning," *The Handbook of Emotions in Education*, September 2013, http://ei.yale.edu/wp-content/uploads/2013/09/Transforming-Students%E2%80%99-Lives-with-Social-and-Emotional-Learning.pdf (accessed

January 30, 2016); John Bridgeland, Mary Bruce, and Arya Hariharan, *The Missing Piece, A Report for CASEL: A National Teacher Survey on How Social and Emotional Learning Can Empower Children and Transform Schools* (Chicago: Civic Enterprises with Peter D. Hart Research Associates, 2013), http://static1.squarespace.com/static/513f79f9e4b05ce7b70e9673/t/526a2589e4b01768fee91a6a/1382688137983/the-missing-piece.pdf (accessed January 30, 2016); Mary Gordon, *Roots of Empathy: Changing the World Child by Child* (New York: The Experiment, 2009); Mary Helen Immordino-Yang and Antonio Damaso, "We Feel, Therefore We Learn: The Relevance of Affective and Social Neuroscience to Education," *LEARNing Landscapes* 5, no. 1 (Autumn 2011): 115–31.

11. Peter Senge, "Taking Personal Change Seriously: The Impact of Organizational Learning on Management Practice," *Academy of Management Executive* 17, no. 2 (2003): 48.

12. For an extended discussion on these philosophies, see Michael Battle, *Reconciliation: The Ubuntu Theology of Desmond Tutu* (Cleveland, OH: The Pilgrim Press, 1997); E. Richard Atleo, *Tsawalk: A Nuu-chah-nulth Worldview* (Vancouver, Canada: University of British Columbia Press, 2005); Robin R. Wang, "Yinyang (Yin-yang)," *The Internet Encyclopedia of Philosophy*, http://www.iep.utm.edu/yinyang/; Martin Buber, *I and Thou* (Mansfield Centre, CT: Martino Publishing, 2010); Kabir Helminski, *Living Presence: A Sufi Way to Mindfulness and the Essential Self* (New York: Jeremy P. Tarcher/Putnam, 1992).

13. For an extended discussion on systems thinking and its wide-scale implications, see Daniel Goleman and Peter Senge, *Triple Focus: A New Approach to Education* (Florence, MA: More Than Sound, LLX, 2014); P. Senge, Otto Scharmer, Joseph Jaworski, and Betty Sue Flowers, *Presence: Human Purpose and the Field of the Future* (New York: Society of Organizational Learning, 2004); Senge, *The Fifth Discipline: The Art and Practice of Learning Organization* (New York: Doubleday, 2006); O. C. Scharmer, *Theory U: Leading from the Future as it Emerges* (New York: Society of Organizational Learning, 2007).

14. Elaine Heumann Gurian, *Civilizing the Museum: The Collected Writings of Elaine Heumann Gurian* (London: Routledge, 2006), 2.

15. Lois Silverman, *The Social Work of Museums* (New York: Routledge, 2010).

16. This category was inspired by Gretchen Jennings's "empathetic museums" discussion: Gretchen Jennings, "The Empathetic Museum: A Pop-up Conversation," *Museum Commons Blog*, June 7, 2013, http://www.museumcommons.com/2013/06/the-empathetic-museum-pop-up.html (accessed January 30, 2016).

perspective taking

& managing emotions

using & managing

emotional intelligence

empathy & perspective taking

1

Teaching Emotion and Creativity Skills through the Arts

Zorana Ivcevic, Nadine Maliakkal, and the Botín Foundation

Empathy is about standing in someone else's shoes, feeling with his or her heart, seeing with his or her eyes. Not only is empathy hard to outsource and automate, but it makes the world a better place.

—Daniel H. Pink

If there is any one secret of success, it lies in the ability to get the other person's point of view and see things from his angle as well as your own.

—Henry Ford

When you start to develop your powers of empathy and imagination, the whole world opens up to you.

—Susan Sarandon

Empathy is one's capacity to understand and share others' feelings. The power of empathy bursts from Picasso's canvas, showing the destruction and suffering after the bombing of Guernica in the Basque country of northern Spain. Empathy is visible when a photographer captures a moment of agony in the face of a refugee and when an actor portrays the distress of a mother who has lost a child. Human capacity for empathy enables and enriches our interaction with others; it motivates altruistic behavior and facilitates many forms of creativity.[1] Major social problems of our time—from income inequality and alleviation of global poverty to conflicts across the world—are not likely to be solved without empathic concern for others and without understanding of others' perspectives. The question thus becomes how to best stimulate and develop empathy. In this chapter, we present a collaboration between the Yale Center for Emotional Intelligence and the Botín Foundation in Santander, Spain, that aims to develop a more empathic and innovative society by teaching skills of emotional intelligence and creative thinking through the arts.

Our work uses involvement in the arts—both art appreciation and art making—to enhance people's well-being, their relationships, and creativity in their everyday and professional lives. Fundamental to this applied educational work is the belief that art provides a suitable medium to teach about emotions and creativity. Works of art convey emotion and are themselves a result of a creative process that is filled with emotions, from anxiety about the unknown to elation of inspiration. Whereas talking about one's own emotions can create inhibiting unease, observing and discussing pieces of art can provide a way to learn about emotions in a psychologically safe way.

Another fundamental premise of our work is that both creativity and emotion skills can be taught and learned by people of different ages. Skills are acquired through feedback and practice, whether one is learning to drive a car or to more accurately read others' emotions. Our approach is rooted in the theory of emotional intelligence, which defines four fundamental emotion skills: accurately perceiving emotions in oneself and others, using emotions to facilitate thinking and problem solving, understanding emotions, and regulating emotions.[2] These skills are at the core of empathy. A person cannot show concern for others if he or she does not accurately perceive his or her emotions, and there cannot be understanding of others without knowledge of the causes and consequences of emotions. Consequently, we created programs and workshops to teach and practice skills rooted in emotional intelligence. In this chapter, we will introduce these programs and highlight those aspects that most explicitly illustrate the relevance of emotional intelligence skills for development of empathy.

We have organized the chapter in three major sections. First, we introduce the Botín Foundation and the Botín Center, along with their vision and philosophy of change. Second, we introduce the concept of emotional intelligence and its relationship with empathy and positive social behavior. Finally, we describe educational programs aimed to teach emotion and creativity skills through the arts at the Botín Center. We introduce the Botín Foundation's art activities for primary and secondary schools and describe workshops developed for children, adults, adolescents, and entire families. We conclude the chapter with a vision for the future and the impact of these programs.

THE BOTÍN FOUNDATION AND THE BOTÍN CENTER

The Botín Foundation was created in 1964 by Marcelino Botín Sanz de Sautuola and his wife, Carmen Yllera, to promote the social development of Cantabria, Spain. Today, although keeping its main focus on Cantabria, the Botín Foundation operates all over Spain and Latin America, contributing to the overall development of society by exploring new ways of uncovering creative talent and supporting it to generate cultural, social, and economic wealth.

In 2014, the foundation celebrated its fiftieth anniversary by tackling its most ambitious project to date, the Botín Center, an art venue envisioned to enrich the city of Santander through the arts and dedicated to the development of creativity as a way to stimulate economic and social growth. The Botín Center was designed by architect and Pritzker Prize winner Renzo Piano as a space for art, culture, and educational activities, as well as a new meeting place in Santander that will link the city center to the bay. The Botín Center and the Pereda Gardens surrounding it will enrich life in the city through art, music, film, theater, dance, and literature. The vision for the Botín Center is for it to be a private art center, point of reference in Spain, and one of the leading art centers on the international art scene.

The Botín Center will extend and strengthen the Botín Foundation's visual arts program, which has been running for over twenty-five years. The visual arts committee, in charge of programming the venue, is led by Vicente Todolí, former director of the Tate Modern in London. The visual arts program consists of three main areas: (1) training in the form of grants for artists and international workshops led by renowned artists; (2) research into drawing by Spanish masters from all historical periods; and (3) exhibitions either directly produced by the foundation or arising from its research and training programs.

The Botín Foundation's art collection is a reflection of its program and its history. It contains works of art by its grantees and workshop directors, complemented by additional works by contemporary artists. The center will encourage people's creative capacities through the arts. It will achieve this by organizing workshops, seminars, courses, and educational activities for children, adolescents, families, and adults. The center will also be a research center for studying the relationship between the arts, emotions, and creativity, as well as an international meeting place for experts and scholars in these fields.

The educational mission of the Botín Center is rooted in the observation that there are two key aspects to human development that are often overlooked or simply left to chance instead of being explicitly and purposefully taught and learned—namely, emotion and creativity skills. Emotions are the driving force of our lives and they help us relate to one another. Similarly, our ability to create allows us to invent, to evolve, and to solve personal and social problems. The educational system has traditionally focused only on the acquisition of knowledge and cognitive development more broadly. We have left emotions and creativity to informal education. Children are not taught how to identify, understand, express, use, and regulate emotions in order to enhance their well-being and direct their thoughts and relationships with others. Nor have we cultivated our ability to generate ideas and to develop and give shape to new ideas or devices.

Moreover, emotions and creativity are connected. Emotions are, in effect, responsible for setting our creativity in motion. Artistic creativity is one of the best examples of this connection. Artists use emotional experiences as inspiration and portray them in their work; they aim to evoke a wide range of emotions in their audience, from enjoyment to confusion and disgust.[3] Thus the educational goal of the Botín Center is to fill the need for explicit education and development of emotion and creativity skills and to do this through the medium of art that they have in common. At the Botín Center, people will learn how to use visual arts, literature, music, and the performing arts to develop an approach to being and thinking that leads them to discover and explore new ways of transforming problems into opportunities for improvement and growth and develop skills for greater empathy.

EMOTIONAL INTELLIGENCE AND EMPATHY

Empathy can most simply be defined as "the heightened responsiveness to another's emotional experience."[4] After five decades of research, psychologists agree that empathy includes both an emotional and a cognitive component.[5] The emotional component of empathy is often termed *empathic concern* and is described as feeling what the other person is feeling, as well as feelings of compassion and concern for others. The cognitive component of empathy pertains to perspective taking defined as one's tendency to put themselves in another person's shoes and take into account their point of view. Furthermore, empathy is related to positive social behavior; it is a social skill that enables people to understand and anticipate others' behavior, which is critical for successful social interactions.[6] Empathy is related to unselfish concern for others and it is an important motivator of helping behavior, even when it involves a cost to the helper.[7]

Thus we know that empathy is desirable. Research also shows that it is acquired and increases with age.[8] But how do we teach and build empathy? What do we teach to enable a person to show empathic concern and be able to put themselves in someone else's shoes? What are the necessary ingredients for empathy? Psychological research points to two sets of attributes: the interest or desire to connect with others and skills on how to do this successfully. Whereas the desire to connect with others pertains to the domain of personality dispositions that are difficult to modify, the "how to" component can be taught and learned.[9]

We base our thinking and teaching of "how to" skills of empathy on the theory of emotional intelligence, which defines four abilities: (1) accurately perceiving emotions in oneself and others, (2) using emotions to facilitate thinking, problem solving, and creativity, (3) understanding emotions, and (4) managing emotion in oneself and others.[10] Together the abilities of emotional intelligence promote high-quality relationships, health, academic, and work performance.[11] We will discuss each of the four abilities in more detail later in the chapter and specifically focus on how they build emotional, cognitive, and behavioral aspects of empathy.

The ability to accurately perceive emotions in oneself and others is based on successful reading of signals from one's body (e.g., sweating, racing heartbeat), social environment (e.g., others' facial expressions, body language, vocal tone), and the physical environment (e.g., lighting in a restaurant can create an emotional atmosphere of relaxation and serenity).[12] Accurately perceiving emotions provides information that something important is happening in the environment and should be attended to.[13] For example, one can only show concern and try to help a friend if they notice that the friend is sad.

The ability to use emotions to facilitate thinking and problem solving involves purposefully channeling emotions to accomplish one's goals.[14] People use emotions when they realize how to match their emotions to tasks for which they are useful. For instance, when feeling pleasant and energized people are better able to generate many ideas and be more flexible in their thinking.[15] Thus when one is happy or exuberant they can use these feelings to work on brainstorming tasks. People also use emotions when they intentionally make themselves feel what others are experiencing in order to help them better relate to someone. Actors use this skill when "getting into character." They use memories of personal experiences to create feelings similar to those of the character they are portraying and thus create a more realistic and believable individual.[16] Role playing exercised through acting training enhances empathy in both elementary school children and college students.[17]

The ability to understand emotions includes acquiring a rich body of knowledge on the causes and consequences of emotions, as well as a rich emotion vocabulary that enables successful communication of emotion.[18] An ability to describe personal experience and the experiences of others using nuanced emotion words (e.g., distinguishing among irritation, frustration, and anger) makes it possible to more effectively understand others and show one's concern.

Finally, managing emotions refers to the ability to come up with strategies to manage the thoughts, feelings, and behaviors related to an emotional experience and evaluate the effectiveness of different strategies in achieving goals.[19] Emotions are managed for different goals, from preventing an emotion (e.g., avoiding stage fright), reducing the intensity of an emotion (e.g., lessening frustration when learning a difficult skill), or prolonging an experience (e.g., maintaining interest when working on a long-term project). Importantly, managing emotions does not mean keeping negative feelings at bay. Rather, this skill involves confronting and contending with a full range of positive to negative and from activated to relaxed emotions. Managing emotions requires one to accurately perceive emotions and understand the course of emotions. To achieve empathy, one needs to manage their emotions successfully, such as having to dampen elation after gaining acceptance to a prestigious college in order to comfort a friend and offer support after a romantic breakup.

TEACHING EMOTIONAL INTELLIGENCE AND EMPATHY THROUGH THE ARTS

Enriching the School Curricula

The Botín Foundation supports two groups of programs that are implemented through the foundation's art exhibitions and art collection (figure 1.1). The first is a school-based program called *Responsible Education* and it involves two hundred primary and secondary schools (serving more than seventy thousand students and seven thousand teachers). The second is a series of workshops developed in collaboration with the Yale Center for Emotional Intelligence for the new Botín Center.

Responsible Education aims to enhance students' physical, emotional, intellectual, and social growth, promote communication, and improve school climate by working with teachers, students, and families. The quality of students' education is improved by introducing the concept of emotional intelligence and development of creativity in schools. An important aspect of *Responsible Education* includes art, music, and literature resources. For the purposes of this chapter, we focus on the visual art resources that are centered on children visiting an art exhibit.

The visual art resources (*ReflejArte*) help students identify and express emotions, feelings, ideas, and opinions by learning and engaging in art appreciation at the Botín Foundation and a series of related art-making activities. *ReflejArte* includes three stages. First, the foundation education staff informs the teachers about the exhibition and present activities to be

Figure 1.1.   The exhibition space at Villa Iris in Santander, Spain.

shared with students to spur their curiosity before they visit the exhibition. During the exhibition session, a facilitator walks the group of students and their teacher through the exhibition room, putting students in contact with art using visual-thinking methodology.[20] Students are asked to focus especially on the emotions that the artwork elicits. This engagement with the art develops empathy through active listening, respect for others' opinions, and identification and expression of emotions (the artist's emotions, their own emotions, and their peers' emotions). Finally, after the session at the exhibition room, the teacher facilitates individual reflection and the creation of a piece of art produced by all the students. Students' creations are showcased at an exhibition titled *Somos Creativos* (We Are Creative) that is open to the public.

Workshops at the Botín Center

With the support of the Botín Foundation, the Yale Center for Emotional Intelligence designed and tested workshops teaching emotion and creativity skills aimed at different age groups. We built on the well-established approach to teaching skills of emotional intelligence in the schools (e.g., the RULER approach)[21] and designed workshops using art-based and museum-based activities as teaching vehicles. The premise of our work is that development of all skills, from handwriting to driving a car to perspective taking, is a process that takes time and practice. Thus all workshops involve multiple sessions and provide opportunities for people to practice and get feedback relevant to skill building. In each session, participants practice emotion skills from previous sessions, are introduced to new skill elements, and take part in the final wrap-up activity in which the lessons are reviewed and discussed. Learning is infused with examples from everyday life to help participants see the immediate value and applicability of learned skills. Although the workshops aim to teach both emotion and creativity skills, for the purpose of this chapter we will focus on building empathy-relevant emotion skills.

The workshops are led by a trained facilitator who guides participants through learning activities. Although the facilitator's role is not to teach art history or art-making techniques, he or she has knowledge both about art and the skills being taught. In this way, the facilitator is able to be a mediator between the art and participants in the process of learning and practicing emotion and creativity skills (figure 1.2). The facilitator stresses that the workshops are not art classes and that participants do not need any prior art background. Rather, the workshop goal is to teach participants to be more skillful at identifying emotions, using and managing them to achieve greater personal well-being, and more successfully address their relationships and educational or professional goals.

Look Again: Workshop for Adults

The adult workshop consists of eight sixty- to seventy-minute sessions. Emotion skills are taught using five techniques (table 1.1). The skills are introduced and built gradually. In the first session, participants are familiarized with the exhibit and asked to sustain observation of one preselected piece of art for ten minutes. After five minutes of uninterrupted

Figure 1.2.   A training session for the workshop for adults.

observation, participants are guided in perspective shifting. The facilitator asks observers to get very close to the art or to look at it from the other side of the room. Each time, participants consider whether they notice anything different about the piece of art and how their emotional reactions change with different perspectives.

The technique of visualization is introduced next and participants are asked to enter the work of art and imagine being in a world in which it comes to life. Then they consider how each of their five senses would experience the piece. What does the environment look like? What physical sensations do they have? What are the smells and sounds? Could one touch anything? As sessions go on, participants are given less direction in visualization and perspective shifting in order to increase participant autonomy.

We introduce the Mood Meter, a tool developed at the Yale Center for Emotional Intelligence to facilitate identification and understanding of emotions.[22] The Mood Meter is a grid created after crossing two main axes describing emotions: pleasantness (ranging from unpleasant/negative to pleasant/positive emotions) and activation (from low to high activation/energy). The four resulting quadrants distinguish distinct groups of emotions: (1) unpleasant high activation emotions, such as fear or anger (the red quadrant on the Mood Meter); (2) unpleasant low activation emotions,

Table 1.1.   Five Techniques to Teach Emotion Skills

Techniques	Definition	Empathy Application
Sustained Observation	Looking at a piece of art for a longer period of time than one might otherwise look (five to ten minutes), allowing one to notice details and gain insights.	Moving beyond initial impressions (for example, from dislike to interest) in interactions with others.
Perspective Shifting	Purposeful changing of observation positions (inches from the piece of art or across the room), angles (below or from left/right side), or roles (as a person in a painting or an art critic) in order to view an object from a different point of view.	Shifting one's position to imagine a situation someone is describing (based on their experience and environment).
Visualization	Imagining that one is somewhere else (for example, within the scene of a painting) to more deeply examine sensations and feelings.	Imagining oneself in a situation someone is describing to recreate their experience (sensations, emotions).
Reflection	Looking back on an experience with openness and curiosity to describe and clarify what happened, noticing patterns and building insight.	Examining one's strong reaction to someone to better understand reasons for the reaction and its origins.
Mood Meter	The tool for describing the quality and intensity of emotions; composed of a grid created by the intersection of two dimensions that describe emotional experience: positive vs. negative and high vs. low activation/energy.	By examining components of the emotional experience (for example, How negative is it? How activated is the person?), one can more successfully identify and describe others' emotions.

Note: Table 1.1 is an overview of techniques teaching empathy-relevant emotion skills using visual arts. This table was generated for the purposes of this chapter.

such as sadness or boredom (the blue quadrant); (3) pleasant high activation emotions like happiness or pride (the yellow quadrant); and (4) pleasant low activation emotions, like serenity and contentment (the green quadrant). By examining the qualities of pleasantness and activation of an emotional experience, one is able to more easily and accurately identify what emotion they or someone else are experiencing. The participants first practice using the Mood Meter by identifying their present emotion and then use the tool to identify emotions evoked by art.

The Mood Meter is used across workshop sessions to build and strengthen the skills of labeling emotions. For instance, in one session participants first observe a piece of art and are then presented background information about the artwork. Facilitators share the name of the artist, title of the work, materials used, year when the piece was created, its historical context, ownership history, estimated price, or other details. As they receive this information, participants are asked to use the Mood Meter to identify any changes in their reaction to the artwork. The activity is discussed to draw a parallel with everyday situations in which it is possible to change first impressions after gaining more knowledge about the different circumstances or a person. More information often increases one's ability to understand others and empathize with them. In other sessions, the Mood Meter is used with different pieces of art and art forms (from paintings to photography to sculpture, and both representational and abstract art).

The workshop puts an emphasis on the informational value of emotions and encourages openness to a wide range of emotions. That is, the goal is not to eliminate unpleasant emotions, but rather to learn from them and understand them better. In one session, participants are explicitly asked to identify a piece of art that evokes difficult or challenging emotions (e.g., anger, fear, disgust) and engage in sustained observation and reflection about the origins of these feelings by exploring personal associations and perceived meanings. Emotions are discussed as potentially directing behavior and thinking, such as when confusion that is not ignored can motivate information seeking. In another session, participants identify pieces of art that embody a personal problem (through emotions it evokes) and another piece of art that embodies the ideal solution to that problem. Working in pairs to describe the emotions associated with the problem and the solution, a person is able to gain a different perspective on a challenge in one's personal life and take a perspective of the other person when they present a personal problem. In the final session, participants are challenged to envision a path by which the problem can be transformed into a solution. They are asked how emotions could change and what strategies they can use to achieve the desired solution.

We performed an initial test of the workshop effectiveness, which will be followed by a more in-depth study of changes in participants' thinking both immediately after their last session and also two months later. For the initial evaluation, participants completed a questionnaire before the first workshop session and after the last session.[23] Participants were asked about their attitudes and beliefs about emotion skills, as well as their evaluation of emotion skills. After the workshop, participants agreed more strongly that identifying feelings accurately and understanding where they come from can be improved with practice, and they showed being more aware that unpleasant emotions can be useful for noticing and solving problems in everyday life. Participants also thought that they were better able to sustain attention when observing a piece of art, better able to use multiple perspectives when observing a piece of art, and better able to discuss emotional experiences with others.

One participant succinctly summarized the lessons learned: "To observe a work that makes me feel, identify emotions, visualize, look for solutions to a problem, and empathize with another person." Open-ended responses showed that participants found learning emotion skills the most useful aspect of the workshop (e.g., "the use of the Mood Meter to be able to describe a mood"; mentioned by 53 percent of participants), followed by art appreciation (e.g., "extrapolating art to personal life"; 41 percent of participants) and self- and social knowledge (e.g., "to share experiences" and "to improve personal abilities you generally don't work on"; 29 percent of participants).

When asked about the most interesting parts of the workshop, one participant stated: "To be able to put myself in the emotion. Awareness of how a work of art makes me feel and be able to identify the emotions that it produces. Find ways to solve problems, empathize with others to try to find a solution to their problem."

Overall, participants found that the most interesting aspects of the workshop pertained to art appreciation (e.g., "analyze the art with another perspective and see what emotions it creates in me"; 72 percent of participants), followed by the self- or social knowledge (e.g., "empathize with others to try to find a solution to their problem"; 56 percent of participants) and emotion skills (e.g., "recognizing emotions in myself"; 33 percent of participants).

How to Use Emotions: Workshop for Children

The child workshop uses art-based activities to teach emotion and creativity skills to children ages six through twelve in six, seventy-five-minute sessions. Sessions one through five follow a similar format, starting with a warm-up activity, followed by an art observation exercise and an art-making activity to represent target emotions. Each session is concluded with a final discussion of the lessons learned. Five sessions focus on a specific emotion: calm, sadness, anger, fear, and happiness. Finally, the last session is an art show that displays all the children's artwork from the workshop.

During each session, children learn to identify emotions, and they engage with pieces of art that evoke different emotions (figure 1.3). For instance, when examining the emotion of fear, children break into groups and go on a treasure hunt to find as many pieces of art in the exhibit that portray the emotion (e.g., fire, stormy sky, an object hiding behind something else). The facilitator then engages children in identifying how fear can be expressed in faces, body postures, vocal tone, behavior, and symbols, and they think of many words or descriptions for target emotions.

Figure 1.3. A session from the workshop for children.

Children are thus guided to build an emotion vocabulary (e.g., describe fear with words like afraid, frightened, nervous, tense, and others) and to explore associated feelings (e.g., feeling not supported, alone or helpless when one is afraid).

After identifying target emotions in art, children are engaged in a discussion about what happens when experiencing different emotions and taught that both pleasant and unpleasant emotions can be useful or detrimental for different purposes. For example, being angry is detrimental if one explodes and yells or hits another child, but it can be useful when channeled into playing a soccer game or standing up for oneself when being treated unfairly. Being sad is not helpful when trying to think of fun ideas for a birthday present for a friend, but it is helpful when having to work on detail-oriented tasks or when trying to understand and comfort a friend whose pet died. Similarly, being very happy anticipating a trip to Disneyland is not helpful when having to take a test at school, but it is quite helpful when trying to think of new games to play with one's friends. When a child understands both potential harm and benefits of different emotions, they will be more likely to stay open to a broad range of emotions and be able to use emotions to enhance their social interactions through sharing, listening, and empathizing with others.

We evaluated the initial effectiveness of the workshop by administering pre-workshop and post-workshop surveys.[24] We measured children's knowledge of how emotions can be used to facilitate thinking and problem solving in social situations using vignettes that described hypothetical everyday situations relevant to children's lives. For example, "Let's pretend that a friend's birthday party is coming up and you need to think of a really good idea for a birthday present. Which mood would make it easiest for you to think of some good ideas for your friend's present?" followed by three choices: "happy," "sad," or "scared." Children were also asked to describe their subjective experience of the workshop.

After the workshop, children had greater knowledge of how emotions can be used to facilitate thinking and actions. In their open-ended answers, most children reported learning emotion skills (e.g., "emotional vocabulary," "how to express myself, to know how others are feeling"; 95 percent of children). Children also reported learning about art appreciation and art making (e.g., "I like art a lot and I didn't know it"; 26 percent of children) and social skills (e.g., "older people [may] know us better and be able to help us"; 5 percent of children). Children also positively evaluated their experience after the workshop and expressed strong interest in future workshops at the Botín Center.

Expressing Oneself: Workshops for Adolescents and Families

Skills of emotional intelligence that are at the core of empathy can be learned throughout one's life. The workshops for children and adults tested the effects of the workshops using the visual arts as a medium and teaching tool. Workshops have also been developed for adolescents and families and are currently being tested. Here we illustrate elements of these workshops that are relevant to empathy development.

Adolescence is a time of strong emotions; from anxiety about fitting in with one's peers to the desire to be unique, to excitement in achieving greater independence, to fear of the unknown, adolescence is a time of experiencing mixed and complex emotions. Adolescence is a time of transition from dependence to autonomy and from childhood to adulthood and a time of great opportunity for learning and personal growth.[25] Because the central development task of adolescence is identity development,[26] the workshop designed for this age group uses making photographic self-portraits as a way to build emotion and creativity skills.

The workshop developed for adolescents builds skills across six seventy-five-minute sessions. Let us illustrate development of empathy through one activity about complex social emotions. Split into small groups, adolescents are asked to find works of art that represent one of four emotions: empathy, jealousy, embarrassment, and pride. Adolescents form definitions for the target emotions and discuss potential causes and consequences of those emotions. For example, a group of adolescents could describe empathy as "sharing the same emotions as another person" and its consequences as "closer relations with someone." Then participants transition to the exhibition space where they find examples of art with content related to the target emotions. The works of art are not intended to be direct representations of these emotions, but rather to be symbolically related or to show a cause or consequence of the emotion. Adolescents share the pieces of art they identified and the facilitator leads a discussion focused on the variety of emotions expressed in art and the emotions elicited through engaging with art, as well as the different ways emotions are conveyed.

The art observation activity becomes an inspiration for art making. Participants start working in pairs and making photographic portraits of each other. While modeling, each person is asked to represent a complex emotion of their choice. Participants are reminded that facial expressions are not the only tool to convey an emotion. The person taking photographs is encouraged to use all techniques for portraying emotions learned in the workshop (e.g., perspective taking, symbolism) and capture what they see in their model. After taking pictures of each other, participants review the photographs and discuss the perceptions of the photographer and intentions of the model, with the goal of gaining an appreciation of discrepancies that often arise between a private experience of emotion and what is observed from the outside. Following this discussion, participants continue working on a series of self-portraits that connect all workshop sessions. The focus of self-portraits is complex social emotions; the represented emotions do not need to be what the adolescent is experiencing in the moment, but something they find meaningful or are curious about. As they are planning their photographs, participants are encouraged to consider the artwork they observed in the exhibition space (e.g., How did the artists portray complex emotions?), as well as the lessons about inner experience and outward expression of emotions. The final guided reflection asks participants to consider how the emotion they portrayed in the self-portraits relates to their selves and their sense of identity.

The final workshop we developed is aimed at whole families (six- to twelve-year-old children, six sixty-minute sessions). Families are the first context for socialization and parents are crucial for the development of emotion skills. Children's social skills and positive social behavior are related to parental warmth and empathy.[27] When a caregiver shows love and gives children opportunities to convey feelings about being loved, the child becomes more capable of communicating care and empathy for those around them.[28] Inviting both parents and children to participate in a workshop enables family members to learn about each other and to acquire skills that can improve relationships within families.

Over the course of the workshop, families engage in activities that encourage them to think about their emotions, label those emotions, and understand the causes and consequences of emotions. The goal is for family members to apply these emotion skills with each other and gain the confidence to carry out these skills beyond the workshop. For instance, in a series of exercises parents and children work together to create a family collage focusing on their emotions and their role in family life. Are the parents frustrated and touchy after coming home from work? Are the children inspired by their day at school? What do family members enjoy doing individually and together?

Family members depict their typical emotions and share these illustrations with each other. In the process, they step into each other's shoes and gain a deeper understanding and appreciation of each other. The facilitators stress that pleasant feelings do not have to be the focus of the collage. Rather, concern for each other or understanding of each other in times of anxiety or sadness could be what connects and describes a unique family. After creating the collages, families are lead through a discussion about memories that can arise while working on the project, how they talk about emotions while working on the collage, and whether they portrayed a range of both positive and negative emotions.

CONCLUSION: ENHANCING EMPATHY THROUGH ENGAGEMENT WITH THE ARTS

Central to the mission and philosophy of the Botín Center is the belief that engagement with the arts, both in the forms of art appreciation and art creation, is a powerful tool in teaching emotion skills at the core of empathy. Pablo Picasso described artists as receptacles for emotions sensed everywhere and in everything, from the earth to fleeting shapes.[29] While artists often intuitively change perspectives and imagine themselves in others' places or feel others' emotions, our goal is to do so deliberately and purposefully by bringing teaching and developing emotion skills outside of the classroom and into the museum.[30]

In this chapter, we described the educational program of the Botín Foundation that aims to teach emotion skills in an art center. In collaboration with the scientists at the Yale Center for Emotional Intelligence, workshops were designed for children and adults, adolescents and families. In multiple sessions, each of the workshops furthers art appreciation and teaches emotion and creativity skills through guided art observation, art making, and reflection. When people are challenged to examine art from multiple perspectives and observe the emotions it evokes, they become more skilled in the language of emotions and more likely to use that language and understanding in everyday interactions and relationships.

ACKNOWLEDGMENTS

The work on this chapter was funded and supported through a collaboration between the Yale Center for Emotional Intelligence and the Botín Foundation, Santander, Spain (Emotions, Creativity, and the Arts grant; principal investigators Zorana Ivcevic and Marc Brackett).

NOTES

1. Daniel C. Batson, Nadia Ahmad, and David A. Lishner, "Empathy and Altruism," in *Oxford Handbook of Positive Psychology*, ed. Shane J. Lopez and Charles R. Snyder (New York: Oxford University Press): 417–26; James C. Kaufman, Jason C. Cole, and John Baer, "The Construct of Creativity: Structural Model for Self-Reported Creativity Ratings," *The Journal of Creative Behavior* 43 (2009): 119–34.

2. John D. Mayer and Peter Salovey, "What Is Emotional Intelligence?" in *Emotional Development and Emotional Intelligence: Educational Implications*, ed. Peter Salovey and David Sluyter (New York: Basic Books, 1997), 3–31.

3. Paul J. Silvia, "Looking Past Pleasure: Anger, Confusion, Disgust, Pride, Surprise, and Other Unusual Aesthetic Emotions," *Psychology of Aesthetics, Creativity, and the Arts* 3 (2009): 48; Pablo P. L. Tinio, "From Artistic Creation to Aesthetic Reception: The Mirror Model of Art," *Psychology of Aesthetics, Creativity, and the Arts* 7 (2013): 265.

4. Albert Mehrabian and Norman Epstein, "A Measure of Emotional Empathy," *Journal of Personality* 40 (1972): 525–43.

5. Mark H. Davis, "Measuring Individual Differences in Empathy: Evidence for a Multidimensional Approach," *Journal of Personality and Social Psychology* 44 (1983): 113–26; Jean Decety and Philip L. Jackson, "The Functional Architecture of Human Empathy," *Behavioral and Cognitive Neuroscience Reviews* 3 (2004): 71–100; Nancy Eisenberg, "Prosocial Development in Early and Mid-Adolescence," in *From Childhood to Adolescence, A Transitional Period*, ed. Raymond Montemayor, Gerald R. Adams, and Thomas P. Gullotta (Thousand Oaks, CA: Sage, 1990), 240–68; Nancy Eisenberg and Richard A. Fabes, "Emotion, Emotion-Related Regulation, and Quality of Socioemotional Functioning," in *Child Psychology: A Handbook of Contemporary Issues*, ed. Lawrence Balter and Catherine Susan Tamis-LeMonda (New York: Psychology Press, 1999), 318–35.

6. Mark H. Davis and Stephen L. Franzoi, "Stability and Change in Adolescent Self-Consciousness and Empathy," *Journal of Research in Personality* 25 (1991): 70–87; Seymour Feshbach, "The Environment of Personality," *American Psychologist* 33 (1978): 447–55.

7. Daniel C. Batson, *The Altruism Question: Toward a Social-Psychological Answer* (Hillsdale, NJ: Erlbaum, 1991); Nancy Eisenberg, Richard A. Fabes, and Tracy L. Spinrad, "Prosocial Development," in *Handbook of Child Psychology: Social, Emotional, and Personality Development*, ed. Nancy Eisenberg (Hoboken, NJ: John Wiley and Sons, 2006), 646–718.

8. Nancy Eisenberg, "Prosocial Behavior," in *Children's Needs III: Development, Prevention, and Intervention*, ed. George G. Bear and Kathleen M. Minke (Washington, DC: National Association of School Psychologists, 2006), 313–24.

9. Joseph A. Durlak, Roger P. Weissberg, Allison B. Dymnicki, Rebecca D. Taylor, and Kriston B. Schellinger, "The Impact of Enhancing Students' Social and Emotional Learning: A Meta-Analysis of School-Based Universal Interventions," *Child Development* 82 (2011): 405–32; Nicole A. Elbertson, Marc A. Brackett, and Roger P. Weissberg, "School-Based Social and Emotional Learning (SEL) Programming: Current Perspectives," in *The Second International Handbook of Educational Change*, ed. Andy Hargreaves, Michael Fullan, David Hopkins, and Ann Lieberman (Dordrecht: Springer Netherlands, 2012), 1017–32.

10. Mayer and Salovey, "What Is Emotional Intelligence?"

11. Marc A. Brackett, Susan E. Rivers, and Peter Salovey, "Emotional Intelligence: Implications for Personal, Social, Academic, and Workplace Success," *Social and Personality Psychology Compass* 5 (2011): 88–103.

12. Hillary A. Elfenbein and Nalini Ambady, "When Familiarity Breeds Accuracy: Cultural Exposure and Facial Emotion Recognition," *Journal of Personality and Social Psychology* 85 (2003): 276–90; John D. Mayer, Maria DiPaolo, and Peter Salovey, "Perceiving Affective Content in Ambiguous Visual Stimuli: A Component of Emotional Intelligence," *Journal of Personality Assessment* 54 (1990): 772–81.

13. Paul Ekman, *Emotions Revealed* (New York: Henry Holt, 2003).

14. Mayer, DiPaolo, and Salovey, "Perceiving Affective Content in Ambiguous Visual Stimuli."

15. Matthijs Baas, Carsten K. W. De Dreus, and Bernard A. Nijstad, "A Meta-Analysis of 25 Years of Mood-Creativity Research: Hedonic Tone, Activation, or Regulatory Focus?" *Psychological Bulletin* 134 (2008): 779–806.

16. Konstantin Stanislavsky, *My Life in Art* (Moscow: Foreign Languages Publishing House, 1950).

17. Thalia R. Goldstein and Ellen Winner, "Enhancing Empathy and Theory of Mind," *Journal of Cognition and Development* 13 (2012): 19–37.

18. Mayer, DiPaolo, and Salovey, "Perceiving Affective Content in Ambiguous Visual Stimuli."

19. Nancy Eisenberg, Richard A. Fabes, Ivanna K. Guthrie, and Mark Reiser, "Dispositional Emotionality and Regulation: Their Role in Predicting Quality of Social Functioning," *Journal of Personality and Social Psychology* 78 (2000): 136–57; John D. Mayer, and Peter Salovey, "Emotional Intelligence and the Construction and Regulation of Feelings," *Applied and Preventive Psychology* 4 (1995): 197–208.

20. Abigail C. Housen, "Aesthetic Thought, Critical Thinking and Transfer," *Arts and Learning Research Journal* 18 (2002): 99–131.

21. Susan E. Rivers, Marc A. Brackett, Maria R. Reyes, Nicole A. Elbertson, and Peter Salovey, "Improving the Social and Emotional Climate of Classrooms: A Clustered Randomized Controlled Trial Testing the RULER Approach," *Prevention Science* 14 (2013): 77–87.

22. Marc A. Brackett and Janet Pickard Kremenitzer, *Creating Emotionally Literate Classrooms: An Introduction to the RULER Approach to Social Emotional Learning* (Port Chester, NY: National Professional Resources Inc., 2011); Marc A. Brackett and Susan E. Rivers, "Transforming Students' Lives with Social and Emotional Learning," in *International Handbook of Emotions in Education*, ed. Reinhard Pekrun and Lisa Linnenbrink-Garcia (New York: Routledge, 2014), 368–88.

23. Marina Ebert, Jessica D. Hoffmann, Zorana Ivcevic, Christine Phan, and Marc A. Brackett, "Creativity, Emotion, and Art: Development and Initial Evaluation of a Workshop for Professional Adults," *International Journal of Creativity and Problem Solving* 25 (2015): 47–59.

24. Marina Ebert, Jessica D. Hoffmann, Zorana Ivcevic, Christine Phan, and Marc A. Brackett, "Teaching Emotion and Creativity Skills Through Art: A Workshop for Children," *International Journal of Creativity and Problem Solving* 25 (2015): 23–35.

25. Laurence Steinberg, *Age of Opportunity: Lessons from the New Science of Adolescence* (New York: Houghton Mifflin Harcourt, 2014).

26. Seth J. Schwartz, "The Evolution of Eriksonian and Neo-Eriksonian Identity Theory and Research: A Review and Integration," *Identity* 1 (2001): 7–58.

27. William Roberts and Janet Strayer, "Empathy, Emotional Expressiveness, and Prosocial Behavior," *Child Development* 67 (1996): 449–70; Janet Strayer and William Roberts, "Children's Anger, Emotional Expressiveness, and Empathy: Relations with Parents' Empathy, Emotional Expressiveness, and Parenting Practices," *Social Development* 13 (2004): 229–54; Qing Zhou, Nancy Eisenberg, Sandra H. Losoya, Richard A. Fabes, Mark Reiser, Ivanna K. Guthrie, Bridget C. Murphy, Amanda J. Cumberland, and Stephanie A. Shepard, "The Relations of Parental Warmth and Positive Expressiveness to Children's Empathy-Related Responding and Social Functioning: A Longitudinal Study," *Child Development* 73 (2002): 893–915.

28. Kevin Swick, "Preventing Violence Through Empathy Development in Families," *Early Childhood Education Journal* 33 (2005): 53–59.

29. Pablo Picasso and Dore Ashton, *Picasso on Art: A Selection of Views* (New York: Da Capo Press, 1988).

30. Marc A. Brackett, Susan E. Rivers, Maria R. Reyes, and Peter Salovey, "Enhancing Academic Performance and Social and Emotional Competence with the RULER Feeling Words Curriculum," *Learning and Individual Differences* 22 (2012): 218–24; Susan E. Rivers and Marc A. Brackett, "Achieving Standards in the English Language Arts (and More) Using the RULER Approach to Social and Emotional Learning," *Reading and Writing Quarterly* 27 (2011): 75–100.

solidarity → curiosity → attention → imagination → listening → empathy

2

Nurturing Empathy between Adults and Children

Lessons from the Children's Museum

Susan Harris MacKay

CREATING CONDITIONS

A young toddler is drawn toward a baby doll in the museum's Kids Care *exhibit and picks it up from the cradle it's resting in. Seeing his interest, his mother gives a gentle assist and he discovers how to place the baby in a small wooden high chair. His mother shows him how to pull the tray from behind the baby, up over its head, and set it in place, ready for a meal, perhaps in the very same way that they do at home. This young child, too young to have a conversation with words, engages in a different kind of dialogue with the materials available to him. He lifts the tray back over the doll's head, takes it out of the chair, then puts it back in and returns the tray to the front of the high chair. And again. And again, several times before he looks up at his mother who has been patiently observing this game of repetition. He claps his hands, eyebrows arched in delight, and a smile peeks out from behind the green plastic pacifier he has in his mouth. His mother returns the smile and nods, confirming the value of his idea, and waits for him to decide what to do next.*

This small moment was captured during one very busy evening at Portland Children's Museum as this family had joined many others for the monthly "Free Friday" programming. In the bustle of a busy museum, it would have been easy to miss this rather small and decidedly ordinary moment, but museum staff were nearby and ready to capture the experience with a camera and notebook, intent on looking for these small moments, eager to better understand the value and complexity within them. The museum staff creates the environment and then pays attention to what happens there, seeking to understand and to uncover curiosities that will propel the work forward with new questions and new possibilities. Poet Mary Oliver has written that paying attention is our "endless and proper work"—that "attention is the beginning of devotion."[1] The practice of documentation and reflection is this kind of paying attention. This "endless work" can itself reveal the power of paying attention to the observer and in turn can demonstrate to the observed (in this case, the child's mother) the power of her own attention. When we create conditions for sustained attention to children and actively work to find and communicate the value in what we notice, we ultimately create conditions that support adults to develop and strengthen empathy for the child's perspective and experience.

Children's museums are places in our communities where children and families come to play. But unlike playgrounds or other environments intended for and conducive to play, the staff of educators in a children's museum has the opportunity to pay attention to and interpret the kinds of play children and families invent and encounter. Using processes of documentation and reflection, exhibits and programs can be created and continually improved to support adults to recognize the powerful capacity that lives in a child at play, and to learn to value the natural and strong learning strategies with which children come hard-wired into the world. Clearly, the museum environment created conditions that allowed the baby boy in the story to demonstrate his natural learning strategies of curiosity and play. Perhaps the baby boy didn't have dolls and highchairs available to play with at home, and encountering them in the museum allowed him to show and strengthen his own capacity for empathy—to imagine the perspective of the caregiver and to take care of a baby. The conditions of the environment also allowed him to show and strengthen his drive to make predictions and test them out by tinkering with the chair until he was convinced of its functions.

Creativity, curiosity, imagination, and empathy are gifts that we often mourn losing as childhood turns to adulthood. We often ask what would happen if we were intentional about creating conditions that sustained and strengthened these gifts. But what if we chose to focus instead on the conditions necessary to support adults to perceive, pay attention to, and value these gifts of childhood—these natural learning strategies that are our birthright as human beings? Is it possible that these gifts of childhood suffer most from a lack of devotion? Is it possible that in our hurry to teach children all the things they don't already know, we overlook the things they come into the world prepared to do? What role might a children's museum play in this endeavor to help adults pay better attention? If paying attention is a prerequisite for empathy, how do we nurture our own capacity to do so?

SEEKING TRANSFORMATION

When we notice that a mother and her baby so naturally engage with one another in the doll corner, we can shine a light on the exchange and the value it holds. Her attention communicates the kind of love, loyalty, and enthusiasm for a person that characterizes devotion. Adults who care for children are endlessly bombarded by messages telling them to do more, buy more, schedule more, and test more. They are told what children need by "experts" who base their advice on generalizations that have little to do with the rich complexity that lives in a moment of attunement like what happened between mother and child in the doll corner. It is far more commonplace to be told what children need or sold something intended to find out what children can't do so that we can then be sold things that will fix them than it is to be invited to consider what remarkable and powerful things children *can* do—and what rights they might have *because* of what they can do. What looks natural is overlooked, ignored, or diminished. Consider the lack of surprise we have that children learn to talk. And yet few endeavors in a lifetime are more complex.

The children's museum has an important role to play in offering counter-messages steeped in genuine experiences like a simple moment between mother and child. Our attention to what happens in the museum has the power to transform our organizations in the direction of greater attunement with the experience of childhood. When we shine a light on the importance of play within contexts that directly connect adults to the power of play in the process of learning, we'll go a long way toward raising the value of play in our communities. We'll begin to shape a vision for the educational institutions within a society that not only says it values creativity, but knows how to support it as well.

It is the vision of Portland Children's Museum to create transformative learning experiences through the arts and sciences—and this is what is meant by transformative: that the learning experiences children have there serve to transform the world into a place where everyone reaches their full potential. Portland Children's Museum is unique in that it has a program called Opal School, a fee-based beginning school and public charter elementary (K–5) school serving 125 children and their families. These vibrant and thriving classrooms serve as laboratories in which museum professionals of all kinds observe the ongoing development of fresh ideas concerning environments where creativity, curiosity, and the wonder of learning thrive. It is the mission of the school program to use that research in a variety of ways to provoke fresh ideas that strengthen education, including the educational environment of the children's museum.

KEEPING THINGS WHOLE

Children's museums are one of the few places where we can ensure that wide audiences have the opportunity to encounter environments and experiences where creativity, curiosity, and the wonder of learning are invited to thrive for the explicit purpose of transforming our world. At Opal School, a commitment to children's social and emotional personhood isn't set apart from the rest of the curriculum—it's infused into every experience. Like the pre-primary municipal schools of Reggio Emilia that inspired Opal School's formation, curriculum is viewed as a ball toss—a playful back and forth between children and adults. This means that teachers go into the school year with focused intention but without knowing precisely what will happen. Instead, the year's content is emergent and negotiated—cocreated between children and teachers. The teacher tosses a question or materials as a way of provoking the children and pays attention to the reply they throw back. The teacher listens carefully at all stages, documenting what he or she hears the children saying and what he or she sees them doing, and he or she reflects on that documentation with colleagues to make sense of the exchange. That reflection process leads the teacher to make a decision about what might be the best next throw for the group; the back and forth means that the group continually gets stronger and more capable as the game continues. All learning requires exchange and comfort with uncertainty. There is no transmission device that will ever work better than real human experience and exchange when it comes to learning. A willing vulnerability to take the stance of a learner increases the likelihood that an adult will empathize with the perspective of a child. Empathy for the perspective of the learner increases the likelihood that things will be learned and at the same time strengthens the strategies necessary for future learning. If we are to improve our environments for learning—in museums or in schools—we must find a way to prioritize relational exchange over transmitted knowledge.

Documentation offers the opportunity to reflect on conditions that invite, support, and sustain experiences like the one in the doll corner and the one in which an eight-year-old named Angelina told her class, "Working with a partner is sometimes easier because you have lots of ideas, but it's sometimes harder because you have to agree." Angelina spoke these words as she and her classmates were getting ready to launch their final writing project of the school year. These third graders were asked to write this final piece with a partner. The teachers wondered if creating a requirement of partnership would create a genuine context to develop and reflect on the skill set that supports collaboration. In other words, they wanted to find out what might happen if collaboration was the end and writing the means, and not the other way around, as is so often expected. Rather than seeing the writing as an isolated task to be learned, it was placed in a whole experience and acknowledged as a natural part of a real human experience.

At about the same time that Angelina and the other third graders were collaborating on writing projects, there was a meeting elsewhere in the museum attended entirely by people over the age of thirty-five. The topic of conversation was the group's general inability to come up with an effective process for working together on new projects. One participant said, "Well, I think this just isn't working because we get together to share our ideas all the time and nothing ever changes. We've tried collaborating and it just doesn't work."

Back in the classroom, there was a decidedly different tone. Zane, age eight, shared, "I know I can't make everybody happy but I can be flexible and make compromises so everyone can be a little bit happy." And Pritam, age nine, said, "At first my partner had one idea and I had one idea, so [our teacher] suggested we look for inspiration, and we found a new idea. In the end I liked our new idea more than our original ideas."

Ultimately, collaboration is an exercise—a practice—reframing problems and engaging with the world as an innovator, a thinker, a scientist, an artist. At its core, collaboration is an exercise in empathy requiring deep listening and imagination. Here is Devin reflecting on a collaborative drawing with his partner, Camille, both age nine: "I thought up one image but Camille didn't really agree so we went deeper and I asked her what she would like. She added the swirly things which made me think of the fountain of youth, and then we said, 'What if it was just a fountain?'"

Documenting theses reflections from the children allows us to perceive something critical the adults seemed to have forgotten: that collaboration is always an option. It always exists as a possibility, but only when all the players are willing and able to imagine that the process of collaboration itself is more valuable than being the one with the best idea. Only if they can commit to going deeper when they hit disagreement, because disagreement will be a given. Only when we can imagine that we can get somewhere together that we can't get to on our own. But it's important to recognize that all this takes a tremendous amount of practice. So maybe it's not that it was forgotten. Maybe it's that it was never learned. It's possible that the adult colleagues in attendance at that meeting were competent writers who learned to be by practicing endlessly at school. But good writing alone doesn't solve problems. Doing anything alone limits our ability not only to perceive new paths, but also to arrive at entirely new destinations. By creating conditions in which children are inspired to utilize their natural learning strategies of play, curiosity, and empathy, we create opportunity to observe these strategies in process and to reflect on their value. We are then able to learn about how we can do more to nurture these capacities rather than pushing them for more immediate and tangible results that we've likely already predicted. Without paying attention to the children and their processes of learning, we can only see what we already know and we can't remember what we've forgotten.

REFRAMING

When we see our role as creators of conditions for learning rather than as transmitters of knowledge and culture, children's museums can become the place where adults are supported to develop empathy for the experience of childhood. This empathy has the potential to place them in a position of solidarity with children as they engage in the struggle of growing and learning. The mother in the doll corner stood in solidarity with her baby as he explored this one tiny place in his world. A moment of attunement between adult and child creates opportunity for the most significant kinds of relationship building. This mother paid attention to the interests of her child, matching his gaze, offering a hand, and then letting him go so he had the opportunity to experience the joy of mastery. She communicated to him that he was worthy and capable, and she gave him the opportunity to find out that his efforts, at first imperfect, could lead to delight—a delight they could share with one another. A few short moments in the exhibit were enough for this little boy's humanity to be celebrated, building habits of mind that will support him to acknowledge the humanity of others as he grows in this world. Carlina Rinaldi writes, "To be open to others means to have the courage to come into this room and say, 'I hope to be different when I leave, not necessarily because I agree with you but because your thoughts have caused me to think differently.'"[2] We can encourage adults to be open to children in this way in order to nurture the development of this attitude as the child grows. In order to develop this attitude, you must experience it. If you have not experienced it, as so few of us have, you must be active in your attempts to unlearn and to reframe. In her book *The Rise*, Sarah Lewis writes, "Reframing can turn an artist's studio into a laboratory, combining things never before considered."[3] She interviews author James Watson on this topic and quotes him as saying, "Fields die just because no one thinks they can outdo what has been done."[4] Environments that prioritize opportunities for adults to empathize with the experience of childhood are a new field that must be invented. We have our work cut out for us.

Expectations of standardized testing and Common Core curriculum create difficult and risky terrain in which to explore and encourage an empathetic relationship between adults and children. These policies and practices serve to hold us to the belief that control, certainty, and the dehumanization of the children in our care is the way to a more robust economy and stable society. They are not isolated to formal learning environments but serve to frame our work in museums as well. In an article titled "Rich People Just Care Less," Daniel Goleman writes, "A prerequisite to empathy is simply paying attention to the person in pain."[5] A prerequisite to empathy is paying attention. But it's not simple. It takes time and it takes practice.

It requires practice considering and articulating what we think and what we feel. Yet the architect of the Common Core, David Coleman, insists that nobody cares about what anyone thinks or feels.[6]

Children have a unique, spontaneous way of asking, exploring, noticing, seeing, and attempting explanation. There is no passive way to create relationship and children naturally enter into this active, reciprocal process of inquiry and research that requires authentic exchange and results in relationship. We support this willingness to learn by accompanying the children's inquiry and supporting the culture of childhood that is so unlike our own passive adult experience.

If creativity belongs to children, how do adults create favorable conditions in which it can thrive? How do we learn to pay attention if we are never asked what we think and what we feel? How do we learn to be comfortable with the thoughts and feelings of others—which might be so different from our own—if we aren't invited to express ourselves? How do we support all people to care more if we structure our learning environments to suppress and replace our natural strategies for seeking relationship and making meaning? What if we recognized our societal ills not as symptoms and results of an academic gap, but a relational gap? What if museums were seen as places where we could build new visions of society by modeling them after the world we want to live in rather than the one we already do?

THE POWER OF PLAY

This become possible when exhibits and programs prioritize relationship, creative expression through the arts and sciences, open inquiry, listening, and collaboration. An active practice of paying attention, documenting what we see, and reflecting with others on that documentation supports us to sustain these priorities and gives us tools to develop comfort with the inherent uncertainties such priorities create. Without that active practice it is common that as adults create environments for learning, they begin with an enthusiastic nod to creativity, curiosity, and the wonder of learning—and then quickly feel challenged as they perceive difficult choices: Creativity or structure? Curiosity or accuracy? Play or learning? Paying attention helps us understand these to be false choices because they allow us to have empathy for the children's perspective and experience. What happens when we pay attention to the child in process is that we are able to see powerful natural learning strategies at work. Strategies such as telling stories, asking questions, empathy, tinkering, exploring with all our senses, trying things out, and developing hypotheses and theories—observing these strategies at work can help us learn to see how strongly competent we human beings are from our earliest days. We arrive in this world ready to learn, to connect, and to seek belonging and relationship.

It is true that children rely on relationship for their very survival. In his book *The Age of Empathy*, Frans De Waal writes, "Our bodies and minds are made for social life and we become hopelessly depressed in its absence."[7] Childhood relies on its relationship to adulthood. Adults create children and then frame the experience of childhood. It is often difficult for adults to see the child as the protagonist of their own life and learning. This typical relationship between adults and children was written in the *New York Times* magazine in an article called "The Mother of All Problems" by Rachel Cusk. She writes:

> What we are offering our children is a story of life in which they have been given a role. How true is it? It's hard to tell. In a story there's always someone who owns the truth: What matters is that character's ability to serve it. But it is perhaps unwise to treasure this story too closely or believe in it too much, for at some point the growing child will pick it up and turn it over in his hands like some dispassionate reviewer composing a coldhearted analysis of an over-hyped novel.[8]

Strengthening the relationship between childhood and adulthood requires us to see the child as the protagonist in his or her own life story, capable of serving his or her own truth. Adults are unquestionably powerful forces in the unfolding of the story, and so it makes sense to do everything possible to ensure the review will be a positive one in the end. Loris Malaguzzi writes articulately about this struggle: "Each one of you has inside yourself an image of the child that directs you as you begin to relate to a child. This theory within you pushes you to behave in certain ways; it orients you as you talk to the child, listen to the child, observe the child. It is very difficult for you to act contrary to this internal image."[9]

As we create exhibits and programs for the museum, we need to ask ourselves: What environments and experiences communicate to children not only that they *can* be seen and heard, but also that they are *worthy* of being seen and heard? Consider the subtle differences in these photographs. In figure 2.1, the child is clearly valued and welcomed in the activity. In figure 2.2, however, the child is invited to express her own way with the clay and the message to her is that her own ideas matter. In this situation, we can see more of the child as she directs her own exploration. We can see her creativity, her curiosity, her playfulness, her desire to engage with the world. Paying attention allows us to take an empathetic stance. What does she care about? What does she wish to contribute? How can I support her to extend her ideas? What connections can I offer to this exchange?

Figure 2.1. A parent cuts a child's hand from clay. The child is seen, loved, treasured, and also objectified. *Source:* Museum Center for Learning.

Malaguzzi acknowledges that "the adult does too much because he cares about the child; but this creates a passive role for the child in her own learning."[10] The adult that does too much for the child unintentionally communicates to the child that he or she is not capable, and we cannot

Figure 2.2. A child captured in process while directing her own work with clay. Documenting a child in process communicates to the child that she is both seen and worthy of being seen. *Source*: Museum Center for Learning.

develop a belief in our own worth if we do not have the opportunity to flex and explore our own capacity. If we only offer children crayons and coloring books, we'll never have the opportunity to see that they are capable of this (see figure 2.3)—and neither will they.

AGENCY AND EMPATHY

We define ourselves by the things we create, and so within our exhibits and planned experiences we need to ask ourselves what we are supplying children as materials for creation, what opportunities we're giving them for authorship, and what chance we're giving them to develop their strengths and strategies for coping when things don't go as planned.

Figure 2.3. An eight-year-old child works with tempera paint and black line pen to represent a sunflower. We can expand our image of the child by offering materials rich in possibility, and by using those materials, children can grow their understanding of their own capacity. *Source*: Museum Center for Learning.

We need to learn to perceive the pervasive stereotypes our culture tends to hold about children so that we can become increasingly aware of how these stereotypes inform our assumptions. How often do we assume: That they are passive blank slates? That they need things to be simple? That they are just cute? That they are needy? That they are messy? These stereotypes inform our assumptions. We act on our assumptions, and our actions influence the quality of the experience of childhood.

Recently my colleague Matt Karlsen sent this note to Opal School staff after a visiting group from Ecuador had spent a day with us:

The principal from the school in Ecuador was delighted by an interaction she saw between two children, one older, one younger. She came to me and said that she had just watched a child who she hoped would become a teacher— who had asked such supportive questions of this younger author. This older child (Tyler) happened to be walking past at that very moment, so I introduced them. She asked him directly what had led him to respond in that way. Tyler said, "I've watched teachers and those are the kinds of questions they're always asking. I know how much that means to people. And I was really interested in her story."

Teachers at Opal School regularly report that they are challenged every day to expand their image of children—that they are endlessly surprised as they bump into their own, too small image. As we work to see children in the process, we truly do get a fresh view of things. Tyler is far from adulthood. But he offers us a glimpse of what could happen if we were clear that we are interested in the stories the children have to tell us every day. They would know how much that means to people. And they would, in turn, be really interested in the stories that others have to tell.

When we focus on supporting empathy like this to thrive, it is also natural that a sense of agency thrives. Healthy agency is believing that you have the opportunity, the ability, and the right to make meaningful and valuable contributions to your community. Healthy agency is being the protagonist in your own story. When adults choose to empathize with the struggle of becoming human, they can stand in solidarity with children—they can give their story back to them, they can communicate that they are worthy of being seen and heard—as they learn how to live in an uncertain world where everyone else has the right to do the same. When we model empathy, we nurture empathy. Creating environments that support the healthy development of agency and empathy are central to our efforts to sustain our planet and our democracy.

Transformative learning experiences through the arts and sciences are possible in environments that nurture empathy and agency, where adults hold a strong image of children, and where children's expressivity is strengthened and encouraged—where children are not only allowed to be seen and heard, but where they understand they are *worthy* of being seen and heard. The materials really matter. In children's hands, materials can help them realize the novel connections they make as they share their observations about their experiences in the world, observations they likely didn't know they had until they picked up the material. Materials open a flow of exchange and ideas; they host their own kind of dialogue, one that allows children to share what might otherwise have been invisible to them and to others. Materials also ensure that images and language nurture one another. Materials allow us to *see* together and therefore *reflect* together— to *encounter* one another—as human beings seeking to express experience. With materials in hand, I can see my ideas, consider memories and connections, and encounter my own response in the same moment. Materials can teach me to think as their use simultaneously requires convergent and divergent thinking, and to exchange words and images, and to listen to those of others. Materials stir ideas we didn't know were there and breed familiarity with our own thoughts, supporting a development of agency—a belief that our ideas matter. Our ideas have influence. Materials have the power to reflect children back to themselves. So what we offer them to use and ask them to do is of tremendous consequence and full of tremendous potential. Because once we are aware of this, we can *do* something and have confidence that it will have mattered.

So I am wondering, how can children's museum exhibits and programs invite adults to stand in solidarity with children as they exercise and strengthen their own agency? What if our children's museums held, as a first priority, an intention to strengthen our collective image of the child in order to combat the stereotypes of weakness and cuteness and neediness? What if children's museums were designed to support children to be seen and to see themselves as active contributors who deserve to be inspired rather than as consumers needing to be entertained? How can our children's museums strengthen our collective understanding of play—not so much as an activity but as a strategy? We don't have to choose between play and learning because play is our most powerful strategy *for* learning.

Recently, an eight-year-old student at Opal School named Lucius observed that it is our instinct to learn how to live. And he's right, of course. It's our instinct to learn how to live and play evolved to help us do just that. We know that all animal species have play behaviors and that those who have fewer instinctive behaviors play more. So we are the most playful animals—with our one instinct to learn to live and our powerful strategy of play to do that.[11] As Brian Sutton-Smith has observed, "The opposite of play . . . is not a present reality or work, it is vacillation, or worse, it is depression."[12] So what efforts will we make to sustain play by empathizing with the perspective and experience of children? And who is better positioned to do so than the children's museum?

NOTES

1. "Transcript for Mary Oliver—Listening to the World," *On Being*, http://www.onbeing.org/program/mary-oliver-listening-to-the-world/transcript/8051#main_content (accessed October 20, 2015).

2. Carlina Rinaldi, "The Relationship Between Documentation and Assessment," *Innovations in Early Education: The International Reggio Exchange* 11 (2004): 3.

3. Sarah Lewis, *The Rise: Creativity, The Gift of Failure, and the Search for Mastery* (New York: Simon and Schuster, 2014), 189.

4. Ibid.

5. Daniel Goleman, "Rich People Just Care Less," *New York Times*, October 6, 2013.

6. "David Coleman: Bringing the Common Core to Life," *YouTube*, https://www.youtube.com/watch?v=Pu6lin88YXU (accessed January 7, 2016).

7. Frans De Waal, *The Age of Empathy: Nature's Lessons for a Kinder Society* (New York: Three Rivers Press, 2009), 10.

8. Rachel Cusk, "The Mother of All Problems," *New York Times Magazine*, March 19, 2015, MM38.

9. Loris Malaguzzi, "Your Image of the Child: Where Teaching Begins," *Childcare Information Exchange* 3 (1994): 52.

10. Ibid., 53.

11. Susan Harris MacKay, "School is for Learning to Live, Not Just for Learning," *YouTube*, https://www.youtube.com/watch?v=dUHNxaebc8Q&feature=youtu.be (accessed January 8, 2016).

12. Brian Sutton-Smith, *The Ambiguity of Play* (Cambridge, MA: Harvard University Press, 2009), 198.

social dilemma negotiation empathy cooperation sharing

3

Wearing Someone Else's Shoes

The Cooperative Museum Experiences of *Science of Sharing*

Hugh McDonald, Elizabeth Fleming, Joshua Gutwill, and Troy Livingston

In a 2010 article in the *Physics Today*, late New York Hall of Science director Alan Friedman wrote that science museums were born as repositories serving collectors and researchers, but soon began evolving into facilities focused on public education.[1] Perhaps the most obvious illustration of this shift is found in the move away from what many regard as a classic science museum setting—quiet marble hallways lined with artifacts in glass cases—and toward livelier galleries filled with interactive exhibits allowing experimentation with natural and perceptual phenomena. The range of phenomena that visitors can now explore in such places is truly vast: in museums and science centers around the world, people can investigate exhibitions on light, sound, electricity, magnetism, motion, mathematics, cosmology, meteorology, and the biological processes that drive life itself.

However, the social sciences are still rarely explored in science museums. In recent decades, research in social and cognitive psychology, behavioral economics, and the neurosciences has led to tremendous advances in our understanding of cognitive and social development, decision making, stress, aggression, cooperation, and many other areas. Importantly, such research is of interest not only to scientists; work in these areas sheds light on social interactions and moral and economic judgments at the heart of some of the most critical problems facing our world, including sustainable resource use, responses to climate change and environmental damage, income inequality, institutional racism and prejudice, ethnic and religious conflict, and social and political polarization. For individuals and institutions to be part of the solution to such problems, people must understand how complex cognitive and social processes are studied. In fact, the American Association for the Advancement of Science (AAAS) has argued that an understanding of key concepts in social psychology is important for a scientifically literate public.[2] And because social scientists study something of interest to all students—themselves—the social sciences offer an ideal entry point for students to learn about more general scientific concepts and methods, such as controlled observation, experimental design, and hypothesis generation and testing.

But despite the importance of such research in illuminating fundamental social and cognitive processes and generating solutions to sobering societal challenges, museums have not adequately explored opportunities to involve the public in the scientific study of social behaviors such as cooperation, resource allocation, and economic decision making. The *Science of Sharing* project was designed to make social interactions the central focus of the museum experience. Funded by the National Science Foundation in 2011, the project was based on a simple premise: social interactions, and the processes by which people perceive and interpret them, are phenomena, and as such are open to the same kinds of playful inquiry and experimentation modern science museums have long applied to physical phenomena like light, sound, and motion.

WHAT IS *SCIENCE OF SHARING*?

Science of Sharing (SOS) was devised to develop and evaluate exhibits and activities that would create opportunities for the public to experiment with social interactions involving cooperation, competition, collaborative problem solving, negotiation, and resource allocation; to prompt reflection on and discussion of perceptions, judgments, and cognitive processes underlying those interactions, including developing interpersonal trust, perceiving social groups, weighing personal gains against community outcomes, and predicting the behavior of others; and to raise public awareness of concepts and methods involved in the scientific study of human behavior and cognition. More broadly, SOS exhibits were intended to help people link their experiences with larger societal challenges involving elements of cooperative behavior and negotiation, such as resource overuse, environmental destruction, international conflict, and climate change. In essence, the project was designed to create experiences that made people more aware of how they perceive and interact with other people and how, in turn, others perceive them. Through this process of stepping into the shoes (and minds) of others, we hoped that participants would gain a greater understanding of the forces that shape everyday social experiences and perhaps an enhanced ability to empathize with the circumstances and actions of other people.

Between 2011 and 2015, the project brought together a diverse team of social scientists, exhibit developers, educators, and researchers to prototype a broad range of experiences, test the way people used, interpreted, and discussed them, evaluate their potential as learning opportunities, and finally to share those experiences with the public and with researchers and museum professionals. Ultimately, the project developed seventeen multiperson interactive exhibits in a permanent gallery devoted to human behavior in the Exploratorium, San Francisco's "museum of science, art, and human perception" (figure 3.1). In addition, some of the exhibits are being duplicated for installation at the Museum of Life and Science in Durham, North Carolina. In the remainder of this chapter, we describe the project's exhibits and activities, discuss the behavioral and cognitive responses they provoked, and offer evidence that they were successful in promoting empathy among participants.

The *TextFish* exhibit is a simulation of an ocean ecosystem in which visitors must coordinate their behavior to sustain a virtual fish population (figure 3.2). The experience provides an immersive and visceral illustration of the Tragedy of the Commons, a situation that may arise when a group or community shares responsibility for maintaining any common resource—a park, beach, lake, ocean, or the like. Each person in such a community is rationally motivated to maximize their own gain from that resource by, for example, catching more fish than they really need to survive. But when

Figure 3.1.   Entrance to the *Science of Sharing* exhibition at the Exploratorium. *Source*: Exploratorium.

everyone acts in that fashion, the resource may be pushed beyond its ability to sustain itself, and the entire community suffers. Such resources therefore demand that each user balance his or her own short-term goals against the longer-term good of the group as a whole.

At *TextFish*, visitors use their cell phones to text the word *fish* to a phone number provided on the label. With each text, they "catch" a virtual fish. Any number of players can fish at once, and each can fish as slowly or as quickly as they desire. But users quickly discover that if too many people fish too quickly, they destroy the fish population and put themselves on the road to (virtual) starvation. Unlike in the real world, *TextFish* then gives visitors a chance to rethink their social strategies after an environmental catastrophe.

Other exhibits give visitors the opportunity to experiment with the Prisoner's Dilemma, a two-person game that has been a cornerstone of research on trust, communication, and risk for decades. At *Career Criminal*, two players in separate booths are each told that they've been arrested for a joint crime. Each can either confess or remain silent. The best outcome for both occurs when both remain silent, because neither provides evidence to the authorities. In that case, both players receive only a year in jail. However,

Figure 3.2.   Visitors at the *TextFish* exhibit. *Source*: Exploratorium.

keeping quiet also makes a player vulnerable: if one remains silent but the other confesses, the confessor goes free and the silent partner spends five years in prison. Although both players know that keeping silent leads to optimal group outcomes, both are also motivated to protect themselves by confessing—and thus both often end up with moderate three-year sentences. This scenario thus turns on how people determine whether they can trust another to act in the pair's *common* interest or whether they should abandon communal effort and seek only personal protection. A sense of empathy with the plight of one's opponent, of course, may be important in such a decision.

Trust Fountain lets players explore the same scenario in a more playful way (figure 3.3). At this two-person drinking fountain, each player decides whether to give a partner a sip of water or a playful squirt. If both choose

Figure 3.3. The *Trust Fountain* exhibit. *Source*: Exploratorium.

Sip, both get a drink. But each also knows that their partner can choose *Squirt* and deliver a jet of water to their partner's chest. Players are thus forced to wonder if they can trust their partner to provide a drink and to consider choosing *Squirt* as an act of self-protection (or revenge). In the end, many pairs jointly choose *Squirt*, and neither receives anything at all. As with *Career Criminal*, empathy (or lack thereof) for the other person's outcome may be a key element in player choices.

Additional exhibits focus participants on other aspects of social interaction involving negotiation, communication, and trust. *Explorations of Social Behavior* displays films illustrating research on impression formation, social norms, helping, cooperation, and other key topics in the behavioral sciences, as well as depictions of social interaction in humans and nonhumans. The *Give and Take Table* is a visitor-managed commons composed of items they themselves provide. Each day, the exhibit is seeded with an inexpensive item, such as a cheap pair of sunglasses, and visitors are prompted to take the item if they wish but asked to replace it with something of equal or greater value. The exhibit therefore reflects the collective social choices of dozens or hundreds of guests. *Donation with Contemplation* is a simple donation box with a twist: there are *three* charitable institutions to which visitors can donate, each of a different type (e.g., an environmental institution, an arts collective, and an animal welfare organization). At *Helping and Wealth*, a set of graphic panels displays methods of studying helping behavior around the world and research on perceptions of wealth distribution. Other SOS exhibits let visitors explore the ease with which random social associations can lead to intense competition and shifting social alliances (*Red/Blue*), work together to keep a virtual creature alive (*Team Snake*), explore their own stereotypical biases and judgments (*Do You Know Who I Am?*, *Sort and Switch*), attempt to answer a series of questions in the same way as a partner with whom they cannot communicate (*Common Knowledge*), and investigate, reflect on, and discuss other aspects of human social behavior (figure 3.4). Many of these exhibits involve empathy for another person's understanding, viewpoint, or feelings, as we will explore later in the chapter.

The team also created and implemented four "Experimonths" in which participants adopted a new social practice for one month and shared and discussed their experiences in an online community. Experimonths gave people the opportunity to experiment with social situations, form and discuss strategies to meet challenges and solve problems, communicate and perhaps come to empathize with strangers, and learn about the scientific study of human behavior. One of the most powerful benefits of the Experimonth model is the increased awareness of how one thinks about social interactions and decisions that occur through exploring a new social behavior for an extended period. By committing to play a public goods

Figure 3.4.   The *Sort and Switch* exhibit. *Source*: Exploratorium.

game every day for a month, for example, participants may think more deeply about their own beliefs about issues of ownership and community and notice connections to those phenomena in their everyday lives.

Experimonths also provided access to a "confessional," an online space where participants could anonymously share their thoughts and feelings. These confessionals established a safe space for community members to express themselves and learn about the actions and emotional responses of others; they also provided much of the data we used to assess the effects of these experiences on participants. (Selected confessional responses to Experimonths are presented later in this chapter.)

Like the *Career Criminal* and *Trust Fountain* exhibits, *Experimonth: Frenemy* (implemented in February 2014) was inspired by the Prisoner's Dilemma (figure 3.5). In this game, players were paired with unknown partners each day. Equipped with only one piece of information about each other and

Figure 3.5. **Payoff matrix for *Experimonth: Frenemy*.** *Source*: Exploratorium.

no way to communicate directly, players decided whether to be "friends" or "enemies." But these choices came with point values: *friending* someone who *friended* you gave each player fifteen points; *friending* someone who *enemied* you gave the enemy-er a whopping twenty-five points but lost the friend-er five points; and if both players *enemied* each other, both got five points. Players thus had to decide whether the risk of playing nicely with a stranger was worth the potential cost and had the opportunity to reflect upon and discuss their choices and reactions through the confessional.

Do You Know What I Know You Know? (April 2014) was conceptually similar to the *Common Knowledge* exhibit. As with *Frenemy*, this game paired players with a different stranger each day and presented a series of questions to each pair (e.g., a map of a wilderness area with the question "You are lost in the woods. Where do you go to be rescued?"). Players needed to come up with the same answer without communicating before proceeding. *Freeloader* (July 2014), based on the Free Rider problem explored in social psychology and behavioral economics, randomly grouped players into teams and gave each player the choice of staying with their teams or leaving to join another group as the month progressed. Each day, players were given one dollar and asked whether or not they wanted to invest their funds in a communal pot that would later be divided equally. As all players—even those who chose not to invest—shared the pot, "freeloading" became an attractive option for some. And in *Belonging* (September 2014), participants posted notices in their communities (primarily clustered in Durham, North Carolina), asking passersby to indicate how much they felt they "belonged" in that spot, and then used those data to create a map illustrating average levels of perceived inclusiveness in that community.

(In addition to exhibits and Experimonths, SOS also generated a set of classroom activities based on core project ideas for free distribution to educators and the public through the project website. More information can be found at http://www.exploratorium.edu/visit/west-gallery/science-of-sharing. Additional information about Experimonths can be found at http://science.experimonth.com/history.)

COGNITIVE RESPONSES TO *SCIENCE OF SHARING*

Approximately one hundred thousand museumgoers have visited the *Science of Sharing* exhibition since it opened at the Exploratorium in October 2014. Museum visitors spent an average of over nine minutes engaged at exhibits, typical for a science museum exhibition of its size. Nearly six hundred people participated in one or more of the project's Experimonths. Results from the project's independent summative evaluation (conducted by Visitor Studies Services) confirm that users found SOS exhibits and Experimonths engaging and thought provoking. Many participants thought extensively about social behaviors, cognitive processes, and perspectives regarding competition, collaboration, and resource sharing, and considered links between these experiences and larger societal challenges involving cooperation, negotiation, and trust. Many users were deeply engaged in personal and social *metacognition*—thinking about how we interpret interpersonal situations, make social decisions and judgments, and categorize people into social groups, cognitive activities that often unfold without conscious awareness. The project's summative evaluation found that 88 percent of exhibition visitors thought about cognitive processes in themselves, friends, family, and even strangers while using the exhibits, and all thirty Experimonth participants interviewed during summative evaluation reported engaging in these metacognitive behaviors as well.

Moreover, we found evidence that Exploratorium visitors in the SOS exhibition engaged in social metacognition more than visitors using exhibits elsewhere in the museum. During the summative evaluation process, the team interviewed two hundred visitors, half in the SOS area and half in galleries devoted to light, sound, and other physical processes. SOS visitors evidenced significantly more metacognition about their own and others' cognitive processes than visitors to the physics exhibits.

Creating experiences that prompted people to become aware of, analyze, and even discuss their own cognitive processes is an end in itself, but *Science of Sharing* was also designed to help people connect these experiences with societal challenges involving cooperative behavior and negotiation, such as resource overuse, environmental destruction, international conflict, and climate change. Evidence from the summative evaluation suggests that SOS exhibits and Experimonths did indeed prompt thinking and discussion about such issues, a process we've called "scaling up" that depends on people examining their own approaches to complex issues like fairness and trust. In addition to learning about current research on cognition and social interaction, SOS thus created new opportunities for the public to investigate factors affecting their own and others' behavior in situations presenting important challenges for our communities.

SCIENCE OF SHARING AND EMPATHETIC RESPONSES

As noted earlier, we found evidence that SOS experiences prompted users to think about their own cognitive processes in social situations and to link their exhibit and Experimonth experiences with larger societal challenges. But does this mean that SOS experiences promoted empathetic responses? Merriam-Webster's defines *empathy* as "the action of understanding, being aware of, being sensitive to, and vicariously experiencing the feelings, thoughts, and experience of another." We argue that two of the key findings from our study of these experiences—social metacognition and scaling up—do indeed demonstrate aspects of empathy related to awareness, understanding, and perhaps even sharing of the thoughts, feelings, and experiences of others.

For example, in addition to exploring their own cognitive and emotional responses to SOS experiences, some exhibition visitors and Experimonth players talked specifically about trying to understand the feelings of others. (Some of the quotations below are from Experimonth confessions; others were obtained in participant interviews during the project's summative evaluation.)

> I found myself getting caught up in [the kids'] anxiety about getting enough fish and there was someone else texting who I couldn't see anywhere which raised the anxiety level. (*Textfish*)

> [Everyone] was coming together or just feeling more good will toward all the other players. (*Frenemy*)

> What I'm learning about this game is that people are just a$$holes. They are mean. I'm friending you and you friend me . . . why not keep it going? You keep me as your enemy even after you clearly see that I'm trying to be friends?? What I'm trying to tell you is that you should not be selfish and friend me next time so we both win. But no, you decide to make me your enemy until the game ends. Why? What have you gained besides more points? Is the objective for you to win at this or to feel good about humanity? You may win at this game, and you clearly beat me, but are you winning in life? Are you winning inside your heart? Do you have compassion for others? (*Frenemy* confession)

> I feel like I see other people as possibly more friendly. . . . There's a lot of bad stuff in the world right now. Definitely the number of people playing that game who played from a friendly state surprised me. And I thought, "Oh, maybe people on the internet are less aggressive than I would have assumed." (*Frenemy*)

Other respondents revealed their attempts to understand other people's thoughts and actions in contexts involving competition, cooperation, and sharing:

> [I learned] that we're all a lot more competitive in our family than I realized. . . . Just that all the kids were really rooting for the team they were on. (*Red/Blue*)

> I think that people probably act differently in this game than they would in real life. I learned that at least in my group of friends that everybody was really good-natured. . . . But, I [had] thought because it's a game they might be more self-serving. (*Freeloader*)

> I also found myself thinking "What was the other person thinking?" I had to make sure she would be cooperative. I had a feeling she would be. (*Career Criminal*)

[I learned] that people you trust are more likely to be nicer. For example, [at the] Trust Fountain—if they're not some random person, but someone you know, you're more likely to get a drink of water rather than a squirt in the face. (*Trust Fountain*)

Some participants focused on the possible effects of kindness on others or on situations in which people appeared to need help, showing their "sensitivity to and vicarious experience" of others' feelings:

I guess putting myself in that position. . . . The person that needed help—I would want someone to help me if I were in that situation and I was surprised that people don't help more . . . because the person is in such obvious need of help. I expected people to be more willing. (*Explorations of Social Behavior*)

Everyone thinks they are quite kind but then you see what they really do like with the Donation Station and Rewind, and they aren't that kind. (*Be Kind, Rewind*)

A friend of mine died the other day. She just got sick and never recovered. It's not supposed to be like that!!!! [My condolences for your friend.] I have only "enemied" once after they chose enemy, and ya know what? I let myself down. I was going to be a friend to all but instead I chose enemy in a moment of REACTION. I'm ashamed of myself. (*Frenemy* confession)

Several SOS experiences were designed to focus users on their own stereotypical judgments and responses. In these cases, participants surveyed in the summative evaluation often thought of how stereotyping and prejudice play out in real-world social situations, showing their "awareness of the thoughts, feelings and experiences of another":

I think there was one where the person drove an SUV or something, and I'm a bus commuter. And I know it's a stereotype of SUVs being selfish, gas-guzzling people, but they were friendly the whole time. But it made me wonder what—who's on the other end of this computer thing. (*Frenemy*)

There were definitely times that it definitely didn't [make me wonder about my opponent], and there were a couple times I was like, "Oh, they're like me," that I definitely felt more sympathetic towards them. I'm not sure that it actually changed my moves, but I definitely felt a kinship to the person who also bicycled to work or a person who had the same political leanings as myself. (*Frenemy*)

During a round, you would see one, like if they're Democratic or Republican or whatnot. And then what kind of car they drive. . . . But I was like, Ach! No, you know, that's why people love tabloids and stuff. It's garbage. I should be focusing on things that are really changing in our world, and how we can change the world for better—no, we like to watch tabloids about Kim Kardashian. It's ridiculous. But that said, it's human nature; we just want to know about the people around us. (*Frenemy*)

In addition to focusing on what others were thinking and feeling in situations like those exemplified by exhibits and Experimonths, some visitors' responses centered on the ethical dimensions of social interactions and how such ethical choices arise in everyday life, again indicating the potential for empathetic awareness of others:

> When they sent out the statistics about the game, I was like, oh, more people want to be friends than they do enemies. I do think about that sometimes. In the news you obviously hear terrible things, but you can always think like more people want to be friends than they do enemies. So there are essentially more good people than there are bad people. We just hear about them. (*Frenemy*)

> I decided to see if over an entire month of games if I could stick with the "high road" and always choose Friend. I have only been mildly tempted to choose Enemy a few times. I am hoping to use this to reinforce my efforts in the real world to do the nice thing vs. the expedient or vengeful thing. (*Frenemy*)

> I freeloaded and feel TERRIBLE. My inbox got out of control at the end of last week and I must have missed the daily report/reminder. I went to play today and saw I was a freeloader. For the first time, I drew comparisons of this game to my work. If I slack off and don't get my part of a project completed, someone else is likely to do it for me, or I just don't get it done. Supporting others or a team requires collective action and responsibility. And in order to do that, I need to stay organized and on top of email apparently. (*Freeloader* confession)

Frenemy players were especially likely to reflect on how they and others thought about competition and cooperation, and how those social interactions played out on broader scales:

> One of the reasons why I was drawn to Frenemy is I feel like it speaks to something that we see in our lives every day. . . . I don't have my own office, I share an office with four other [people], and we work very closely together, and there's a lot of competition. And I guess it sort of made me think about, we all have a choice, whether we choose to engage positively and supportively. . . . I think the more we try to put ourselves ahead individually, it kind of detracts from the movement of the team.

> There was something that happened in the news that did make me think about playing the game, which was that it was, we played the game right around the time that the Olympics were being broadcast, and I thought several times about different interviews I saw with athletes, and how interesting it is that teammates seem to be so close, and there wasn't a whole lot of focus—none that I saw, really—on sort of like nasty competition between teammates. But it did kind of make me think about how, you know, surely they've got [to be competitive]—especially thinking about the Team USA and how supportive athletes appear to be of each other, and I don't know if that's just how the media portrays it; otherwise it's just not a very nice story.

There's a lot of times where we think of situations and we're like, "Oh, if those people get [more], then I won't have as much," but that's usually not really true. Usually, if everyone's doing pretty well, we're all doing better. . . . I was thinking about that while we were playing. . . . There's so much right now that's so polarized—in politics and social policy and people's outlooks. I feel like it's really easy to go down a rabbit hole of, "My side needs to win," or you're looking at ways to mitigate poverty, and people are thinking, "But I'm not gonna have as much if we help people who are destitute." I think it's a really sad approach. When people see it as, "If you have anything, I have less." There's a lot going on now in the world that feels that way.

These comments reveal participants' attempts to make sense of how they themselves and their partners viewed and interpreted complex social experiences. Taken together, they suggest that the interactive exhibits and Experimonths elicited not only analytical interest in the way others think and act, but also empathetic responses, including emotional engagement with others and awareness that people may see and interpret the same experiences quite differently.

Even more optimistically, the comments imply that at least some respondents not only experienced empathy, but also saw the *value* of empathetic responses. Perhaps coming to understand that actively seeking to adopt the perspective of others can lead to better emotional and practical outcomes for all concerned, both in the museum context and in the wider world, can be thought of as a kind of "meta-empathy":

I realized that sometimes you have to take a step back and see how other people feel . . . that you can't just rely on yourself. . . . I think sometimes you have to anticipate how other people think and be open to hearing their ideas and be willing to change.

Science of Sharing showed that it is indeed possible to create museum-based experiences that prompt people not only to experiment with social interactions, but also to seek to understand how others experience those situations and ultimately to feel more connected to them in the process. As one respondent noted during the *Belonging* Experimonth:

I am still that sad person stuck in a small Wyoming town, 500 miles from fitting in. Finding my confession front and center was a little disconcerting. Oddly, I don't know that I felt a part of some community, but taking part in Experimonth does make me feel a part of something. . . . I also have recently begun working in Social Media for a Maker Faire and so seeking out blog posters and editing submissions and posting them, does make me feel a part of that community.

EMPATHY-PROMPTING ASPECTS OF *SCIENCE OF SHARING* EXPERIENCES

What aspects of these activities fostered empathy in participants? Are specific design features critical for promoting or maintaining a sense of empathy in such experiences? We believe at least two aspects of SOS exhibits and Experimonths were key to participants' empathetic awareness or understanding of others' attitudes or thinking processes.

Social interaction is required. These experiences all involve exploring and investigating one's own real-time interactions with others. We believe this may naturally prompt thinking about one's own emotional responses and perhaps generate empathy for the responses of others. How is this achieved? Nearly every SOS exhibit and Experimonth is designed to require two or more people to interact, and their interaction is the explicit focus of the experience. Moreover, many of the exhibits use physical design to communicate that focus on social interaction. For example, many exhibits use a face-to-face architecture in which players sit or stand opposite one another. Cooperative exhibits employ semicircular layouts to promote a mindset of teamwork. Experimonths also employed digital design to convey social interaction, including left-right iconography similar to the face-to-face structure of exhibits.

A safe space for social and emotional exploration. Simply creating opportunities for social interaction is probably not sufficient to generate empathy; participants also need to feel a sense of safety to explore social phenomena openly and nondefensively. We believe that several aspects of SOS exhibits and Experimonths helped to promote feelings of well-being. Exhibits were designed to communicate a spirit of playfulness and whimsy. For example, *Trust Fountain* involves being squirted with water, *Red/Blue* requires slapping large buttons with a satisfying *whap!* to score points, *Be Kind, Rewind* shows a funny animated film, and *Team Snake* requires fast, coordinated action and lively communication for the group to keep the video snake alive. This spirit of fun may take a bit of the sting out of feelings of betrayal, selfishness, and loss that may be elicited at the exhibits, perhaps allowing for more openness to those negative experiences.

Other exhibits support safety through allowing players to see multiple perspectives and thus come to understand that there may be more than one reasonable way to perceive a given situation. At both *Public/Private* and *Making Meaning*, participants sort or choose cards based on their opinions, then reveal their choices to spark a discussion. There are explicitly no right answers; instead, players are given an opportunity to openly share differing values and beliefs. On the other hand, Experimonths created safety through a design feature ubiquitous in the digital world: anonymity. *Frenemy* and *Do*

You Know What I Know? never reveal the identity of players' opponents, and confessionals were completely anonymous. We believe that these design elements—playfulness, multiple perspectives, and anonymity—may help participants relax, open themselves to the underlying social phenomena, and thus build a sense of empathy for others.

These findings offer a compelling and optimistic starting point for the development of new social experiences for museums and other contexts. Ultimately, we also hope that continued experimentation with experiences prompting self-reflection and empathy will assist people in making more cooperative and beneficial choices in their everyday lives.

ACKNOWLEDGMENTS

We would like to thank the members of the *Science of Sharing* team for their work and dedication represented in this chapter. This material is based upon work supported by the National Science Foundation under Grant No. 1114781. Any opinions, findings, and conclusions or recommendations expressed in this material are those of the author(s) and do not necessarily reflect the views of the National Science Foundation.

NOTES

1. A. J. Friedman, "The Evolution of the Science Museum," *Physics Today* (October 2010): 45–51.
2. American Association for the Advancement of Science, *Science for All Americans Project 2061* (Oxford: Oxford University Press, 1990).

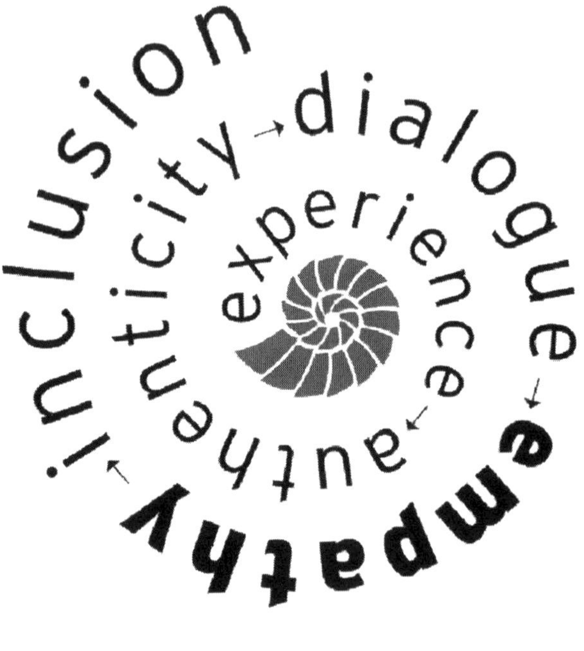
empathy
inclusion
authenticity
dialogue
experience

4

Social Fiction and Catalysts of Change

Enhancing Empathy through *Dialogue Exhibitions*

Orna Cohen and Andreas Heinecke

Let's start from the end. How do we produce evidence that exhibitions at museums or science centers can foster empathy?[1] The importance of fostering empathy is theoretically well understood and broadly discussed, but the question remains: What concrete examples measure an exhibition's impact on visitors in terms of behavioral change, mutual understanding, inclusion of marginalized groups, or openness toward minorities? *Empathy* is a buzzword across all sectors. Exponents in politics (Barack Obama),[2] economics (Jeremy Rifkin),[3] universities (Daniel Goleman),[4] and social entrepreneurship (Bill Drayton)[5] emphasize the importance of empathy to close societal gaps and create open-mindedness, tolerance, and cohesion, especially in times when social bonds seem to be becoming looser and egoism and selfishness more often rule behavior within our society. Empathy as an educational objective is clearly recognized, and since 1994, UNICEF has seen empathy as a basic skill that every child should acquire.[6] Therefore empathy needs to be taught as much as literacy. Why, then, is it so hard to find impactful approaches when the topic is so evident? And why can we identify only a few examples of exhibitions that address the topic and, most importantly, track the impact in the community?

Albert Einstein, well known as a Nobel Prize Laureate in physics, a talented musician, and a devoted fighter for peace and anti-violence, also had important insights into education, but they have remained unknown to the broader public. This is a real pity because we believe that Einstein's statements are fundamental to highlighting the quintessence of education. Some quotes attributed to Einstein may underscore the importance of his findings. Consider these three quotes:

1. "No problem can be solved from the same level of consciousness that created it."
2. "The only source of knowledge is experience."
3. "Education is what remains, after one has forgotten what one has learned in school."[7]

NO PROBLEM CAN BE SOLVED FROM THE SAME LEVEL OF CONSCIOUSNESS THAT CREATED IT

Let's start with the first quote. According to Einstein's insight, and translated in the museum world, a new museology needs to be presented. Objects and showcases have limited capacity to convey behavioral changes, so we need to find a new methodology to design and operate exhibitions. We considered this paradigm shift using the following components:

- At the center is the human being.
- On view are social processes.
- The ruling factor is the dialogue between diverse communities.
- Exhibitions become platforms for encounters.
- Experiences happen in real time and refer to real life.
- Learning intends to change attitude rather than improve knowledge.
- Mediation happens through people of diverse backgrounds.
- The ultimate goal is behavioral change in terms of values, self-conceptualization, and cross-cultural communication.

We describe this new type of exhibition with the overarching term *Dialogue Exhibition* because dialogue is the basic methodology and final objective for fostering empathy and strengthening social relations. Like *empathy, dialogue* is a buzzword, so we need clarification. David Bohm helps us to understand the real meaning of dialogue in his essay *On Dialogue:*

> I give a meaning to the word "dialogue" that is somewhat different from what is commonly used. The derivations of words often help to suggest a deeper meaning. "Dialogue" comes from the Greek word *dialogos. Logos* means "the word," or in our case we would think of the "meaning of the word." And *dia* means "through"—it doesn't mean two. A dialogue can be among any number of people, not just two. Even one person can have a sense of dialogue within himself, if the spirit of the dialogue is present. The picture or image that this derivation suggests is of a *stream of meaning* flowing among and through us and between us. This will make possible a flow of meaning in the whole group, out of which will emerge some new understanding. It's something new, which may not have been in the starting point at all. It's something creative.

And this shared meaning is the "glue" or "cement" that holds people and societies together.

Contrast this with the word "discussion," which has the same root as "percussion" and "concussion." It really means to break things up. It emphasizes the idea of analysis, where there may be many points of view. . . . Discussion is almost like a ping-pong game, where people are batting the ideas back and forth and the object of the game is to win or to get points for yourself. Possibly you will take up somebody else's ideas to back up your own—you may agree with some and disagree with others—but the basic point is to win the game. That's very frequently the case in a discussion.

In a dialogue, however, nobody is trying to win. Everybody wins if anybody wins. There is a different sort of spirit to it. In a dialogue, there is no attempt to gain points, or to make your particular view prevail. Rather, whenever any mistake is discovered on the part of anybody, everybody gains. It's a situation called win-win, in which we are not playing a game against each other but with each other. In a dialogue, everybody wins.[8]

As conceived by Bohm, dialogue is a multifaceted process, looking well beyond typical notions of conversation. It is a process that explores an unusually wide range of experiences and reflects our values, patterns of thought, emotions, or biases. Hence the major challenge of a *Dialogue Exhibition* is to ensure a dialogue between societal groups that usually don't have a chance to meet and give them an opportunity to enter into an open-minded exchange. Because "everybody wins," the speakers have to be guaranteed mutual benefit. Dialogue can be seen as a meta-methodology in the learning process. This refers to Martin Buber's education learning theory. He stated that "the learning community should embody diversity, ambiguity, creative conflicts, honesty, humility, and freedom. However, this can only be achieved with a dialogical method that allows conflicting viewpoints to implicate—highlight and challenge—each other. This inter-human reality signifies a place (mutuality) and calls for an interaction (dialogue)."[9] Bohm and Buber worked closely together to develop a theory of dialogue. It is our attempt to use exhibitions as platforms for encounters to create the prerequisites for a dialogue: a dialogue to foster empathy.

THE ONLY SOURCE OF KNOWLEDGE IS EXPERIENCE

Moving to Einstein's second quote, we already know from Aristotle that "for the things we have to learn before we can do them, we learn by doing them."[10] Benjamin Franklin's famous proverb varied the importance of active involvement: "Tell me and I forget. Teach me and I remember. Involve me and I will learn."[11] This means that the learner plays an active role and isn't a passive receiver. He must be open to being actively involved in the process and able to reflect upon the experience. Hence the learning process is based on two pillars: the emotional part, with an immersive experience, and the cognitive part, where an analysis takes place to conceptualize the experience. For museums, certainly, John Dewey became one of the most famous proponents of hands-on or experiential learning. He argued that "if knowledge comes from impressions made upon us by natural objects, it is impossible to procure knowledge without the use of objects, which impress the mind."[12] The combination of experiential learning and dialogue-based reflection are the two main components of *Dialogue Exhibitions*, which we describe in the following section.

It might be of interest for the reader to know that the initial motivation for creating *Dialogue Exhibitions* didn't come from people who were working in or for museums. The beginning of the development was based on the assumption that exhibitions may work as catalysts to change people's general biases when it comes to disability. As a matter of fact, people with disabilities are still second-class citizens who face discrimination and exclusion, lower income, higher unemployment rates, and unequal education, etc.[13] The interaction between people with and without disabilities is often hindered by stereotypes, fears, avoidance, and prejudice. There is a gap between *us* and *them*, so it is of utmost importance to reverse these deeply held prejudices and the pity harbored for people with disabilities. Hence, in developing the *Dialogue Exhibitions*, it was key to include affected people as facilitators and to bring them into a position where they could act as ambassadors for their own cause. This guarantees an authentic encounter and a dialogue that goes beyond the pure experience in the exhibition. Thus the social impact comes first. We started from the end and the only objective was to generate social change for people with disabilities and for the general audience, who usually isn't affected directly or indirectly by disability. The origins of this social venture with *Dialogue Exhibitions* date back to the late 1980s and so have enriched the social and cultural landscape for the last twenty-eight years. It hasn't lost its attraction in that time. *Dialogue Exhibitions* have spread to 170 cities in thirty-nine countries and have been a catalyst for several people to invest in the idea by opening their own museum-like centers to host *Dialogue Exhibitions*. Every year, approximately seven hundred thousand people experience *Dialogue Exhibitions*; the impact on these people will be described later.[14] But first, what do *Dialogue Exhibitions* look like?

Dialogue in the Dark: An Exhibition to Discover the Unseen

The concept of *Dialogue in the Dark*[15] is simple: visitors are led by guides who are blind in small groups through specially constructed dark rooms in which scents, sounds, wind, temperature, and textures convey the characteristics of daily environments; for example, a park, a city, a boat cruise, or a bar (figure 4.1). Daily routines become a new experience. A reversal of roles is created: people who can see are taken out of their familiar environment. People who are blind provide them with security and a sense of orientation by transmitting to them a world without pictures.

Dialogue in the Dark is not supposed to convey what it is to be blind. To say *blind means black* would be a gross oversimplification and would not at all correspond to the real-life situation of people who are blind, as only 5 percent worldwide see pure black. The other 95 percent have extremely different forms of blindness and impaired vision. Hence the darkness has to be understood as a metaphor referring to the social reality of people who are blind and experience discrimination; social exclusion; prejudice; and unequal opportunities in society, education, and the labor market. Thus they are also a representative example for other fringe groups *who stand in the dark*. Darkness, however, is also an ideal medium for communication. In the darkness, appearance and status symbols don't count, and this makes room for unprejudiced encounters. *Dialogue in the Dark*'s visitors are also connected through the strong emotionality of the experience, something that gives rise to mutual support and a shared basis for communication. Dialogue is of utmost importance because whoever does not speak does not exist. Social distance disappears and solidarity is born: people are not judged and labeled quickly but are instead given the chance to express themselves and their values during conversation. This happens naturally

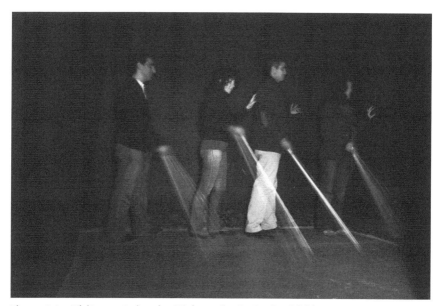

Figure 4.1. Visitors entering the *Dialogue in the Dark* exhibition. *Source*: DSE.

first and foremost with people who are blind, as they are the people visitors talk with most in these surroundings. Participants in the exhibition develop empathy for and understanding of people with disabilities and gain an expanded awareness of human variety.

Apart from this social dialogue, *Dialogue in the Dark* strives to stimulate reflection about identity and perception. Dialogue with oneself starts no later than when a visitor enters the complete darkness, leaves familiar ground, and experiences limitations. Frustrations arise and this makes room for new assessments, whether of the experience of strong emotional feelings, one's own limitations, or the discovery of other senses. There is also the humbling joy of fresh appreciation for one's eyesight. A mere one-hour visit is often enough for visitors to discover several unexpected things inside them.

Dialogue in Silence: An Exhibition on Nonverbal Communication

The second exhibition, *Dialogue in Silence*,[16] follows the same principles as *Dialogue in the Dark*. The setting is a soundproof room in monochromatic white and visitors wear a sound-canceling headset (figures 4.2–4.4). Total silence cannot be simulated in the same way as total darkness, but with soft carpets, sound-absorbing wall surfaces, and the highly efficient headset, the immersion works. The hearing audience is instructed before entering the exhibition not to speak but to enter into only nonverbal dialogue with the guide, who is deaf. People quickly learn to listen with their eyes and express themselves with their hands, face, and body. *Dialogue in Silence* does not intend to simulate deafness or teach sign language. The objective is to widen the understanding of communication, improve visual perception, and bring together people who are deaf and who are hearing to demonstrate that they can communicate against all odds. People who are deaf are the ambassadors of deaf culture and experts in nonverbal communication. The exhibition doesn't present deafness as a deficit. Rather, it conveys the beauty and potential of visual-based communication and helps the hearing public to sneak into the shoes of people with deafness. The exhibition itself is structured with different rooms, each dedicated to one topic in nonverbal communication and titled *Dance of the Hands*, *Gallery of Faces*, *Play of Signs*, and *Forum of Figures*. The last room of this one-hour journey is the *Dialogue Room*. Here visitors take off their headset and, with the support of a sign-language interpreter, can dialogue with the guide. A lively discussion starts about the guide's life, background, daily opportunities and challenges of being deaf, and hopes and ambitions.

Dialogue in Silence forces people to move out of their comfort zone. It's challenging to follow the visual instructions, capture signs, and improve facial expressions. However, with the support of their guide, people gain more and more self-esteem and communicate nonverbally in a joyful way.

Figure 4.2. Visitors working on their facial expressions in the *Gallery of Faces* of the *Dialogue in Silence* Exhibition. *Source*: G2 Baraniak.

Figure 4.3. A guide who is deaf presenting the *Play of Signs* of *Dialogue in Silence*. *Source*: G2 Baraniak.

Figure 4.4. Young visitors with a guide who is deaf in the *Dialogue in Silence* Exhibition. *Source*: G2 Baraniak.

A completely different communication system is conveyed, and people who had never before had contact with a deaf individual are encouraged to overcome their hesitations and insecurities about talking in a different way.

In some locations, both *Dialogue in the Dark* and *Dialogue in Silence* are displayed. This generates another level of inclusion because it's quite rare for people who are deaf and people who are blind to work together. Thus not only is empathy fostered between people with and without disability, but mutual understanding is also enhanced across different disability communities.

Dialogue with Time: An Exhibition on the Art of Aging

The third *Dialogue Exhibition* tackles the topic of aging. *Dialogue with Time*[17] intends to foster intergenerational dialogue and overcome prejudices, wrong assumptions, or stereotypes regarding old age. Guides, age seventy and above, lead visitors through the exhibition and act as facilitators with their expertise in various aspects of aging (figures 4.5 and 4.6).

Growing old is primarily perceived as a decline, and the broader understanding highlights the downside of old age, such as physical and mental limitations, isolation, dependency, and irreversible illnesses. But old age can also be seen as an asset, and we believe that exhibitions can convey a new understanding and change the mindset. *Dialogue with Time* has the

Figure 4.5. Visitors sharing their opinions about happy aging in the *Dialogue with Time* exhibition. *Source*: G2 Baraniak.

potential, on one hand, to act as an important basis for raising awareness of the basic human conditions that elderly people deserve, and on the other hand, to reduce the fear of growing old in a society focused on youthfulness.

The same design principles as in the first two *Dialogue Exhibitions* come into play. *Dialogue with Time* is an immersive environment and the facilitation is through affected individuals. Like the others, it is a walk-through exhibition, and the audience is led in small groups through different stations that address various topics of aging and allow visitors to grasp a different understanding of age and aging far beyond textbooks. But more importantly, the stations in *Dialogue with Time* give the facilitators great entry points to start the dialogue. Six rooms refer to different facets of age and aging:

- Prologue: Aging is a natural process.
- Dialogue room 1: Aging as a personal matter.
- The yellow salon: The diversity of aging—limitations.
- The pink salon: The diversity of aging—assets.
- Dialogue room 2: The future of aging.
- Epilogue: It's never too late.

The senior citizen guides guarantee an authentic encounter and stimulate dialogue by sharing their experience of growing old.

Figure 4.6. A young visitor experiences limitations in walking with the help of a senior guide in the yellow salon of the *Dialogue with Time* exhibition. *Source*: Bert Bostelmann.

Dialogue Exhibitions in a Nutshell

All *Dialogue Exhibitions* have in common an immersive environment, the visitor as both object and subject of the exhibition, and a role reversal where people marginalized because they are blind, deaf, or elderly become superior in the setting while the visitors have to cope with their limitations. The final objective is to set up a platform for encounters where people feel comfortable to dialogue.

Due to the dissemination of *Dialogue Exhibitions* around the world, approximately ten million people's perspectives toward *otherness* may have been changed. And at least ten thousand people with disabilities and senior citizens have been given a stage to enter into dialogue and foster empathy with an audience.[18]

EDUCATION IS WHAT REMAINS, AFTER ONE HAS FORGOTTEN WHAT ONE HAS LEARNED IN SCHOOL

Finally, let's take Einstein's third quote and set it in relation to exhibitions and the impact on visitors. What remains after visitors have been to an exhibition? As we know, exhibition goers are mainly motivated to share time

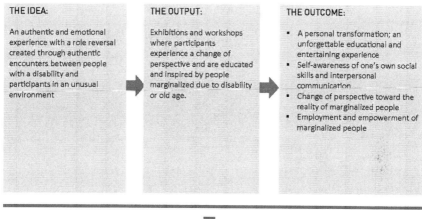

THE IDEA:	THE OUTPUT:	THE OUTCOME:
An authentic and emotional experience with a role reversal created through authentic encounters between people with a disability and participants in an unusual environment	Exhibitions and workshops where participants experience a change of perspective and are educated and inspired by people marginalized due to disability or old age.	• A personal transformation; an unforgettable educational and entertaining experience • Self-awareness of one's own social skills and interpersonal communication • Change of perspective toward the reality of marginalized people • Employment and empowerment of marginalized people

THE SOCIAL IMPACT:

• Awareness about people with disabilities and elderly people, their needs, potential, and contributions, leading to inclusive behavior
• Improvement of the socio-economic conditions of marginalized people.

Figure 4.7. Social Value Chain of *Dialogue Exhibitions*.

with friends and family while visiting an exhibition, and they are eager to learn more about interesting topics. But what remains after an exhibition visit, especially when the topic is about empathy? How do we track the impact and measure how visitors develop more empathy for marginalized people? What's the distinction between outcome and impact?

In our understanding, and related to the museum context, the outcome reflects a visitor's feelings, thoughts, and insights immediately after visiting the exhibition, whereas the impact goes beyond. Impact tracks changes in a visitor's behavior as a result of visiting the exhibition. Impact can lead to direct actions. The tools to measure outcome are well known: questionnaires, evaluation forms, or face-to-face interviews. Some of us analyze guestbooks and other spontaneous expressions after visitors have been to an exhibition. The tools to measure impact generally need more resources, such as the comparison of a visitor's answers before and after the visit or a long-term survey with follow-up phone calls, interviews, and questionnaires from one to five years after the exhibition visit. An important component is to compare the answers of visitors with a control group (nonvisitors).

In the last fifteen years, we have been working on measuring the outcome and impact of *Dialogue Exhibitions* and have used most of the tools described here. Currently, we have received data from more than forty surveys administered in ten countries (United Kingdom, Germany, France, Finland, Denmark,

Israel, India, Hong Kong, Japan, and Mexico) with more than five thousand people contributing to the results. We have accumulated enough data to enable us to draw a social value chain of *Dialogue Exhibitions* (figure 4.7).

Dialogue Exhibitions Are a Transformative Experience

The countless *Dialogue Exhibition* guestbooks slumbering in our archives are irrefutable proof of the fact that visitors, after coming out of the exhibition, have a strong need to voice their feelings and thoughts. More than 98 percent of all comments are positive. The adjectives used to describe the exhibition are mostly superlatives: super, fantastic, marvelous, indescribable, unforgettable, unusual, fascinating, sensational, and unique. Other general comments include "an intensive experience," "an exceptional experience!" "demanding, but enjoyable!" "another dimension, a thought-provoking experience!" and "impressive encounter!"

Many visitors record the transformative nature of the experience. After experiencing *Dialogue in the Dark*, visitors have written "an impressive experience which moves seeing into a different dimension" and "this experience has enriched me tremendously."[19] Comments following *Dialogue in Silence* have included "it is not the same any more," "it opens another world," "it gives me wings," "it pushes me to reflect," "I feel enriched," "this show is changing my life," and "I understood something completely new that was totally impossible one hour ago."[20]

We see two main reasons being responsible for this transformation, namely that *Dialogue Exhibitions* raise self-awareness and offer authentic encounters.

Dialogue Exhibitions Raise Self-Awareness

In *Dialogue with Time*, 40 percent of visitors declare that the exhibition serves as a catalyst to rethink their way of life.[21] They think about their presence and future ("What can I do now to prepare for this phase of my life?"), start planning for the future ("How to live a good life in the future? How to prepare for retirement?"), and reflect upon the process of aging with its positive and negative outcomes. Most importantly, the fear of aging is reduced, as shown in visitor feedback: "Age is not a number but a state of mind." "I'm sorry that our society defines old age according to number and not according to skills and abilities." "Aging has a lot of faces. How amazing it is to stay young at 75." "Aging is a phase of life and I am ready to face it." "With all the fears regarding being old, it is more frightening not to become old."[22]

In *Dialogue in Silence*, visitors discover their capability to express themselves nonverbally: "I did not know that my hands could be so talkative."

"I discovered a hidden part of myself." "We are hearing but our bodies are dumb." "It is the discovery of the day! My eyes spoke, it's true." "What a pleasure to talk differently and what a richness!"[23]

Through the temporary withdrawal of sight in *Dialogue in the Dark*, visitors gain a deep understanding about the value of vision and the importance of one's eyesight: "Only now do we appreciate being able to see." "I hope I always remember how happy I am to be able to see." "I feel a deep gratitude to have the gift of sight."

This immersion into darkness awakens the discovery of nonvisual senses: "I could feel so many things by touch, quite wonderful." "It was very impressive, seeing without looking!" "In future I shall be more conscious of my other senses (they don't come as a matter of course)."[24]

Furthermore, the experience in the dark stimulates a deep self-reflection of one's own social skills and interpersonal communication: "Being in the dark opened my eyes to seeing many qualities in me and others that I didn't know." "It's highly recommended to everyone, especially for those who don't listen well [to experience this] unique way in which to learn about different means of communication." "It is a unique experience that enhances the understanding of the rapid changes in environment."[25]

Dialogue Exhibitions Offer Authentic Encounters

Almost 50 percent of visitors express their deepest gratitude after leaving a *Dialogue Exhibition*. This need to express gratitude is rare compared with feedback from other types of exhibitions. For example, 78 percent of *Dialogue in the Dark* visitors explicitly mention the individual who was guiding them through the dark: "Thank you very much, Jürgen. I was afraid when I went in, and found I could relax in a dark world." "Many thanks, Mandy! The tour was super! It was nice to get to know you a little better." "Jens, the guide, was really cool and friendly! I shall come again! Don't forget me."[26]

In *Dialogue in Silence* and *Dialogue with Time*, more than 40 percent of guestbook entries show deep appreciation for the tour guide: "Very nice tour by the wonderful Mrs. Schneider!" "Thank you! The guide has been very friendly, competent, and authentic." "Many thanks for this interesting, innovative exhibition! Mrs. Mönch has guided me very professionally and endearingly. Thank you."[27]

The interaction with the senior citizen guide is a personal and crucial experience in *Dialogue with Time*. We found that 85 percent of the audience rate the encounter as "excellent," and 30 percent explicitly appreciate Dialogue room 1 and in particular the guide's personal presentation and the shared time. This authentic encounter connects people and creates an emotional bond, as all *Dialogue Exhibitions* show: "It is an interactive experience with 'experts' who know what they are talking about." "Sometimes people are more convincing than things." "To have the senior guide at our side is a good idea. It makes sense that especially younger people understand what will change in the future regarding demographics."

The authentic encounter remains the key experience for visitors over the long term. Five years after visiting *Dialogue in the Dark*, 76 percent of visitors remember talking to the guide and have very clear memories about the encounter, and 11 percent even remember their guide's name.[28]

Dialogue Exhibitions Enhance Empathy

Using exhibitions as a platform for an authentic encounter in an immersive environment can change people's perspectives about *otherness* and help them develop empathy. *Dialogue in the Dark* is a physical and intellectual tour of discovery in the world of people who are blind. After experiencing the exhibition, 46 percent of the audience expresses empathy for people with blindness. Visitors gain insight into the difficulties faced and better understand what it means to *survive* without eyesight in a visually dominated world. We have received such comments as: "1,000 steps in the dark have brought me a big step closer to the world of the visually impaired." "Thank you for the impressions which have shown me a lot, and what difficulties there are if you can't see." "After this visit I have a better understanding of the blind people with whom I have to deal through my job." "For the first time I imagine having a blind child . . . from now on I can imagine it." "This exhibition is more important for a mutual understanding than one can guess beforehand." "The exhibition is an excellent contribution when it comes to dealing with disability. I got a lot out of it."[29]

Dialogue in Silence generates an equal impact. Some visitors go further in their reflection and point out that this exhibition is a "lesson in tolerance." Their comments include considerable reflection about stereotypes and prejudice and show that *Dialogue in Silence* helps to raise empathy and respect for people who are different. For example: "We should be more open to each other." "A great lesson of humility, that helped us overcome the prejudices of the hearing people." "I will understand better human kind after leaving this place." "This helps us to see the conditions under which a deaf persons lives."[30]

In *Dialogue with Time*, 25 percent of visitors' reflections are about empathy and the recognition of old people. Those who experience *Dialogue with Time* gain a clear understanding of age being an asset, as well as a sense of the possible limits: "I learnt to appreciate the values of the senior citizens." "Old people are an asset in the society and need to be respected accordingly." "The exhibition shows in a nice way that old people are still part of the society and it is very important to understand that."[31]

These outcomes aren't only for the short term. As our long-term surveys show, *Dialogue Exhibitions* lead to a shift in mindset and to inclusive behavior. Five years after visiting *Dialogue in the Dark*, 58 percent of visitors confirm that their attitude and behavior toward visually impaired people, and the handicapped population in general, have changed since visiting the exhibition. Seventy-six percent state that the encounter with their guide stays forever in their memory, while 88 percent remember in detail the conversation with their guide in the dark bar.[32]

The long-term survey for *Dialogue in Silence* shows the same results. The exhibition is recognized as important for society, with 90 percent of visitors stating that the exhibition achieved the objective of changing stigmas and prejudices concerning the deaf.[33] Specific comments have included "this helps us to see the conditions under which a deaf person lives" and "this handicap must be hard to bear in our society."

Visitors define deafness differently before and after experiencing *Dialogue in Silence*. In a survey before entering the exhibition, 81 percent state clearly that deafness is a disability and use words like handicap, loneliness, exclusion, difficulty, and emptiness. After the tour, only 39 percent define deafness as a disability, and new words are used, such as communication, expression, observation, another world, difference, and even asset.[34]

On behalf of the Israeli Ministry of Social Affairs and Social Services, we facilitated another research study because the Ministry questioned whether visitors to *Dialogue in the Dark* actually change their attitude toward people who are blind. Hence they asked for a study that included a control group of nonvisitors to determine any differences in views about people with blindness in terms of social and labor integration.

The research shows clearly that individuals who had visited *Dialogue in the Dark* were much more open to hiring a blind lawyer, accepting a blind manager, or being friends with a person who is visually impaired. People who haven't experienced the exhibition primarily felt pity and couldn't imagine having any interaction with the blind.[35] This research gives proof that the public's perceptions regarding disability can be changed through an exhibition.

Dialogue Exhibitions Improve Life for Guides

Last but not least, it is important to underscore the fact that *Dialogue Exhibitions* fundamentally change the way people with disabilities or senior citizens view themselves. *Dialogue Exhibitions* have great influence in developing the personalities and identities of staff members. Being a guide changes an individual's self-perception and their relationship with the population and also increases self-esteem. People who are blind, deaf, or elderly gain strength from acting as a guide, increase their competence

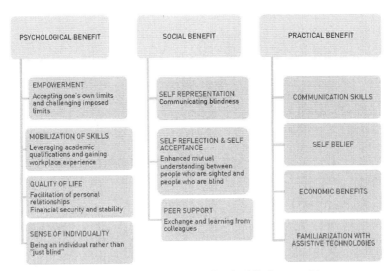

Figure 4.8.   Benefits of *Dialogue in the Dark* for the blind tour guides.

at communicating, take responsibility, work together in a team, and learn to defend their interests. Earning an income helps them to be independent and strengthens respect from family and friends. For many guides, working for *Dialogue in the Dar*k or *Dialogue in Silence* is their first paid job. They gain experience and qualifications, which can be useful in the labor market independent of *Dialogue Exhibitions*. Disabled people change from passive receivers of welfare to active contributors to society and are able to live a self-determined life. For the elderly guides, there is the chance to share their experience with the younger population, as well as increase their income.

An international survey by SHM Social Science Survey Institute in London, England, tracked the long-term impact for forty-five blind guides of *Dialogue in the Dark* in six countries: Israel, Mexico, Germany, Austria, the United Kingdom, and Italy. The study traced the guides' histories over ten years starting from before they were involved in the exhibition to figure out what had changed for them through their engagement with *Dialogue in the Dark*. The social and economic improvement results are shown in figure 4.8.[36]

CONCLUSION

We have provided evidence that *Dialogue Exhibitions* are a catalyst for social change, and they can foster more than just empathy. Measurable achievements are:

- Employing people with disabilities in the regular workforce through *Dialogue Exhibitions*;[37]
- Encouraging people with disabilities and senior citizens to start their own social ventures;[38]
- Attracting the capital of private investors to build their own museums for *Dialogue Exhibitions*;[39]
- Increasing the number of permanent Dialogue centers;[40]
- Increasing the number and range of "copycat" or similar events;[41]
- Receiving more than twenty-five awards and recognitions;
- Contributing to scientific reflection and publications; and
- Realizing an international rollout over all continents.

Even after twenty-eight years of operating *Dialogue Exhibitions*, the peak has yet to be reached. For us, it is of utmost importance that the exhibition not be self-referential. It is crucial to track subsequent activities to prove that social change can happen through exhibitions.

Let's start from the beginning: Originally, museums were seen as temples for the Muses to worship beauty and inhale the holy breath. This sounds a bit outdated, and we quickly imagine a Greek pantheon with stone sculptures, mainly of strong bearded men and half-naked women. Yet this image comprises the quintessence of a museum's present responsibilities. Museums are places to inspire people, but not only in terms of the arts, literature, or science. A museum's contemporary function should be to inspire reflection on one's inter- and intrapersonal skills and to open perspectives about how to benefit society and commit to social responsibility. This function includes promoting empathy, which shouldn't stay just as an aspirational objective.

Exhibitions offer untapped potential for communicating social information, correcting misconceptions, and improving attitudes, emotional intelligence, and cognitive skills. As Chandler Screven writes, "Learning is voluntary and self-directed in such informal settings. There are no grades, no top-down control, and there is no reason to pay attention except for its own sake. Learning is foremost driven by curiosity, discovery, free exploration and the sharing of experiences with companions."[42] An increase of knowledge and skills happens in a playful manner, and the serious and critical content is not obvious. Consequently, there is no pressure to understand anything, and a change of attitude, shift of perspective, or overcoming of prejudices may happen automatically. But often museums are an optional resource in education. Exhibitions are nice and good to have, but not "must-haves." Formal and informal education run concurrently, and the intersections between educational institutions and museums have space for improvement. Two plausible scenarios for the future of museum education can be shaped, according to Katherine Prince, senior director of KnowledgeWorks, as "a *vibrant learning grid* in which all of us who care about learning create a flexible and radically personalized learning ecosystem that meets the needs of all learners, or a *fractured landscape* in which only those whose families have the time, money and resources to customize or supplement their learning journeys have access to learning that adapts to and meets their needs."[43]

In a vibrant learning grid, museums, libraries, and other cultural institutions and community-based learning providers work together. Supported by social enterprises, social services, nongovernmental organizations, the municipality, and corporations, such important subjects as the promotion of empathy can be leveraged. Museums have an additional task: they are stakeholders in an expanded educational ecosystem and influence learners and teachers by offering new learning landscapes. Learning agents from a variety of backgrounds support the learners and teachers in customizing and carrying out their learning journeys. These learning agents represent diverse communities and guarantee authenticity in the mediation of content. This content isn't focused on knowledge or skills though. Rather, the mediation aims to change behavior and foster empathy, which lead to an inclusive society.

According to Paula Gangopadhyay, chief learning officer for the Henry Ford Foundation and member of the National Museum and Library Service Board, "the power of museums as a whole isn't harnessed yet. The landscape of museums, libraries, and traditional or nontraditional learning spaces is still fragmented. Many efforts are running concurrently without any coordination."[44] Efforts need to be streamlined to enhance empathy, stimulate compassion, and utilize exhibitions as catalysts for social change. Hopefully this book will give an overview of the many initiatives working to reach a single goal: to encourage executives from museums and inspire exhibition makers to use their influence and creativity to foster empathy. But museums cannot do it alone. A new educational ecosystem is needed with new players and innovative ideas. Museums can widen their scope. They can become social labs, promote social fiction, and serve as resource centers for community work. We leave you with a quote from Henry Ford, one that we found appropriate to the work we have gathered: "Coming together is the beginning. Working together is progress. Staying together is success."[45]

NOTES

1. As empathy is often used as a synonym for sympathy or compassion, we need to give a definition. Here are two: "Empathy has been proposed to be the ability to perceive the meaning and feelings of another and to communicate those feelings to the other person" (Jane Stein-Parbury, "Patient and Person: Developing

Inter-personal Skills in Nursing," *Western Journal of Nursing Research* no. 8 [2005]: 329–42). "Empathy furthermore is the state of perceiving the internal frame of reference of another person, with accuracy and with emotional components and meanings that pertain to it, as if one were with the other person, but without the loss of the as-if condition" (Carl Rogers, "A Theory of Therapy, Personality, and Inter-personal Relationships, as Developed in the Client-centered Framework," in *Psychology: A Study of a Science*, ed. Sigmund Koch [New York: McGraw Hill, 1959], 111–28).

2. An article in *The Guardian* stated, "According to Barack Obama, the 'empathy deficit' is a more pressing political problem for America than the federal deficit and holds the key to the success of his second term as he seeks to build bridges with Republicans and tackle the wave of horrific shootings that last year disfigured American communities from Colorado to Connecticut." Mark Honigsbaum, "Barack Obama and the 'Empathy Deficit,'" *The Guardian*, 2013, https://www.theguardian.com/science/2013/jan/04/barack-obama-empathy-deficit (accessed January 15, 2016).

3. Rifkin considers the latest phase of communication and energy regimes—that of electronic telecommunications and fossil fuel extraction—as bringing people together on the nation-state level based on democratic capitalism, but at the same time creating global problems, like climate change, pandemics, and nuclear proliferation. Rifkin extrapolates the observed trend into the future, predicting that Internet and mobile technology along with small-scale renewable energy commercialization will create an era of distributed capitalism necessary to manage the new energy regime and a heightened global empathy that can help solve global problems. See Jeremy Rifkin, *The Empathetic Civilization: The Race of Global Consciousness in a World in Crisis* (New York: Penguin Group, 2010).

4. Goleman writes, "Self-absorption in all its forms kills empathy, let alone compassion. When we focus on ourselves, our world contracts as our problems and preoccupations loom large. But when we focus on others, our world expands. Our own problems drift to the periphery of the mind and so seem smaller, and we increase our capacity for connection—or compassionate action." Daniel Goleman, *Emotional Intelligence: Why It Can Matter More than IQ* (New York: Bantam Books, 1996), 54.

5. In a public speech, Bill Drayton said, "The single most important skill that every person must have today is empathy" (June 23, 2014, Ryerson University, Toronto, Canada).

6. World Health Organization, Division of Mental Health, *Life Skills Education for Children and Adolescents in Schools. Pt. 1, Introduction to Life Skills for Psychosocial Competence. Pt. 2, Guidelines to Facilitate the Development and Implementation of Life Skills Programmes* (Geneva: World Health Organization, 1994), http://apps.who.int/iris/handle/10665/63552#sthash.QX9Es6Lb.dpuf.

7. The origins of the three quotes could not be clearly established. Our only reference is Brainy Quote, http://www.brainyquote.com/quotes/authors/a/albert_einstein.html (accessed January 15, 2016).

8. David Bohm, ed., *On Dialogue* (London: Routledge, 1996), 6.

9. Kenneth Paul Kramer, *Learning Through Dialogue: The Relevance of Martin Buber's Classroom* (Lanham: Rowman and Littlefield Education, 2013), 14.

10. Aristotle, *Nicomachean Ethics*, trans. J. A. K. Thomson (London: Penguin Group, 1953), 159.

11. There are some who say this is originally a Chinese proverb, but it is generally attributed to Benjamin Franklin.

12. John Dewey, *Democracy and Education: An Introduction to the Philosophy of Education* (New York: WLC Books, 2009), 217–18.

13. "Disability and Socioeconomic Status," *American Psychological Association*, 2006, http://www.apa.org/pi/ses/resources/publications/factsheet-disability.pdf (accessed January 15, 2016).

14. The annual impact is tracked through different performance measurement tools, such as SRS (social reporting standard) or SROI (social return on investment), as well as, for example, number of visitors, number of sites, employees, media coverage, revenues, and special acknowledgments.

15. *Dialogue in the Dark* is the brainchild of Andreas Heinecke. Since its launch in 1988, the exhibition has been disseminated by social franchises throughout the world. Hundreds of copycats have built up their own ventures based on *Dialogue in the Dark* and have enhanced the social impact significantly. http://www.dialogue-in-the-dark.com (accessed January 15, 2016).

16. *Dialogue in Silence* is a cocreation of Orna Cohen and Andreas Heinecke. After various pre-versions, it was launched in 2006 at Cité des Sciences et l'Industrie in Paris and has since been showcased around the world. http://www.dialogue-in-silence.com (accessed January 15, 2016).

17. *Dialogue with Time* is a cocreation of Orna Cohen and Andreas Heinecke. It was first presented at the Israeli Children's Museum in Holon in 2012. The concept was then adapted for Germany and shown in Frankfurt and Berlin. In March 2016, the first presentation in Asia took place at the National Taiwan Science Education Center, Taipei. http://www.dialogue-with-time.com (accessed January 15, 2016).

18. The dissemination across the world was steered by a social entrepreneurial mindset without governmental support or private donations. In 2015 alone, *Dialogue Exhibitions and Workshops* were hosted in Europe (Germany, Austria, Switzerland, the United Kingdom, Italy, Russia, Turkey, Greece), Asia (Israel, India, Malaysia, Philippines, China, Hong Kong, Taiwan, South Korea, Japan, Thailand, Singapore), the Americas (the United States, Brazil, Argentina), and Africa (Rwanda, Kenya). In 2016, the launch of *Dialogue in the Dark* in Australia is scheduled.

19. Orna Cohen, *Dialogue in the Dark: What Are Its Consequences and How Can They Be Proved? An Evaluation of the Exhibition Dialogue in the Dark* (Hamburg: 2006): 22, www.dialogue-in-the-dark.com/files/DiD_VisitorsEvaluation_2006.pdf (accessed January 15, 2016).

20. Orna Cohen and Andreas Heinecke, "Scenes of Silence: An Exhibition to Break Down Mental Prejudices," *Visitor Studies Today* 8, no. 3 (2004): 15, http://vsa.matrix.msu.edu/vst.php (accessed January 15, 2016).

21. Dialogue Social Enterprise, *Dialogue with Time, Visitors' Feedback* (Frankfurt: Museum of Communication, 2015).

22. Orna Cohen, *Dialogue with Time, The Outcome: First Results at the Israeli Children's Museum*, Evaluation Report (2012), 20.

23. Cohen, "Scenes of Silence," 15.

24. Cohen, *Dialogue in the Dark*, 22.

25. Dialogue Social Enterprise, *Dialogue in the Dark Workshops: Long Term Survey*, Evaluation Report (2010).

26. Cohen, *Dialogue in the Dark*, 22.

27. Dialogue Social Enterprise, *Dialogue with Time: Guestbook Analyzed Quotes* (Frankfurt: Museum of Communication, 2014).

28. Cohen, *Dialogue in the Dark Exhibition: Long Term Survey*, Evaluation Report (2005).

29. Cohen, *Dialogue in the Dark*, 22.

30. Cohen, "Scenes of Silence," 15.

31. Cohen, *Dialogue with Time*.

32. Cohen, *Dialogue in the Dark Exhibition*.

33. Midgam, *Visitors' Stands and Satisfaction from Dialogue in Silence Exhibition*, Submitted to the Israeli Ministry of Social Affairs and Social Services (2008).

34. Sophie Pité, *Scénes des Silence—Y-a-t-il changement de représentations des sourd?* Master's thesis (Paris VIII, 2004).

35. Midgam, *Impact Research Report: Dialogue in the Dark*, Submitted to the Israeli Ministry of Social Affairs and Social Services (2008).

36. Maurice Biriotti, *Keeping the Dialogue Going. An Evaluation and Outcomes for Guides Employed by Dialogue in the Dark Worldwide* (London: SHM London, 2007).

37. In 2015, *Dialogue in the Dark* India placed 1,500 people with disabilities in the work force, http://www.dialogueinthedarkindia.com/take1/about-take-1.html (accessed January 10, 2016).

38. The best example is the dark restaurant *Blinde Kuh* in Zurich, Switzerland. A team of people with blindness, who had worked for *Dialogue in the Dark*, established their own venture more than ten years ago, http://www.blindekuh.ch/restaurant-in-the-dark-blindekuh-zurich.html (accessed January 15, 2016).

39. In Seoul, the founder of Naver Corporation, Kim Sang-Hun, built a museum from scratch for *Dialogue in the Dark*, http://www.dialogueinthedark.co.kr/index.nhn (accessed January 15, 2016). Other private investors are in Hong Kong, Tokyo, Hyderabad, and Istanbul.

40. Permanent *Dialogue Exhibitions* are operating in Hamburg (since 2000), Frankfurt (2005), Holon (2004), Milan (2005), Hong Kong (2010), Tokyo (2001), Seoul (2010), Bangkok (2010), Singapore (2009), and Hyderabad (2011).

41. There are countless events, workshops, and dinner activities that take place in the dark around the globe. Darkness has become a movement, and the impact goes far beyond our own activities.

42. Chandler Screven, *Museums and Informal Education*, CMS Bulletin 1, no.1 (1993), http://www.infed.org/archives/e-texts/screven-museums.htm (accessed January 15, 2016).

43. Katherine Prince, "Glimpses of the Future of Education," in *Building the Future of Education: Museums and the Learning Ecosystem* (Center for the Future of Museums, American Alliance of Museums, 2014), 14–15.

44. Paula Gangopadhyay, "Time for a Perfect Storm!" in *Building the Future of Education: Museums and the Learning Ecosystem* (Center for the Future of Museums, American Alliance of Museums, 2014), 26.

45. Ibid.

Compassion
imagination
art → imagination
art making
response art
response
empathy

5

Response Art

Using Creative Activity to Deepen Exhibit Engagement

Jordan S. Potash

Museums have the potential to serve as communal gathering places in which visitors encounter new perspectives, challenge preconceived notions, and develop personal connections to social issues.[1] Implied in these ideas is that viewers must be able to understand another's circumstances, appreciate their emotional state, and perhaps feel moved to take action. In other words, the bridge between viewer and subject is empathy. According to His Holiness the Dalai Lama and Howard C. Cutler, empathy is a process defined as "our ability to connect with others, our ability to relate to them, understand their feelings, to share their experience and so on."[2] Empathy is the foundation for compassion and ultimately actions intended to alleviate another's suffering. In this chapter, I describe a theoretical framework and review practical examples of having exhibition visitors create art to foster empathy.

ART THERAPISTS IN MUSEUMS

To some it may seem unusual for an art therapist to write about museums. The American Art Therapy Association defines art therapy as a mental health profession that makes use of visual art making for expression, communication, and insight.[3] However, Silverman demonstrated that museums in partnership with helping service professionals have the opportunity to involve the public by widening an individual's perspective, enhancing relationships, and contributing to community development.[4]

Although I was trained as a mental health clinician, from my earliest days in graduate school I was interested in finding ways to make use of the principles of art therapy in service to community work. I am always amazed how art therapists help nonartists feel comfortable making art to stimulate awareness of self, others, and the world, as well as to make meaning of their artworks. In thinking how to use these skills outside of clinical settings, museums are a natural fit. Art therapists undertake an integrated training in studio arts and psychology, which allows us to work in a variety of environments. For me, partnering with museum educators and exhibition curators has allowed me to introduce the vast abilities art therapists have to offer to their communities.

It has been heartening to me to join others in these pursuits. Art therapists have positioned themselves in a diverse range of museums such as the Tate Britain,[5] Phillips Collection,[6] Memphis Brooks Museum of Art,[7] and Museum of Intolerance.[8] The museum offers a stimulating environment to affect psychosocial change,[9] in part because clients temporarily shift their identities and those of others to see themselves as museum attendees and artists.[10] Art therapists can facilitate audiences to express and transform emotions,[11] which can lead to increased well-being.[12] By participating in art therapy visitors know more about other people, cultures, and social issues.[13] Visitors appreciate the shared nature of their experiences,[14] learn from fellow museum attendees,[15] and reflect on social change implications.[16] Whether as co-hosts of exhibitions with therapeutic potential or partners in educational workshops, museum professionals and art therapists have much to offer one another.[17]

STRUCTURING THE MUSEUM EXPERIENCE FOR EMPATHY

Although empathy may be a naturally occurring emotion, it often requires opportunities and frameworks in which it can be fostered. Museums have taken up this call by offering engaging and innovative programs designed to allow viewers to appreciate the subject matter, consider their emotional response, and reflect on their relationship to it. Bedford reminded curator-educators,* "The aesthetic experience is not about teaching—the didactic telling—but closer to facilitating—the experiential showing or doing."[18] In order to work this way, she described the importance of focusing on three factors: storytelling, imagination, and art as experience. *Storytelling* entails the curator-educator presenting a coherent narrative that informs visitors, but also considers their role as an active listener in shaping the story being told. With *imagination*, curator-educators encourage viewers to make meaning of an exhibit by offering thought-provoking metaphors and

---

*Museum curators and educators are two distinct fields, but Bedford described that her work did not differentiate these roles. As such, I use the term *curator-educator* to refer to both.

integrating their own associations, reflections, and bodily reactions. Based on John Dewey's philosophy and infused with Maxine Greene's social advocacy, *art as experience* focuses visitors to pay attention to the emotions evoked by the exhibit to deepen their understanding and develop meaningful connections to the subject matter. These three core factors lead to practical strategies. First, objects, artifacts, and artworks can be displayed to stimulate narratives, while also being presented in such a way as to stir imagination. Second, a single object can invoke imagination and lead a visitor to consider the story as descriptive of a particular group or social issue. Third, building in multisensory interactions and creative uses of technology promotes engagement and invites curator-educators to consider exhibits as theater or performance art, thereby putting the visitor in the role of actor. Lastly, the success of an exhibit can be evaluated based on how well the exhibit and associated activities provided a meaningful experience.

There can be a fine line between providing opportunities for emotional connection and stepping into the bounds of indoctrination or propaganda. A way to avoid this is to offer a structure that respects a range of possible visitor responses. Behavioral economics theorists Thaler and Sunstein describe the essential role of *choice architects*, those who "have the responsibility for organizing the context in which people make decisions."[19] The emphasis here is on scaffolding situations to help direct attention, but in which individuals still exercise free will. Museum scholars Falk and Dierking articulate a similar process in emphasizing the necessity of *free-choice learning* as part of exhibition design. [20] The idea is that by providing a structured experience, visitors can be given an opportunity to experience an emotional connection and at the same time have the freedom to arrive at their own conclusions.

With these ideas in mind, museum guides can prompt empathy by focusing attention on the subjective circumstances of the subjects of an exhibit. For example, Modlin, Alderman, and Gentry reported on the essential role of docents in their ethnographic study of tour guides at Destrehan Plantation (near New Orleans, Louisiana).[21] Guides, by determining what to focus on and which stories to tell, have the opportunity to instill "historical empathy" that promotes connection to the realities of slavery and extends the historical narrative to the present for healing discussions.[22] Even in the absence of guided tours, Villeneuve and Viera demonstrated how supportive interpretation, such as suggested reflective questions and experiential activity, can help visitors make meaning of exhibits and identify connections between the presented material and one's own lived experience.[23] This occurred even when there was a cultural difference between subject and viewer. In a similar study, Arnold, Meggs, and Greer found that providing specific writing prompts to frame reflection led viewers "to discover and express deep empathy and strong emotions" and "to connect vicariously with the subjects depicted."[24]

RESPONSE ART: EXPERIENCE AND EMPATHY

The aforementioned examples demonstrate how guided discussion and reflective experiential activity can promote empathy. Visual art making provides another opportunity. Situating empathy at the center of art making was the philosophy of Bauhaus-inspired art educator Friedl Dicker-Brandeis.[25] Dicker-Brandeis was influenced by the notion that "artistic development and expression entail inner knowledge that reflects the maker's experience of an object more than the object itself."[26] Such sustained attention fosters the artist's familiarity with the subject matter, which in turn cultivates connection, resonance, and intimacy. Wix described this philosophy as "using art to know a thing firsthand through examining it before visually recording it is a way to relate closely with both the object and the observing self."[27] Being able to intimately envision and relate to another is central to Dicker-Brandeis's definition of beauty. Dicker-Brandeis's ideas are especially poignant because she taught them to children while interned in the Terezin ghetto prior to dying in Auschwitz. Before she was detained, she was able to pass her ideas on to her student Edith Kramer, who later became one of the founders of art therapy in the United States.

One of the ways in which Dicker-Brandeis's teachings have been implemented in art therapy is through the concept of *response art*. This type of art making refers to when an art therapist makes art about a clinical session in an attempt to understand the client better.[28] Response art can promote "empathic resonance"[29] with another by acting as an imaginative or "*interpretive* dialogue."[30] Whether created in the presence of a client or privately after a session, response art allows art therapists to make art for personal reflection and to clarify their feelings about the client. It also may inform the direction of future art therapy sessions.

Due to my interests in art making for social change, I have attempted to translate response art into community work in an approach I describe as *guided relational viewing*.[31] This process includes intentionally offering a structured viewing process and opportunities for art making to encourage exhibition visitors to experience empathy. Grounded in the tenets of nonviolence resistance philosophy, the aim is to foster an environment in which participants open themselves to hear another's story as portrayed in art, engage their imaginative faculties through art making, and experience a meaningful encounter in order to adopt a new perspective or behaviors that can lead to social change. The practical steps include viewing directives, art making, and reflection. The viewing directives encourage visitors to freely identify one artwork or object that is personally meaningful, thereby applying a relational frame to the museum experience. Viewers are then given time to create response art based on the thoughts and feelings evoked by their selection. Ideally, the art making occurs in the presence of the selected artwork or artifact to sustain the imagined relationship. At the end, visitors are encouraged to reflect on their imagery through individual writing and discussion. The overall process combines a structured process with free-choice learning in order to promote art making as a vehicle for engagement and empathy.[32]

GUIDED RELATIONAL VIEWING EXAMPLES

I will now describe how my colleagues and I used response art to foster empathy in a museum and in community exhibitions. The community exhibitions included art created by amateurs in order to raise awareness on particular topics. These exhibitions differ greatly from a professional collection in a museum, but I include them to demonstrate various ways in which creative activity can be used to enhance the viewing experience for the purpose of stimulating empathy. Each example included a research component designed to collect both quantitative and qualitative evidence.

Intensifying Responses to the Holocaust

Response art can be used in conjunction with a historical exhibit in order to help visitors have empathy for historical events. In a partnership with the US Holocaust Memorial Museum (USHMM) in Washington, DC, we designed a workshop intended to foster and understand visitors' empathic responses to the museum.[33] Twenty-two visitors were allotted two hours to take an individual self-guided tour of the museum's permanent exhibit. When finished, half were randomly selected and directed to a classroom where an art therapist instructed them to create art with the directive, "Please use the materials provided to make a picture of your emotional reaction to the Holocaust Museum permanent exhibition." Despite the fact that only three identified as artists, all participants created personally meaningful images and accompanying reflective writing. After art making, participants wrote a description of their art and then discussed it with the group.

Although the visitors were asked to focus on general feelings, several of them described their artwork as related to specific images, artifacts, and stories such as a train car used to transport prisoners, gravestones used to pave a road, or a collection of shoes from victims (figure 5.1). Seven of the participants specifically described responses related to empathy. Ten indicated a desire to participate in social change. As an exa, a middle-aged Hispanic

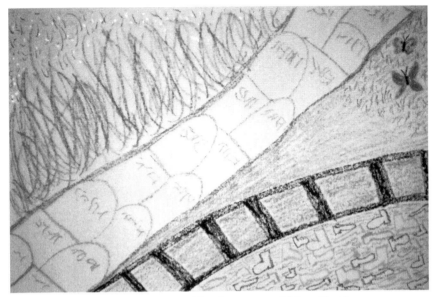

Figure 5.1. USHMM response art (with reference to exhibit artifacts).

man created an image of a face looking out of oversized glasses; one lens contained fire and the other water (figure 5.2). He wrote, "The initial image that I saw when I entered the exhibit brought a hurt feeling of sadness, to the point that I started to get teary-eyed." From this empathic response, he continued, "I was struck by the two elements of fire and water—they both have very creative aspects and also very destructive aspects, but together they can create earth, living. When these two elements come together, they are hopeful." Reflecting further on the "creative" and "destructive" aspects in his drawing, he imagined whether he might have the capacity for the kind of hate that leads to violence. "Where does that live in me and what do I need to do to see that in myself for that not to happen?" This example demonstrates how the visitor matched the feelings of the museum, reflected on them, and arrived at an insight about his personal responsibility for furthering suffering. Such a compassionate attitude can be a foundation for prosocial activity.

In addition to the qualitative account, we assessed and compared the changes in empathy experienced by the eleven visitors who participated in the art making workshop with the additional eleven who did not participate in the workshop. The Interpersonal Reactivity Index measures empathy using twenty-eight items as a global personality trait by looking at four areas: emotional empathy, cognitive perspective taking, ability to adopt the perspective of a fantasy character in a book or movie, and level of personal distress upon hearing of another's pain.[34] Immediate state empathy—how

Figure 5.2. USHMM response art.

the participant felt at the moment—was measured using a shorter scale of eight items divided between empathic concern and personal distress.[35] Participants in the art-making group, as well as those in the control group, were found to have comparable levels of trait and state empathy prior to beginning their visit. However, only the group that participated in art making had a significant increase (pre = 8.55, post = 11.58; F [1, 20] = 11.58; p = 0.00) in state empathy. What is important about these results is that the increase in empathy was measured after the visitors individually made art and wrote their reflections but before the group discussion. The finding indicates that the opportunity to engage in creative activity has an important role when targeting empathy.

Fostering Understanding of Mental Illness

Incorporating response art into exhibitions can also be used to foster awareness of current social issues. We organized two separate and independent exhibits aimed to increase awareness and challenge stigma toward people living with mental illness in Hong Kong. Clients in art therapy groups created the exhibits to tell their personal stories. They were guided by the theme "something I want to share about my life with someone else." We selected this theme to allow the artists to showcase any aspect of their lives, whether directly related to mental illness or not. Visitors to the exhibit toured all of the artworks, selected one that was meaningful, answered questions regarding their selection, created response art, engaged in reflective writing, and participated in discussion groups.

Some of the examples of empathy included: "The artwork and I shared something in common, it struck a chord with me" or "I felt that way, too."[36] One woman deliberately recreated a painting from the exhibit in her response art, stating, "Because I don't know the artist, I can only do a sketch of her painting so that I can stand in her shoes and try to understand her better" (figure 5.3).

Many participants did not have direct declarations of empathy, but there were indications of empathy in their response art. Visitors included colors, symbols, and compositions in response art that mirrored selected artwork from the exhibit. We described these occurrences as "graphic empathy."[37] In a painting titled *Stresses from Earth . . . The Fruit of the Solar System*, the artist attempted to portray the isolation that he felt as a result of living with mental illness (figure 5.4). It contained a blue-green earth, a circle to represent the artist, and a purple nebula to serve as protection from the hot red sun that symbolized stress. One of the drawings in response to this piece was intended to offer advice to the artist: "When facing problems and obstacles, which you can't bear, one may try to look at it from another perspective or other resolution methods, like the amoeba." The comment was offered

Figure 5.3.   Mental illness awareness: Exhibit (left) and response (right).

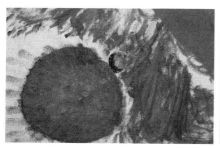

Figure 5.4. Mental illness awareness: Graphic empathy exhibit (left) and response (right).

in consolation, but does not indicate empathy. However, a careful look at the art indicates similar color patterns between the exhibit and response pieces. In the response art, the only purple shapes divide the drawing in half similar to the purple nebula. The only red and blue shapes are in the same areas as the corresponding colors in the original art. The color used to represent the amoeba is similar to the one used to represent the moon. The participant did not indicate if this was intentional, but it demonstrates mirroring of the exhibit art. This careful attention to the art reflects Dicker-Brandeis's theory. These examples indicate how empathy may be activated even if it is not readily evident.

Quantitative analysis utilized two scales designed to assess stigma toward people living with mental illness. Stigma measures do not directly indicate empathy. Instead, they measure parallel concepts related to understanding, perspective taking, and compassion. The Attribution Questionnaire 9 (AQ-9) uses nine items to determine stigma as classified by attitudes, behaviors, and emotions.[38] The Social Distance Scale (SDS) contains eight items designed to assess comfort interacting with people living with mental illness.[39] Results suggested that the exhibit combined with the workshop increased comfort associated with people living with mental illness, as evidenced by the SDS, and decreased stigma, as measured by the AQ-9. These results offer hope that the response art and associated activity can lead to empathy and compassionate actions.

As a way to connect empathy to specific social change behaviors following the response art, visitors who created response art engaged in conversation with each other about what they learned, but also possible initiatives that could alleviate stigma associated with mental illness. They identified formal education curricula, ongoing public awareness campaigns, and recreational activities in which people without mental illness could interact with those with mental illness. Additional discussion groups composed of workshop participants and people living with mental illness further discussed these ideas to create concrete programs.

Appreciating Doctor Empathy for Patient Suffering

In a final example, we paired response art with an exhibit intended to evoke empathy for medical illness. We worked with eighty-one third-year medical students in Hong Kong to create art and poetry that reflected their experience of witnessing patient pain and suffering.[40] From the resulting art and poetry, my colleagues and I curated an exhibit of twenty pieces that best represented portrayals of empathy. The assembled exhibit was displayed twice to two different groups of visitors.

The exhibit was first viewed by fourteen Korean medical students on a study trip as part of their medical humanities curriculum.[41] Medical humanities is a field that uses the arts, literature, and mindfulness practices to help doctors increase self-awareness and improve patient relationships. Students viewed the whole exhibit and then selected one artwork that was personally meaningful, answered questions regarding their selection, created response art, and completed reflective writing. One of the students selected an artwork about a young man who was wheelchair bound as a result of kyphoscoliosis (a spine deformity). The artist statement from this artwork read, "He reminded me of a moth, which I drew flying towards the moon (the source of light), just like him being hungry for knowledge despite that he might not live long." The viewer described her response art as (figure 5.5):

> I want him [patient portrayed in the art] to approach knowledge about the disease and pain. So, I drew the moth near the yellow knowledge and one moth is so lonely, so, I drew a couple of moths. One moth is [the] patient and the other is me. . . . That is a process, to know the disease with me (doctor).

The visitor responded to the pain portrayed by envisioning a relationship with the patient. Although this was an imaginary exercise, it may serve as a reminder when she works with patients in the future. As a further demonstration of empathy, the immediate state empathy scale revealed a numerical increase in empathic concern (pre = 1.46, post = 2.43),[42] but the sample size was too small for statistical analysis. The workshop demonstrated the possibility that response art could help doctors in training become more empathetic.

The exhibit was viewed a second time in a public hospital in Hong Kong.[43] This time we only displayed eight images due to space limitations and a desire to remove images that may have been too disturbing to patients, such as those depicting death. This exhibition provided an opportunity to see if response art could be used as a brief reflective tool in a natural setting. The exhibit audience was composed of patients, visitors, and staff. As they approached, an exhibit attendee randomly assigned them to one of three viewing directives: guided direction (select an artwork that was meaningful), guided relational direction (select an artwork that

Figure 5.5. Doctor-patient understanding: Exhibit (left) and response (right).

was meaningful and create a sketch or poem in response), or no direction (viewing as usual). Ninety-seven people participated in the study with a near even distribution among the three directives. Of the thirty-three people assigned to the guided relational direction condition, four of them selected the image of the boy in the wheelchair previously described. The drawing responses included images of a physically able boy engaged in activity or in nature, as well as a comment by a hospital employee who wrote, "I feel understood through the painting" (figure 5.6).

Instead of measuring empathy, this study measured the effect of the art exhibit and creative activity on mood, as that is a primary concern in a hospital. Participants completed the Brief Mood Introspection Scale before and after viewing the exhibit.[44] The scale is composed of sixteen items rated on a Likert scale that can be combined in different ways depending on the subscale of interest (namely pleasant–unpleasant, arousal–calm, positive–tired, and negative–relaxed). The results indicated moderate support that the guided and guided relational directions could increase mood. Even though we did not measure empathy, the scale included two related items, loving and caring. There were nonsignificant differences on both. However, among the three viewing directives, the increase in loving (pre = 4.55, post = 5.25) was the highest for those who created response art compared to those who did not. The study demonstrated that response art could take the form of a short reflection when a one-hour art-making workshop is unfeasible, but it is unclear what effect this brevity may have on empathy.

Figure 5.6.   Hospital exhibit: Response art.

IMPLICATIONS FOR CREATIVE ACTIVITY TO
DEEPEN EMPATHY IN EXHIBITIONS

As is evident through these examples, promoting creative activity as part of the exhibit helped to foster empathy. Returning to Bedford's factors (storytelling, imagination, art as experience),[45] we can see how creating response art intensifies exhibit experiences by repositioning the viewer from passive to one who is emotionally involved in the exhibition.

The response art enhanced the storytelling to position viewers as cocontributors to the presented material. The exhibits told historical narratives or current viewpoints to transmit particular lessons regarding cruelty, discrimination, and suffering, as well as understanding, resilience, and triumph. Audiences were instructed to pay attention to their reactions and use them as guides to interpret the exhibit instead of relying only on expert testimony. The example of the gentleman at the USHMM demonstrated how response art may even help reframe distress into an opportunity for meaning making. Being part of the storytelling lets participants know that their experiences are important components of the exhibition and encourages them to be inquisitive.

Creating art heightened imagination as participants experimented with line, color, shape, and symbol in myriad patterns, compositions, and styles. The focus on response art kept visitor's responses central to understanding the exhibit. Audiences used what they saw as a foundation for creating art that was both thoughtfully reimagined and deeply connected to the selected artwork.[46] The response art became the record of their viewing experience and provided a starting point for further learning and meaning making.

Both of these applications of storytelling and imagination are embedded in the third factor, art as experience. For a brief period of time, response art helped visitors identify with the exhibit by adopting the presented perspective or noticing an emotional connection. In essence, the exhibits fostered empathy by employing intentionally designed activities along the traditions of supportive interpretation and free-choice learning.[47]

CONCLUSION

Art making can aid museums in their quest to help visitors increase self-reflection, reimagine relationships, and promote social change. Through art making informed by art therapy, audiences are given permission to reflect on their thoughts and feelings within a supportive structure. Whether drawings, paintings, or poems, such activity can inform viewers about their own values, leading them to recognize shared moments with others and to conceive possible actions to alleviate suffering. Translating emotions in art and adopting another's perspective are the seeds that cultivate empathy. Perhaps it is through the experiential nature of doing that art making allows for an imaginative meeting between the public and others who are not present or who might not even exist in the same historical context. Inviting viewers to take a few moments or an hour to create response art may be the first step in the ultimate aim of helping visitors understand another's lived experience and be moved to take action.

NOTES

1. Graham Black, *Transforming Museums in the Twenty-first Century* (New York: Routledge, 2012).

2. Dalai Lama and Howard C. Cutler, *The Art of Happiness in a Troubled World* (London: Hodder and Stoughton, 2009), 304.

3. "What Is Art Therapy?" *American Art Therapy Association,* http://arttherapy.org/aata-aboutus/ (accessed December 1, 2015).

4. Lois Silverman, *The Social Work of Museums* (New York: Routledge, 2010).

5. David Shaer, Kirstie Beaven, Neil Springham, Silke Pillinger, Alan Cork, Jane Brew, Yvonne Forshaw, Pauline Moody, and Chris "S.," "The Role of Art Therapy in a Pilot for Art-based Information Prescriptions at Tate Britain," *International Journal of Art Therapy* 13 (2008): 25–33.

6. Brooke Rosenblatt, "Museum Education and Art Therapy: Promoting Wellness in Older Adults," *Journal of Museum Education* 39 (2014): 293–301.

7. Karen Peacock, "Museum Education and Art Therapy: Exploring an Innovative Partnership," *Art Therapy: Journal of the American Art Therapy Association* 29 (2012): 133–37.

8. Debra Linesch, "Art Therapy at the Museum of Tolerance: Responses to the Life and Work of Friedl Dicker-Brandeis," *The Arts in Psychotherapy* 31 (2004): 57–66.

9. Andree Salom, "Reinventing the Setting: Art Therapy in Museums," *The Arts in Psychotherapy* 38 (2010): 81–85.

10. Geoffrey Thompson, "Artistic Sensibility in the Studio and Gallery Model: Revisiting Process and Product," *Art Therapy: Journal of the American Art Therapy Association* 26 (2009): 159–66.

11. Donna J. Betts, Jordan S. Potash, Jessica J. Luke, and Michelle Kelso, "An Art Therapy Study of Visitor Reactions to the United States Holocaust Memorial Museum," *Museum Management and Curatorship* 30 (2015): 21–43; Carolyn B. Treadon, Marcia Rosal, and Viki D. Wylder, "Opening the Doors of Art Museums for Therapeutic Processes," *The Arts in Psychotherapy* 33 (2006): 288–301.

12. Rosenblatt, "Museum Education and Art Therapy."

13. Linesch, "Art Therapy at the Museum of Tolerance."

14. Shaer et al., "The Role of Art Therapy."

15. Betts et al., "An Art Therapy Study of Visitor Reactions."

16. Jenny Jones, "Crossing the Meniscus: Art Therapy and Local Agenda 21," in *Art Therapy, Race and Culture,* ed. Jean Campbell, Marian Liebman, Frederica Brooks, Jenny Jones, and Cathy Ward (London: Jessica Kingsley, 1999), 209–25.

17. Peacock, "Museum Education and Art Therapy."

18. Leslie Bedford, *The Art of Museum Exhibitions: How Story and Imagination Create Aesthetic Experiences* (Walnut Creek, CA: Left Coast Press, 2014), 115.

19. Richard H. Thaler and Cass R. Sunstein, *Nudge: Improving Decisions about Health, Wealth, and Happiness,* rev. and expanded ed. (New York: Penguin, 2009), 3.

20. John H. Falk and Lynn D. Dierking, *Learning from Museums: Visitor Experiences and the Making of Meaning* (Walnut Creek, CA: AltaMira Press, 2000).

21. E. Arnold Modlin Jr., Derek H. Alderman, and Glenn W. Gentry, "Tour Guides as Creators of Empathy: The Role of Affective Inequality in Marginalizing the Enslaved at Plantation House Museums," *Tourist Studies* 11 (2011): 3–19.

22. Ibid., 4.

23. Pat Villeneuve and Alicia Viera, "Multiculturalism and the Supported Interpretation (SI) Model," in *Multiculturalism in Art Museums Today,* ed. Joni Boyd Acuff and Laura Evans (Lanham, MD: Rowman and Littlefield, 2014), 81–94.

24. Alice Arnold, Susan Martin Meggs, and Annette G. Greer, "Empathy and Aesthetic Experience in the Art Museum," *International Journal of Education through Art* 10 (2014): 331–47.

25. Linney Wix, *Through a Narrow Window: Friedl Dicker-Brandeis and Her Terezín Students* (Albuquerque, NM: University of New Mexico, 2010).

26. Ibid., 8.

27. Ibid., 24.

28. Barbara J. Fish, "Response Art: The Art of the Art Therapist," *Art Therapy: Journal of the American Art Therapy Association* 29 (2012): 138–43.

29. Michael Franklin, "Affect Regulation, Mirror Neurons, and the Third Hand: Formulating Mindful Empathic Art Interventions," *Art Therapy: Journal of the American Art Therapy Association* 27 (2010): 160–67.

30. Bruce L. Moon, *Existential Art Therapy: The Canvas Mirror*, 3rd ed. (Springfield, IL: Charles C. Thomas, 2009), 119.

31. J. Potash, "Art Therapists as Intermediaries for Social Change," *Journal of Arts for Life* 2 (2011): 48–58.

32. J. Potash, Rainbow T. H. Ho, Jess K. Y. Chick, and Friendly S. W. Au Yeung, "Viewing and Engaging in an Art Therapy Exhibit by People Living with Mental Illness: Implications for Empathy and Social Change," *Public Health* 127 (2013): 735–44.

33. Betts et al., "An Art Therapy Study of Visitor Reactions."

34. Mark H. Davis, "Measuring Individual Differences in Empathy: Evidence for a Multidimensional Approach," *Journal of Personality and Social Psychology* 44 (1983): 113–26.

35. Jay S. Coke, C. Daniel Batson, and Katherine McDavis, "Empathic Mediation of Helping: A Two-Stage Model," *Journal of Personality and Social Psychology* 36 (1978): 752–66.

36. Potash et al., "Viewing and Engaging in an Art Therapy Exhibit," 738.

37. J. Potash and R. T. H. Ho, "Drawing Involves Caring: Fostering Relationship Building Through Art Therapy for Social Change," *Art Therapy: Journal of the American Art Therapy Association* 28 (2011): 74–81.

38. Patrick W. Corrigan, Amy C. Watson, Amy C. Warpinski, and Gabriela Gracia, "Stigmatizing Attitudes about Mental Illness and Allocation of Resources to Mental Health Services," *Community Mental Health Journal* 40 (2004): 297–307.

39. Bruce G. Link, Francis T. Cullen, James Frank, and John F. Wozniak, "The Social Rejection of Former Mental Patients: Understanding Why Labels Matter," *American Journal of Sociology* 9 (1987): 1461–500.

40. J. Potash, Julie Y. Chen, Cindy L. K. Lam, and Vivien T. W. Chau, "Art-making in a Family Medicine Clerkship: How Does It Affect Medical Student Empathy?" *BMC Medical Education* 14 (2014).

41. J. Potash and Julie Y. Chen, "Art-mediated Peer-to-Peer Learning of Empathy," *The Clinical Teacher* 11 (2014): 327–31.

42. B. Coke and McDavis, "Empathic Mediation of Helping."

43. R. T. H. Ho, J. Potash, Fanny Fang, and Judy Rollins, "Art Viewing Directives in Hospital Settings Effect on Mood," *Health Environments Research and Design Journal* 8 (2015): 30–43.

44. John D. Mayer and Yvonne N. Gaschke, "The Experience and Meta-Experience of Mood," *Journal of Personality and Social Psychology* 55 (1988): 102–11.

45. Bedford, *The Art of Museum Exhibitions*.

46. Wix, *Through a Narrow Window*.

47. Thaler and Sunstein, *Nudge*; Villeneuve and Viera, "Multiculturalism and the Supported Interpretation (SI) Model"; Falk and Dierking, *Learning from Museums*.

6

From Indifference to Activation

How Wonder Fosters Empathy In and Beyond Informal Science Centers

Mary Beth Ausman, Michele Miller Houck, and Robert Corbin

HOW DO WONDER AND EMPATHY
RELATE TO ONE ANOTHER?

Wonder is an innate human response to the world around us. It is an emotion or state of mind that we all experience, and our shared experience of wonder unites us as thinking and feeling beings. At its core is curiosity, for without being curious, one cannot succumb to wonder. A lack of curiosity toward our surroundings isolates us and makes us indifferent to the role we play in our society, cultures, and the grander ecosystem.

Empathy is the archenemy of indifference, so empathy and wonder make good bedfellows. To wonder is "to think or speculate curiously" or "to be filled with awe, admiration or amazement." Wonder also demonstrates the spectrum of human intellectual and emotional awareness because it also can mean "to doubt."[1] When people experience wonder, they respond emotionally—their facial expressions change, they gesticulate, they verbally respond to the experience, they might even move closer in proximity to the experience or another person. These social cues serve as invitations to others to coexperience that moment of wonder. At the very root of the word *empathy* is the Greek definition *empátheia*, or affection. When one experiences empathy, there is a "psychological identification with or vicarious experiencing of the feelings, thoughts, or attitudes of another."[2] As wonder is an emotional response, and empathy relies upon sharing another's emotions; the two are inextricably linked.

Empathy takes wonder to a higher level because it is a sharing of experience and reaction with another individual, which can result in a response and subsequent dialogue about the experience. Taking the risk of sharing one's wonder with another person is a vulnerable position, and yet it is a key element in the cycle of wondering and learning. As e. e. cummings writes, "We do not believe in ourselves until someone reveals that deep inside us something is valuable, worth listening to, worthy of our trust, sacred to our touch. Once we believe in ourselves we can risk curiosity, wonder, spontaneous delight or any experience that reveals the human spirit."[3]

WHY ARE INFORMAL SCIENCE CENTERS GOOD AT IGNITING WONDER?

Museums of all kinds have always been a natural environment for experiencing wonder. Though object collections date to ancient cultures around the globe,[4] a revival of object collecting occurred with the sixteenth-century *Kunst- und Wunderkammer*, or cabinet of curiosities, which individuals used to display their private collections of natural, scientific, aesthetic, historical, and industrial objects, among others.[5] Over the centuries to follow, those cabinets and rooms would expand to become museums—separate buildings with collections specializing in particular themes or content areas. The ultimate goal of displaying these collections, or "wonders," was to induce a sense of awe or astonishment in the viewer, all while educating them on the vast complexities of the world. Without context, these wonders provided little else to the viewer than a mostly passive experience of observing, absorbing, and possibly responding to the objects' uniqueness or rarity with relation to their daily lives. As museums have evolved, so has the definition of wonder: it is no longer merely an object at which to marvel; instead, it is an experience that motivates and inspires.

Today's informal science centers and museums play a critical role in evoking wonder. We make science accessible through hands-on, interactive, inquiry-based exhibits and experiences that bring difficult concepts into context and focus. Informal science centers encourage social behavior with activities that require collaboration, communication, and innovative thinking. The collaborative spirit of informal science centers makes us natural conveners of shared experiences, which not only promote opportunities for empathic interaction, but also depend upon them. General audiences of science centers and museums are not as likely to link emotion, empathy, and science together. Nevertheless, science informs our knowledge base and our opinions, which often can be quite emotionally charged. Consider evolution, climate change, conservation, vaccinations, and fossil fuels, just to name a few. So shouldn't informal science centers play a role in introducing our communities to the wonders of our world, especially if those wonders might inspire our visitors to activate their own participation in science careers, advocacy, or even simply coconstructing their own understanding of science? Empathy and wonder drive activism. Richard Dawkins might agree, as he writes, "There is an appetite for wonder, and isn't true science well qualified to feed it? It's often said that people 'need' something more in their lives than just the material world. There is a gap that must be filled. People need to feel a sense of purpose. . . . Just study what is, and you'll find that it already is far more uplifting than anything you could imagine needing."[6]

Experiencing wonder within the informal science center context is not guaranteed because it requires visitor investment. In order to wonder, one must make the conscious effort to be engaged and involved. All too often, indifference dominates the human impulse of engagement; we live in an age in which we engage more with our personal electronic devices than with the people and the world around us, as voiced by Sherry Turkle in *Alone Together*, among others. A lack of engagement comes from a lack of awareness and inspiration. Informal science centers and museums can combat indifference from two angles: by presenting information in an engaging fashion and by motivating visitors to use that information to improve the world around them. In "The 95 Percent Solution," John Falk and Lynn Dierking posit that the majority of science knowledge among Americans is not derived from formal classroom experience, rather from informal experiences in nature, at museums, zoos, and even on television or via the Internet.[7] Informal science centers and museums carry a significant responsibility to educate the public, and the door to knowledge and its application opens more readily when our visitors engage in wonder-filled experiences. Though wonder is a universal experience, every informal science center employs different strategies within their unique contexts to elicit wonder in its guests.

To that end, Discovery Place and Carolina Raptor Center teamed up in 2015 to examine the impact our institutions have on wonder experiences among our visitors. We were curious to learn whether wonder was present as a result of certain experiences more than others, and to what end our visitors might "utilize" their wonder to activate what they learned beyond our science centers. When we set out to observe visitors in our informal science centers, our focus was purely on wonder. However, the results of the research in both institutions studied point to a significant relationship between empathy and wonder that piqued our interest. The intertwining of wonder and empathy has impacted the way we consider the visitor experience and how we might improve upon it. In order to explain the role of empathy in informal science centers, we begin with our exploration of wonder.

WHAT DOES WONDER LOOK LIKE IN THE INFORMAL SCIENCE CENTER?

Does the size, scope, or mission of an informal science center or museum impact its ability to ignite wonder? Discovery Place, an informal science center in the heart of uptown Charlotte, North Carolina, had not considered that question until one of our local partner institutions, Carolina Raptor Center, expressed an interest in our early exploration of wonder among Discovery Place visitors. In spite of our differing approaches to informal science education, we shared a common interest in wonder-filled visitor experiences. As members of the only statewide consortium of informal science centers and museums in the United States, the North Carolina Grassroots Science Museums Collaborative (NCGMSC), both institutions had contemplated the question, "How do our visitors experience wonder?" and shared a mutual interest in gathering data that would inform the institutions' strategic directions for audience development and visitor experience design and delivery. The NCGMSC leads a statewide effort to demonstrate its members' collective importance to the field and to use its impact on the state economy and STEM career readiness to leverage legislative support for informal science education. With support from the NCGSMC in the summer of 2015, Discovery Place and Carolina Raptor Center conducted an informal research study at both locations with the intent to compare and contrast our findings from a large informal science center with a mission of inspiring curious thinkers to discover the wonders of science, technology, and nature, and an outdoor science center focused specifically on the conservation of birds of prey. As two unique partners convening to answer the same question, we began to explore what measuring wonder would look like at each institution.

THE WONDER QUESTION

As Discovery Place had long been in the business of "igniting wonder," we *wondered*, what exactly does wonder *look* like? And how does it manifest itself in the visitor experience? To answer those questions, we needed to better understand what drives wonder among our visitors. In 2014, we began intentionally observing our guests and their reactions to experiences throughout the museum, convened focus groups among staff that frequently interacted with guests on the museum floor, and sent out surveys to staff, asking them to reflect about their observations of wonder in the museum: When they observed wonder occurring, what did it look like? Where did they see wonder happen most frequently? What prompted wonder-filled experiences? From our data collection, we pieced together an agreed-upon set of wonder "norms" that continuously surfaced among our visitors, and based upon staff responses, where to look for their occurrence. Wonder was becoming observable, but a question remained: Even if we could observe and document wonder, what would be our purpose in doing so?

After months of conversations among Discovery Place staff members and observations of visitors on the floor, we felt that measuring wonder for the sake of measuring wonder was not enough. We wanted to discern how Discovery Place was impacting the visitors' wonder experience and what the visitors were *doing* with that experience. We felt our research question was just out of reach until, in an unexpected moment of clarity during a class observation, the question came into focus before us, like a wonder-filled experience all its own. While observing a museum education program on the fire triangle[8] and the requisite elements that ignite and sustain a fire (fuel, heat, and oxygen), a revelation occurred: igniting wonder is much like igniting a fire (figure 6.1)!

In science centers, wonder typically occurs around an extraordinary experience—something that is otherwise inaccessible to our visitors in their daily lives. In the analogy of a fire triangle, the extraordinary experience is the fuel. It gets the mind turning. What makes the experience extraordinary is its delivery. Informal education affords a variety of entry points, but it relies heavily on activation, inquiry, and interaction. To that end, the fuel within the wonder triangle is not just the topical content of the experience, but also its ability to capture and keep the interest of the learner. What are the sparks that ignite the wonder fire? Two reactions: emotional (affective) wonder and cognitive wonder. Emotional wonder is the heat in the fire triangle. Discovery Place calls it the "Wow!" moment, when a visitor's reaction is obviously visible or audible, but driven by one's prior knowledge, experiences, and the personal connection created with the current experience (figure 6.2). The "Wow!" moment is typically fleeting and can occur repeatedly as the extraordinary experience unfolds.

Because a "Wow!" moment is short lived, it cannot be sustained without additional exploration. Cognitive wonder is the oxygen that allows the fire to continue burning. More informally, cognitive wonder is the "How?" moment, when a visitor asks a question or makes a supposition, either to themselves or to someone else.

"How?" moments of wonder require the learner to make a deeper investment in the extraordinary experience by considering some aspect of the content being taught. Thus as the fire triangle requires three balanced

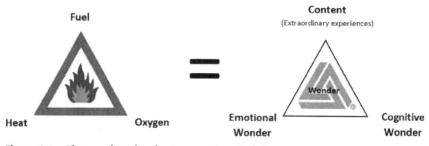

Figure 6.1. The wonder triangle. *Source*: Mary Beth Ausman.

Figure 6.2. Emotional wonder: A boy shows his wonder-filled reaction during a *Nose to Nose* encounter at Discovery Place. *Source*: Mary Beth Ausman.

elements, so does the wonder triangle. As the conversation progressed between Discovery Place and Carolina Raptor Center, what interested us was how we could distinguish between the "Wow!" and the "How?" in observing our visitors' reactions to extraordinary learning experiences—and what the results would tell us about the visitor experience at both science centers.

"WOW!" AND "HOW?": THE IMPACT OF INFORMAL SCIENCE CENTER EXPERIENCES ON WONDER

At Discovery Place, learning experiences can be big, bold, and boisterous or intimate and personalized. The telltale "Boom!" from the stage indicates the introduction to a program about fire and chemistry, while visitors might be encountering a sea cucumber or ball python with a delicate two-finger touch elsewhere in the museum. The goal of all of our educational acts is to engage the visitor, and we use a variety of informal teaching strategies to do so. Many of our experiences lead off with a hook to grab our visitors' attention, evoking frequent "Wow!" responses from their participants. In conducting research on wonder, Discovery Place wanted to know where in the museum people began to transfer that "Wow!" experience to a "How?" experience, in which they ask questions that demonstrate a desire to explore the answer further (figure 6.3). To that end, we wanted to observe visitors throughout the museum to determine whether there were any patterns and trends in visitor attitudes and behaviors, and what those trends might tell us to help design future exhibitions, programs, and even staff training. Furthermore, if the "How?" moment encourages questioning, which likely results in dialogue, could we observe where wonder was being shared—and perhaps *cultivating empathy*?

In contrast to the flash of Discovery Place, Carolina Raptor Center has been described as a quiet walk in the woods—with birds. Carolina Raptor

Figure 6.3. Cognitive wonder: A family engages in dialogue during their visit to the rainforest at Discovery Place. *Source*: Candy Howard.

Center's setting in Latta Plantation Nature Preserve lends itself to a contemplative connection with the natural world and its avian inhabitants. Our history as a bird rehabilitation center further shapes our audience's impressions, as people have often viewed us through a lens of sympathy and sadness. To them, we are a facility filled with injured birds to be protected and rehabilitated. To us, there is so much more to experience and to take away. Carolina Raptor Center celebrates natural experiences and the quiet wonder that occurs in its intimate setting. The portion of our audience composed of the prototypical naturalist or bird enthusiast is guaranteed to return repeatedly. That audience is innately comfortable in our environment and finds opportunities to connect authentically with nature on its own. We recognize the need to create an environment in which less comfortable or familiar audiences can also experience the wonders of nature via birds of prey. For these audiences, the Carolina Raptor Center experience must be more than a walk around our Raptor Trail. We want the experience to be "sticky" and lasting, to the point that our visitors are inspired and act to help us spread our mission of raptor conservation, and to return over and over to deepen their relationship with us and our birds.

Historically, Carolina Raptor Center has collected visitor satisfaction surveys that gathered lots of data, but shared very little on how to improve the visitor experience. We already knew our restrooms were clean and what locations people engaged the most with our exhibitions. We could observe that ourselves. Instead, we wanted to gather visitor feedback to inform our strategic direction, which was to grow and diversify our audience, as well as to motivate them to serve as ambassadors for us beyond their visit. We wanted to be a center where people would enter to engage with our mission over and over in different ways and come out changed, inspired, and activated toward a greater goal—spreading the message of raptor conservation. Measuring wonder at Carolina Raptor Center would help us determine how we were activating these growing audiences. Our starting point, however, was different from that of Discovery Place.

After we learned of Discovery Place's wonder triangle, we considered its application at Carolina Raptor Center and observed an intriguing contrast to what Discovery Place was reporting. "Wow!" moments at Carolina Raptor Center are more rare; they do occur when visitors observe a bird in flight or engage in a deeper raptor experience like taking a vulture for a walk. More often, however, the Raptor Center visitor was moving from the "How?" moment to the "Wow!" moment. What happens on the Raptor Trail is more of a slow burn than a dramatic ignition—little sparks along the way move visitors from the "How?" toward the "Wow!" Understanding drives the visitor toward a revelation. Instead of a fleeting "Wow!" moment, visitors' "Wow!" is often the result of a growing base of knowledge that has more significant staying power. Engaging the visitor in the questions of

"How?" first—drawing them in with information about a bird, the touch of a wing, or simply the reality of the bird itself creates curiosity and takes us down the path to "Wow!"

Carolina Raptor Center wanted to gather feedback from our visitors to determine how those encounters transformed their experiences, and to gauge the depth of their impact. How did we attract people to walk in the front door, make connections to our common experiences, engage them in our mission, and then activate them? What would it take to light a "wonder fire" on the Raptor Trail, and keep the fire lit within our visitors long after their departure?

MEASURING "WOW!" AND "HOW?"

In order to determine how we would measure wonder via observation at Discovery Place, we had begun the process by asking our educators to reflect about their observations of wonder on the museum floor: When they observed wonder occurring, what did it look like? Where did they see wonder happen most frequently? What prompted wonder-filled experiences? We assembled their responses, compared them with visitor observations the research team had conducted on the museum floor, and organized them into categories. From those categories, three essential types of observational indicators emerged: expressions, gestures, and verbal responses. We created an observation tool that could be completed on the museum floor by an observer, featuring the three categorical lists of indicators assembled from our own observations and internal conversations.

Observers chose individuals at random throughout the museum, noted the program/exhibition they attended, whether or not it was facilitated, visitor age group, gender, and membership status, marked all the behaviors they observed on the list, and made notes for other comments or reactions not listed on the observation tool. Discovery Place volunteers conducted nearly two hundred observations throughout the summer of 2015 and recorded the observations on a spreadsheet for analysis. Because expressions and gestures typically aligned with fleeting "Wow!" reactions and verbal responses could be categorized as "Wow!" comments or "How?" questions, observational data could be quantified to determine which types of learning experiences were associated with one or both types of wonder. Observations were sorted by learning experience, after which visitor behaviors and reactions were used to create a "profile" of each learning experience. These profiles ultimately provided a basic wonder "heat map" of learning experiences around the museum's floor plan. The profiles indicated areas on the heat map where wonder was "hot" in the museum—during staff-facilitated experiences and in areas where visitors could interact with or observe live animals. This affirmed staff responses that preceded the wonder observations.

At Carolina Raptor Center, the research team spent nearly three months completing over one hundred observations of our programs, exhibits, and visitors. We knew not to expect a lot of wonder moments on a typical day, but when they did occur, a pattern emerged: that of human interaction. In contrast to the busy weekend Raptor Trail that is filled with visitors, docents, and staff, on a weekday, visitors might not see another person apart from the Visitor Service Associate who sold their entry ticket. During the quiet times, to a large degree our visitors are left to be their own facilitators of learning. While visitors often experience wonder without interacting with others at Carolina Raptor Center, we observed that visitors got to "Wow!" more quickly when a human was there to make or share that connection with them. Furthermore, the opportunity to share that connection with others is what motivates the visitor to embrace wonder and act upon it. Empathy really matters in this equation. Considering this observation, we decided that if the ultimate goal was to move visitors from indifference to activation we needed to start asking the following questions: What did visitors *see* when they came to Carolina Raptor Center? What did that make them *think* about? How did that make them *feel*? What were they going to *do* about it? And finally, *who* (or *what*) inspired them during their visit? Once we knew the answers to these questions, we could figure out how to create more wonder-filled moments.

Carolina Raptor Center and Discovery Place worked together to develop a five-question survey that we converted into a facilitated activity—almost a game—near the exit of the Raptor Trail. We placed high school interns at the beginning of the activity to facilitate the game. The interns passed out color-coded Popsicle sticks to visitors in five age categories (children, teens, adults accompanying children, adults, and seniors), which they placed into collection jars to indicate their answers to the five aforementioned questions about their experiences. For example, the question "What did you see that you will remember most?" had the following five choices: Injured Birds, Birds in Cages, Smiling Volunteers, Bird Handlers, or Flying Birds. Answer choices for each question were scored on a Likert scale that indicated the degree to which the visitor identified with feelings of indifference or activation during an experience.

WHERE VISITORS AND WONDER INTERSECT AT OUR INFORMAL SCIENCE CENTERS

After collecting observational data at Discovery Place, we explored the following questions:

1. Where is wonder most abundant?
2. Where can we see visitors moving from the "Wow!" to the "How?"?
3. Do interactive programs and exhibits have higher instances of wonder than noninteractive ones?

Observations of Discovery Place visitors indicate that in general, wonder is abundant in a variety of experiences. As observers noted indicators of wonder behavior on the observation form, each indicator was given a point. The museum experiences that garnered the highest mean in number of points were: animal exhibitions including *Fantastic Frogs* and the *Rainforest,* animal encounters including *Explore More Life* and *Nose to Nose* experiences, *Cool Stuff* (an interactive physics "playground"), staff-facilitated shows and demonstrations at the stage, and *Random Acts of Science* (staff- and volunteer-conducted experiences on the museum floor). The results of the observation tool demonstrate that in general, wonder can be found in both facilitated and nonfacilitated experiences, which may or may not be interactive. For the most part, however, visitor wonder aligns with experiences where our visitors can interact with a Discovery Place staff member, volunteer, and/or live animal.

Where those experiences intersect, the visitor's propensity for demonstrating wonder behaviors is even stronger: for example, in educator-led *Nose to Nose* animal encounters, at the touch tank, or during a stage show involving live animals. Observational data showed consistently higher instances of visitor questions and conversations with educators or among one another during these experiences than others.

In order to further gauge where visitors' wonder experiences shifted from "Wow!" to "How?" observations of visitors around the museums' exhibitions and educational experiences were qualified into "Wow!" and "How?" behaviors to determine where and when each type of reaction occurred. The two most significant indicators of "How?" behavior were visitors talking with others (either visitors or museum staff) and asking questions. Of the 189 observations conducted, 51 percent of observations indicated visitors talked with others and 25 percent asked questions. Among those observed behaviors, 80 percent of visitors who talked with others and 86 percent of visitors who asked questions did so during museum experiences that featured animal encounters, staff facilitation, or both. Discovery Place concluded from the observation tool results that wonder does indeed occur more frequently in interactive experiences during the museum visit.

In order to determine if the data pattern was isolated to this observation tool, Discovery Place compared the data to the results of tracking guest "linger time" in the museum's lab spaces over the summer and guest comments on what they enjoyed the most about their visits. In both cases, experiences involving biological sciences continued to outperform other experiences in the museum. Average lab linger times in *Explore More Stuff* (physics and chemistry) and *Explore More Collections* were almost half the nearly ten-minute average linger time of *Explore More Life*. More than half of guests' responses to what they enjoyed most related to live animals in the museum (figure 6.4).

Discovery Place can conclude from this preliminary research that there is much more to study with respect to visitor wonder behaviors and which museum experiences specifically trigger the "How?" moments that lead to richer sharing of wonder through questions and dialogue. What is most interesting, perhaps, is considering the degree to which those experiences

Figure 6.4. A mother and daughter experience the touch tank together at Discovery Place. *Source:* Candy Howard.

truly activate our visitors into a stronger relationship with one another as they explore what fills them with wonder. The process of observing wonder helped us to realize the important role empathy plays in activating those conversations, questions, and mutual sharing of moments, ideas, and motivation to be active learners and advocates.

Because the programmatic goal at Carolina Raptor Center is to enhance experiences that result in activating the visitor, we weighed the degree to which visitors demonstrated wonder on a scale that represented the spectrum of indifference to activation (figure 6.5). The Raptor Center considered our data in two ways, including a mean score out of five for each question and the top answers by percentage for the question. Looking at the most popular answers gives us clues about what we need to tweak to reach the highest level of engagement, represented on our question scales as scoring a 4 or 5.

What did visitors see at Carolina Raptor Center? Nearly three-quarters of visitors chose the two lowest answers on the wonder scale: Injured Birds and Birds in Cages, and the average score for SEE was 2.11 out of 5, indicating a low "Wow!" factor among respondents. These results indicate that many visitors are still stuck in the sympathy mode and have not moved away from thinking of us as a sanctuary for injured birds. As a result of this visitor feedback, our interpretation and programs are now deemphasizing the disabilities of the animals and focusing on the positive natural history and science discovery that can be realized by observing and interacting with large birds of prey. We believe focusing on building a positive bird-human interaction will move our scores toward a more engaged result on the wonder scale.

What are people thinking about on the Raptor Trail? Visitor responses echoed the first scores on the wonder scale, as one-third of respondents were thinking about eating lunch instead of the weighty issues of conservation

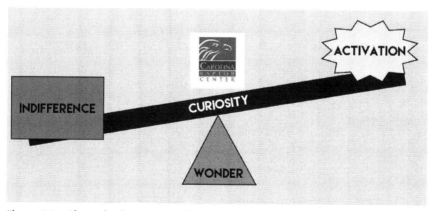

Figure 6.5.   The activation teeter totter. *Source*: Michele Miller Houck and Mary Beth Ausman.

or habitat preservation. The mean score of visitor responses landed slightly higher than the first question at 2.46 out of 5. As wonder moments are currently more abundant in weekend programming, increased opportunities to see flying birds, experience raptors up close, and engaging with birds with trainers during the week could have a huge impact. Through this research we have identified the need for more programs (and more humans) daily on the Raptor Trail. Interactions with Carolina Raptor Center staff will also encourage visitors to become more aware of the concerns at the forefront of raptor protection and conservation.

When visitors were asked to reflect on the impact of the Carolina Raptor Center experience itself, the resulting responses scored more favorably toward the activation end of the wonder spectrum. The "How do you feel?" question received the highest scores in all five age groups: 3.31. Nearly two-thirds of responses were on the higher end of the scale, and only one-tenth of visitors said that they were indifferent. These results indicate that we are inspiring people to experience the "Wow!" moment in much the same way other informal science centers do. Responses to our "What will you do?" question earned a mean score of 2.52, which is likely the most significant question to dissect in order to understand how we move people toward activation. In essence, we are halfway to our goal of an activated result on the wonder scale. More than one-third of visitors engaging in the activity answered "Learn More" and another one-quarter answered "Tell the World"—the highest-rated answer. As a result, Carolina Raptor Center will look for ways and create experiences to move the visitor toward true activation.

So how do these results point to empathy in the museum experience? Our contention is that the connection between wonder and empathy is natural. When you experience a wonder moment and then share it with others (empathy), you are moving up the wonder scale to activation. This interaction enhances your experience and magnifies your wonder moment (figure 6.6).

Observations of visitor behavior and reactions during animal encounters at Discovery Place also demonstrate another interesting finding: visitors are more likely to experience a "Wow!" moment *and* a "How?" moment during these particular programs. Categorical sorting of visitor reactions on the wonder observation tool indicated a higher instance of visitors asking questions and engaging in dialogue during encounters with specimens from our live collections and our educators. Still, visitors approach animal encounters with a range of emotions, from trepidation to enthusiasm. Recognizing that one of the definitions of wonder is *to doubt*, we noted that often the hesitant visitor experiences a broader spectrum of emotions on the wonder scale. In fact, the doubtful visitor frequently demonstrates even more animated reactions to the wonders they experience because they have invested more into the experience than their nondoubting counterparts (figure 6.7).

Figure 6.6. **Father and teen daughter imitate eastern screech owl behavior at a Meet the Raptors presentation at Carolina Raptor Center.** *Source*: Michele Miller Houck.

By taking a risk to experience wonder, the reward is much more signifi-cant. As they traverse the wonder spectrum from doubt to curiosity to awe, these visitors also tend to share their reactions more readily with others. From the outset of the experience, the doubtful visitor must establish a per-sonal connection through trust in order to participate. Visitors extend their trust to the program facilitator and to the animal itself. Animal encounters are naturally empathic because the trust we cultivate with the facilitator and the animal is a two-way street. We often hear visitors channeling their own prior experiences in nature by asking their doubtful companions, "Who is more scared, you or the animal?" When a facilitator offers strategies for being gentle and respectful to the animal, it serves as a reminder to the visi-tor that the experience is an exchange, not a unidirectional experience. The passive experience of the cabinet of curiosities model has been replaced by the learning experience that is sensory, emotional, psychological, intellec-tual, empathetic, and *mutual*.

THE WONDER OF LIFE THAT INSPIRES EMPATHY

Overall, data collected from both sites indicates that wonder is strongest and deepest during interactions with animals or other human beings.

Figure 6.7.   A Mother overcomes her fear of snakes during a *Nose to Nose* encounter at Discovery Place. *Source*: Candy Howard.

Could this be a response rooted in our own biology? Do we as living beings have an affinity for interacting with humans and other animals? How does our common link as bio-organisms impact the depth of wonder we experience, and furthermore, how do we choose to share that moment of wonder with other bio-organisms? Sophia Vasalou theorizes, "The very existence of living beings that appear to us as an ultimate limit to our own egoism awakens wonder at the way in which others embody the ultimate source of all life and vitality."[9] We marvel at life, its fragility, and our participation in it, as *wonderful*; and it seems that sharing in that fascination is as human an impulse as experiencing wonder itself. Vasalou finds common ground with philosopher Martha Nussbaum, writing, "As Nussbaum observes, 'wonder at the complex living thing itself' is what mobilizes our compassion and empathy. Wonder redraws our world of concern, establishing true mutuality with a wider sphere of life."[10]

Observing wonder at our two sites has shown us that whether one starts from the "Wow!" or the "How?" emotional and cognitive wonder are cyclical, feeding off one another. As we already indicated, one can begin the wonder journey in either sphere. What matters is that a "Wow!" moment has the potential energy to inspire a question in a subsequent "How?" moment, whose answer can inspire another "Wow!" moment, and so on and so forth. What constitutes a "Wow!" moment for one visitor might not be nearly as salient or poignant to another, as visitors "assimilate and sort the museum visit experience into mental categories of personal significance, each determined by events in their lives before and after the visit."[11] So where does empathy enter this singular cycle? When the museum visitor transcends their personal "Wow!" moment in an informal science learning experience by asking a question and starting a dialogue with another person (colearner or museum educator), the visitor's isolated experience shifts in two ways: it opens the opportunity to consider the experience from another person's perspective, which impacts how the visitor assimilates those perspectives into a coconstructed understanding. The "How?" moment becomes a potential facilitator of idea exchange, shared understanding, and mutual connection.

Empathy comes from sharing a common experience—being able to place oneself inside the thoughts and feelings of another. When two or more people share a common experience around human or animal interaction, that common experience opens them to opportunities to engage with others and become involved in the deeper exploration of their shared biology. When we explore something more deeply with others, we lose ourselves in the experience and become more open to sharing our thoughts and reactions with others through dialogue. Vasalou states, "By imbuing life with an alluring luster, wonder sustains our desire to connect with the surrounding world. For this reason, the experience of wonder often leads to forms of empathy and selfless concern quite different than would arise in a life shaped solely by the active will."[12] Within the context of our research study, we discovered that the experience of touching, interacting with, or observing another animal brought people together in dialogue and spurred them to let their guard down, ask questions, linger, and engage in visitor-to-visitor and visitor-to-educator interactions. To that end, animal (and human) encounters leveraged potential empathic moments in which we observed increased visitor engagement and involvement in the experience and with each other.

The visitor reaction during a moment of wonder is among the most authentic behaviors observable in the informal science center environment. Because wonder is such a personal emotion, its manifestation in one's expressions, gestures, and verbal responses is typically a very honest lens into the visitor's individual experience. When visitors share their reactions among each other, a community of shared experience naturally occurs, creating the opportunity for that moment to become more than wonder-filled, but also empathic. The visitor's shared authentic response transcends cultural and social barriers, allowing visitors of different backgrounds, knowledge levels, or interests to find a common bond via their experiences. Once an experience establishes a relationship via an exchanged glance, expression, word, comment, question, physical contact, or otherwise, those sharing the experience are linked by their experience. Similar responses to the same experience breed relationships among visitors and cultivate opportunities for empathic dialogue.

Experiencing and sharing wonder around other forms of life not only makes us appreciate our own existence, but also endows an appreciation within us for the complexity of our world ecosystem and the constructive and destructive roles we play in it. Improved understanding of the world around us can potentially incite compassion, which connects empathy and moral development. We consider the consequences of our actions and weigh those differently when equipped with knowledge and wonder of another living being. When informal science center visitors engage in dialogue around a shared experience, the dialogue can deter indifference and spur action. Carolina Raptor Center measured this through visitors' responses to the question, "What will you do?" The 5 answer, "Tell the World!" represents to us true activation—the creation of citizen activists engaged in our mission in the world, the conservation of raptors. Built in relationship with humans and animals, this result is really what we are striving for, and we believe that it can be actualized through the creation of a dynamic visitor experience with empathy and connection at its core. When visitors carry their wonder beyond the informal science center experience, they also carry empathy into the world around them.

Informal science centers play a crucial role in linking wonder and empathy through modeling effective and portable strategies for use beyond their informal learning experiences. Curiosity is an essential ingredient to experiencing wonder, and knowing how to ask the right question to satisfy one's curiosity is at the heart of the pedagogy of informal science centers. We aim to model effective inquiry strategies that can equip visitors with the necessary skills to become facilitators of their own wonder moments. This might occur in demonstrating questions that build upon each other toward a hypothesis, utilizing investigational strategies that help to prove or disprove that hypothesis, or analyzing gathered information to inform one's position. These strategies reflect scientific habits of mind that are essential to creating unique "Wow!" and "How?" moments for every individual. By modeling these habits through extraordinary learning experiences, informal science centers encourage visitors to take ownership of their own wonder. What visitors do as a result of those experiences could become the basis for a future career; a role in advocacy, activism, or fundraising; or, at the most essential level, in coconstructing one's own learning and others'. Developing our visitors' critical-thinking and problem-solving skills and their ability to question and to act upon their research allows them to play a role in social and global issues because they are well informed and invested. Informal science centers are incubators for wonder, empathy, and activation of scientific habits of mind, opening the door to practices and behaviors that can foster empathy within households, families, communities, and the world.

THE IMPACT OF WONDER ON EMPATHY

Throughout our exploration of wonder at Discovery Place and Carolina Raptor Center, we continue to marvel at the ways our visitors engage with us and one another to deepen their knowledge and their connections to the world around them. Our early findings have led us to ask new questions about the nature of visitor interaction during moments of wonder and which interactions result in higher instances of activation than indifference. Already we see our impact on our communities through volunteerism, donor engagement, visitation, as well as the students who become interns and apprentices because of their strong affiliations with our organizations, or the members and repeat visitors who continue to return for programs that have become a part of their families' traditions. As both organizations continue to hone our programmatic efforts to move the empathy dial from indifference to activation, we recognize that our voices are just one in a community dialogue. We aim to motivate our visitors to push our missions forward into their own communities, taking ownership of their learning and becoming active voices in the dialogue about science. When our visitors feel they are empowered with the knowledge and wonder to question and debate the science issues that face our society and our world, their collective voices are louder and stronger. We hope that in those moments they will recall the wonder they experienced as learners at our informal science centers and channel that wonder into a positive impact on our collective future.

NOTES

1. "Wonder," *Dictionary.com*, http://dictionary.reference.com/browse/wonder?s=t (accessed December 11, 2015).

2. "Empathy," *Dictionary.com*, http://dictionary.reference.com/browse/empathy?s=t (accessed December 11, 2015).

3. Goodreads.com, http://www.goodreads.com/quotes/7161-we-do-not-believe-in-ourselves-until-someone-reveals-that (accessed January 26, 2016).

4. "Wonder," *Dictionary.com*.

5. "Heilbrunn Timeline of Art History," *Collecting for the Kunstkammer*, http://www.metmuseum.org/toah/hd/kuns/hd_kuns.htm (accessed December 11, 2015).

6. John Brockman, "Science, Delusion and the Appetite for Wonder: A Talk with Richard Dawkins," *Science, Delusion, and the Appetite for Wonder*, http://edge.org/conversation/richard_dawkins-science-delusion-and-the-appetite-for-wonder (accessed December 11, 2015).

7. John H. Falk and Lynn D. Dierking, "The 95 Percent Solution," *American Scientist* 98, no. 6 (2010): 486.

8. Smokeybear.com,   http://www.smokeybear.com/elements-of-fire.asp (accessed January 16, 2016).

9. Sophia Vasalou, *Practices of Wonder: Cross-disciplinary Perspectives* (Eugene, OR: Pickwick Publishers, 2012), 77.

10. Ibid.

11. J. H. Falk and L. D. Dierking, *Museum Experience Revisited* (Walnut Creek, CA: Left Coast Press, 2012), 215.

12. Vasalou, *Practices of Wonder*, 85.

museums research psyc[h]ology inspires museums empathy

7

The Psychology of Empathy

Compelling Possibilities for Museums

Adam P. Nilsen and Miriam Bader

When it comes down to it, putting oneself in the shoes of another person is a complex social psychological act. Psychologists have published volumes of research that explore exactly what goes on when we try to understand what it is like to be another person, examining factors that both promote and hinder this process. Museum professionals are increasingly seeking to foster empathy through their exhibits,[1] and close attention to current psychological research is key to maximizing the empathic impact of a museum exhibit or program. Given that there are many social benefits to being skilled at taking others' perspectives, including an increase in caring behavior toward others[2] and a decrease in the tendency to stereotype,[3] it is no wonder that many museum professionals have empathy as a goal.

This chapter explores some of the noteworthy research findings about empathy and considers ways in which museum professionals can apply them to their own institutions. This research is paired with examples of how educators at the Lower East Side Tenement Museum in New York City have promoted empathy in their tours. The Tenement Museum is renowned for the idea that fostering empathy with people in other places and times leads us to a deeper understanding of analogous situations in our own context.[4] This chapter begins with a brief background on the Tenement Museum, followed by an overview of concepts relating to empathy. We then turn to seven concrete research findings from studies of empathy and perspective taking, each paired with an example from the Tenement Museum. Because these examples come from a history museum, we conclude with a consideration of how they may apply to other types of museums and informal learning environments. Our hope is to inspire others to look to scholarly research and to get creative in experimenting with its applications.

THE LOWER EAST SIDE TENEMENT MUSEUM

Since its founding in 1988, the Tenement Museum has inspired visitors to connect to the theme of immigration past and present by elevating the stories of everyday people and building exhibits and tours around them. The museum is located in a narrow, five-story tenement on the Lower East Side of New York City at 97 Orchard Street (figure 7.1). Constructed in 1863 to house an influx of new immigrants, the building's apartments were home to seven thousand people from twenty nations over the years. In 1935, a new building code led to the tenement being condemned as a residence, and it continued to serve the community as a commercial space until the museum was established. Today, the museum welcomes over 220,000 visitors each year, including 50,000 K–12 school students. All visitors explore the museum on guided tours, visiting apartments that have been recreated to interpret the lives of families who once lived and worked in the building. To date, eight distinct and thematic tours are offered at 97 Orchard Street (figure 7.2). This educator-led experience allows museum staff to keep both the visitors and the spaces safe and to offer a highly responsive educational experience. All tours strive to engage visitors with history and foster connections between the stories of the residents of 97 Orchard Street, visitors' personal experiences, and larger social, economic, and political contexts. For many visitors, empathy is key to forging such connections.

CONCEPTUALIZING EMPATHY AND RELATED TERMS

It is important to note, however, that scholars have drawn useful distinctions between empathy and several closely related concepts.[5] The most basic of these concepts is *perspective taking*, the effort to explore the thoughts and feelings of another person and to come up with a theory of what is going on in that person's mind.[6] *Empathy* is distinguished as a feeling of *shared emotion* with another person: you feel happy, and I imagine what you must feel like, leading me to feel happy too. Empathy thus may be the result of perspective taking, but not always. *Sympathy*, by contrast, is a feeling of pity for another person. Many people use these terms interchangeably, and in this chapter, when we cite a study, we use the same terminology used by the authors of the study.

RESEARCH FINDINGS

In what follows, we present a number of recommendations for promoting empathy in museums, using the nuances and concepts that psychological

Figure 7.1. Façade of 97 Orchard Street today. Photograph by Keiko Niwa.

Figure 7.2.   Group of visitors in the Baldizzi family's apartment, featured on the *Hard Times* tour. Photograph by Keiko Niwa.

research has revealed. We outline seven actions that may be taken to foster empathy or counteract biases associated with low empathy. Very little of this research has taken place in the context of museums, so we encourage readers to consider ways in which these findings may or may not apply to different kinds of museums and to use the examples from the Tenement Museum as inspiration for other ways in which these ideas may be applied. We begin with one of the most foundational areas of research.

1. *Provide context and guide visitors to reflect on their own positionality in order to avoid egocentric bias and the fundamental attribution error.* It can be difficult to get out of our own heads: to move beyond the *egocentric bias* that leads us to assume that others think the same way we do. Psychologists view perspective taking as a process of modulating egocentric bias by "anchoring and adjusting": we initially project our own perspective onto another person and use that perspective as an anchor, and we then sequentially (and often very rapidly) locate differences between ourselves and the other person. Each time we locate a difference, we adjust our evaluation of how the other person must be thinking.[7] For instance, in thinking about the Salem Witch Trials, one may initially apply his or her own present-day judgment (e.g., "The idea of witchcraft is silly—there is no such thing!") to a person living in seventeenth-century Salem, and then locate differences (e.g., "Unlike me,

these were people living in a strict Puritan culture," "People thought very differently about the 'supernatural' than I do," "Gender dynamics were very different than they are in my own context") and adjust that initial judgment until arriving at a more refined understanding of the other person's perspective.

If something hinders this process, we may be apt to commit the *fundamental attribution error*: we fail to look at the other person's unique context and we attribute the other person's actions to something about his or her *inherent* personality. A classic example is that if a man cuts you off while you are driving, you may assume that he is inherently a jerk and do not consider whether he is perhaps driving someone to the emergency room. When we apply these notions of egocentric bias and the fundamental attribution error to the study of the past, scholars have used the term *presentism*: the tendency to judge people of the past by present-day norms and standards, ignoring differences in context. A key way in which to help people get beyond egocentric bias, the fundamental attribution error, and presentism is thus to provide contextualizing information on which to base more sophisticated perspective taking.

In a museum setting, failing to provide such information may make it impossible for a visitor to entertain the perspective of another person. The Tenement Museum thus strives to provide context to all of the family stories that are presented. Being transparent with visitors about how we know what we know fosters a nuanced understanding of the history. Inviting visitors to investigate primary sources like census records, court documents, and historic photos allows visitors to coconstruct the context with the educator and to use the information they uncover, along with the questions they raise, to gain a deeper understanding of an immigrant's experience (figure 7.3). Doing so also encourages everyone in a tour group to reflect on his or her own experience and life context and to share their unique points of view with each other, exploring how these perspectives differ.

2. *Elicit lists of reasons to combat the hindsight bias.* Another factor that may make it feel easy to pass judgment about people living in other times is the fact that we have a sort of privileged information: the benefit of hindsight. We can look back at a summary of a person's life or read an overview of a historical period and see and know things that a person living in that context could not have seen, known, or predicted. We also know the outcome of historical events: for example, who won and who lost, or who was successful and who was not. A failure to recognize this privileged information is known as the *hindsight bias*, and it may often lead us to think that we could have predicted the outcome of an event, as though the event were inevitable. In relation to perspective taking, this bias reflects a failure to put ourselves thoughtfully into the shoes of another person and take stock of

Figure 7.3. Educators are trained to use primary sources to engage visitors in the material. Photograph by Miriam Bader.

the information that the person was working with. As an example, take the story of miners who came to California during the Gold Rush beginning in 1848. We know today that very few of the miners struck it rich, but that is only because we can look back at the period as a whole. One may think,

"Of course they were not going to get rich! They should have known all along," and for that reason, one may even assume that gold miners were "idiots" for not foreseeing their supposedly inevitable failure.[8] It is easy to lose sight of the fact that, in a gold miner's reality, striking it rich was a true and well-reasoned possibility.

Research has suggested two different ways of attenuating the hindsight bias.[9] One way is to encourage people to come up with a list of reasons why a particular outcome occurred. In the case of the Gold Rush, this would mean coming up with many reasons why gold miners rarely struck it rich, such as widespread illness, crime and lawlessness, racism and prejudice, and competition between miners. The goal with coming up with such a list is to show that many different circumstances came together to lead to a particular outcome: that miners were not inherently "idiots," but that they navigated multiple complex dynamics that guided their fate. It may also be useful to consider how a change in one of these dynamics may have led to a different outcome, supporting the notion that the outcome was not inevitable.

Museum practitioners can thus counter hindsight bias by encouraging visitors to see the many different situations and dynamics that would have guided the thoughts, decision-making processes, and actions of people of the past. At the Tenement Museum, storytelling has proven a powerful tool in this effort. Building a rich narrative filled with details about daily life and worldviews of the time helps visitors to understand the reasons behind particular outcomes. For example, during a tour, visitors are often surprised to hear that tenement families tended to have large numbers of children. Hindsight bias can lead to the assumption that it was ignorant and stupid for parents to have big families, and to the thought that "of course there was overcrowding and poverty—they should have just had fewer children!" This reaction demonstrates a failure to put oneself in the perspective of a person living in the past. To preempt such judgments, educators use their narrative skills to offer visitors a different way of seeing the situation. They discuss the challenges of being an immigrant and leaving one's family in the old country with the hopes of building new family and community by having many children. The importance of the family economy is also essential to understand. The educator shares examples from the 1900 census that underline how important children's wages were to the household. According to the 1910 US Immigration Commission, foreign-born families in general derived 21.1 percent of their household income from children's work, with Russian Jews deriving the most at 30.7 percent. The high child mortality rate in the Lower East Side would also have contributed to a family's decision to have more children. The educator also notes how religious beliefs and access to education about birth control impacted family planning. These details help visitors to see the situation from the point of view of someone from the past and to replace thoughts that are tinged by hindsight bias with a thought that is more empathic: "I can see how, given those many factors, it made sense to have a big family. People in that context had a different way of thinking and reasoning than I do today."

3. *Encourage visitors to make an emotional connection to another person.* Hand in hand with these cognitive needs for contextual information is the usefulness of emotional connection in promoting empathy. In one study, Mendoza compared two different ways of encouraging people to empathize with another person: either through "situation-based" empathy or through "emotion-based" empathy.[10] In his study, romantic couples or pairs of roommates came into a lab, and person A shared a grievance about person B. In the situation-based condition, person B was asked to think about person A's situation and to say how he or she would have felt *in person A's situation.* In the emotion-based condition, person B was asked to describe how person A was feeling and then to recall *an emotionally analogous situation* in which he or she had similar feelings, regardless of whether the situation itself was similar. Mendoza found that the feeling of being *emotionally similar* to each other made the participants in the emotion-based condition more empathic with and understanding of each other than participants in the situation-based condition.

The staff of the Tenement Museum has noted that encouraging visitors to make these kinds of emotional analogies to their own lives is an effective way of guiding visitors to empathize with people of the past and to feel connected to the historical material. An example is the museum's *Irish Outsiders* tour, which introduces the experience of the Moores, an Irish immigrant family struggling with prejudice in 1869. In this tour, an educator may ask visitors to recall a time when they themselves felt like outsiders to get at what emotions they associated with that feeling of being an outsider. As humans, we have all likely experienced some combination of the emotions associated with being an outsider, such as anger, indignation, or disappointment. Creating the space for visitors to see similarities between their own feelings and those of the Moore family makes it easier for visitors to empathize with the Moores even though they lived in very different contexts.

4. *Endow visitors with the role of another person.* Visitors may be able to take these cognitive and emotional components of empathy one step further, into living history scenarios, where they take on the roles of past people in order to gain a deeper and more empathic understanding of a past person's experience and perspective. Unlike theater or reenactment, participants are not observers watching someone else's actions, but rather take an active role in the performance. One of the most robust pieces of research to support this method of teaching empathy through living history is a study

by Stroessner, Beckerman, and Whittaker.[11] The researchers evaluated the effects of the *Reacting to the Past* program in which, over the course of a semester, university students participate in a series of history role playing "games," such as "Confucianism and the Succession Crisis of the Wanli Emperor, 1587" and "The Threshold of Democracy: Athens in 403 BC." Students each receive a role and explore primary sources and contextualizing information, and the instructor's role becomes limited as students build arguments to support a set of objectives based on the historical material. The researchers found that students who took courses using this *Reacting to the Past* methodology demonstrated higher empathy and self-esteem, as well as superior rhetorical skills, in comparison to students who took a course that did not involve *Reacting to the Past*. *Reacting to the Past* is different from a typical museum visit in that it lasts for multiple weeks, but in combination with research on the success of living history in museums,[12] it is reasonable to expect that role playing may elicit empathy in a single visit.

At the Tenement Museum, staff has similarly observed that immersive role play helps visitors to connect empathically. An example is *Meet Victoria*, a program offered to visitors of all ages (figure 7.4). In this program, visitors meet a costumed interpreter playing the role of Victoria Confino, a fourteen-year-old who immigrated with her family from Kastoria, Greece, in 1913. The educator prepares the visitors by assigning them the role of new immigrants from Russia who have arrived in New York City in 1916. Visitors are encouraged to ask Victoria questions that they have as "immigrants" in a new country. In order to help the visitors get into character, the educator shares a variety of resources that provide context, including historical images of the shtetl from which they moved, descriptions of their sixteen-day boat journey, and information about their experience at Ellis Island. As they become an immigrant family starting a new life in America, the visitors take on a role analogous to Victoria's. By creating a scenario in which the visitors need advice from Victoria, they come to see Victoria as a contemporary instead of a stranger from the past—a view that helps them see the world from her perspective. As visitors have written in their comments, "OMG she was so good I forgot she was an actress!" and "This experience has made me appreciate my own ancestors' experience more and those of current immigrants now. I'm usually so comfortable in my shell that I didn't know how this would be, but I was surprised by how much I got into it." Such comments suggest that the immersive and sensory experience of visiting with Victoria in her apartment helps visitors maintain their role, suspend disbelief, and limit egocentric bias.

5. *Give vivid instructions for how to empathize.* The four suggestions mentioned thus far are based on the hope that creating the right circumstances will elicit empathy, but there may be times when a museum educator deems

Figure 7.4. A school group visiting victoria during the *Meet Victoria* program.
Photograph by Miriam Bader.

it appropriate to ask visitors *explicitly* to engage in perspective taking or empathy. In this case, it is important to consider the research of Galinsky, who found that, in order to encourage people to empathize, it may be necessary to give them very vivid instructions for how to do so.[13] In his study, he gave people either minimal empathy instructions (simply to "take the perspective" of another person) or vivid empathy instructions (to "take the perspective" of another person, but also to "think about what it would be like" to be the other person, "imagine what it would be like to" be in the other person's shoes, to "imagine what it would feel like to be in [another person's] situation," and to "try to visualize yourself in the other person's role"). He then gave them a complex task that required them to think through another person's perspective. Those who received the vivid instructions at the start of the study showed deeper consideration of the other person's perspective than did those who received the minimal instructions. Additional instructions mentioned by Galinsky include to "concentrate" on the other person and "in your mind's eye, visualize clearly and vividly how he feels in this situation." In reference specifically to historical perspective taking, Nilsen added additional vivid instructions:[14] "Imagine what it would feel like to see the world with a different set of eyes and living in a different time and place. Try your hardest to question the assumptions you may have that are based on the context you live in." If a museum professional is hoping to promote empathy through an exhibit or a program, it may not be enough to ask visitors to take the perspective of another person; additional, process-oriented instructions such as those used by Galinsky and Nilsen may be necessary.

The *Meet Victoria* program also serves as an example of this strategy. In order to get visitors into the roles they will play, the educator gives explicit instructions, asking the visitor to imagine what it would be like to be living in 1916. Visitors are guided to leave their contemporary perspective behind in order to tap into another era, and they are instructed to imagine what they would hear, smell, and feel at that time. These process-oriented instructions are key to getting visitors into character.

However, in other contexts these kinds of explicit instructions might be awkward, infantilizing, or forced. We thus pose the question: In what situations would it be constructive to give visitors instructions to empathize? This might make sense in museums that are more self-guided than the Tenement Museum, where it could be part of an audio guide, or it could be part of introductory text in an orientation space. Further research would be useful here, but it is productive to recognize that a prompt that may seem straightforward to museum professionals may need to be fleshed out for visitors.

6. *Guide visitors to avoid hot-cold empathy gaps by giving them a small sample of another person's experience.* Another common hindrance to empathy is the notion of *hot-cold empathy gaps*. A "hot" emotional state is one that is emotionally charged, like fear, hunger, anger, or embarrassment, and a "cold" emotional state is the opposite, like sense of security, satedness, calm, or social comfort. Studies have shown that when we ourselves are in a "cold" state, we have a hard time empathizing with or predicting what it is like to be in the opposite (i.e., "hot") state. In one study, participants were told a story of three backpackers lost in the wilderness and asked to predict how uncomfortable the backpackers' thirst would be. Half of the participants had just exercised at the gym (and were thus thirsty themselves), while the other half had not. Participants who had just exercised predicted that the backpackers' thirst would be worse, in comparison to the predictions made by participants who had not just exercised.[15] When a museum visitor is in a comfortable, climate-controlled museum, free of feelings like fear, cold, or thirst, is he or she really able to grasp what it would be like to be terrified, freezing, or parched?

This line of research suggests that a museum could elicit empathy by giving visitors a small sample of the experience of another person. In a study by Nordgren, McDonnell, and Loewenstein, participants were asked to imagine that they were schoolchildren who, as punishment, were being forced to stand outside in the cold without a jacket.[16] One-third of the study participants were asked to stand out in the cold themselves, another third were asked to keep one arm in a bucket of ice water, and the other third were asked to keep one arm in a bucket of warm water. The researchers asked the participants to predict how uncomfortable one of these hypothetical students would feel. Remarkably, those who had an arm in ice water *and* those who actually stood out in the cold themselves both made the *same* estimates about how uncomfortable the hypothetical student would feel. That is, it did not matter whether they were actually experiencing being in the cold or just having an arm in ice water. Just having a "sample" of the situation—having an arm in ice water—led people to empathize just as much as people who were experiencing the full situation firsthand by standing out in the cold.

Visitors to the Tenement Museum may experience these kinds of hot-cold empathy gaps and have a hard time grasping the "hot" feelings that the residents of 97 Orchard Street likely felt. The immersive and dynamic format of the exhibits, however, creates opportunities for visitors to sample aspects of residents' daily life. For example, visitors are asked to crowd into small spaces so they can experience the crowding firsthand. On some tours, they are also asked to lift heavy buckets as residents would have, and to stand in hot rooms without air conditioning. Educators build these components directly into the narrative and encourage visitors to use the experience to gain insight into what it might have been like for the building's residents. Giving visitors samples of crowdedness, strain, and heat can foster deeper empathy than simply describing such feelings to visitors. As one visitor noted in a focus group with regard to the feeling of being crowded, "The thing that I appreciate about something like this is that it makes it a lot more tangible. Again, you can have a sort of theoretical, academic, abstract conversation of, 'people will double up, triple up [in bedrooms]' but when you've seen so many people in a unit, it becomes a very real, personalized kind of experience."

7. *Do not overload your visitors and risk subjecting them to desensitization bias.* With all of the methods we have described so far, an important concept to keep in mind is the *desensitization bias*. Psychologists have found that when a person is repeatedly exposed to some sort of stimulus, he or she may become desensitized and thus have a hard time empathizing with someone who is experiencing the stimulus for the first time. Campbell and colleagues tested this by exposing participants in their study to an annoying noise[17]— some participants heard the noise for forty seconds and some heard it for five seconds. Those who heard the noise for forty seconds, and who had therefore become desensitized to it, found the sound less annoying than those

who heard it for only five seconds. The researchers then asked participants how annoying they thought the noise would be for *another* person hearing the noise for the first time. Those who heard it for forty seconds predicted that the noise would be *less* annoying than those who heard it for only five seconds. In comparison to the five-second listeners, the forty-second listeners *also* said they would feel less bad if another person was forced to hear the noise. The researchers suggest that a way to sidestep this desensitization bias may be to encourage people to imagine how they would have felt the *first* time they heard the annoying noise or to observe the reactions of other people who are experiencing the stimulus for the first time. In a museum, is it possible to give visitors too much of a stimulus—for instance, too many upsetting images of people in danger—such that they become desensitized and no longer empathize with the people in the images?

At the Tenement Museum, desensitization bias can be illustrated through the visitors' experience with the physical layout and size of apartments. Each apartment contains three rooms, which total approximately 325 square feet and housed an average of six people. Windows and doors of one apartment often led directly into those of neighboring apartments, creating few opportunities for privacy from family members or neighbors. Visitors are often shocked by this and feel a sense of discomfort within the physical space. However, after visiting a few of the spaces in the building, visitors sometimes remark at the tour's conclusion that "that was not that bad after all." Such comments highlight how visitors became desensitized to the physical layout of the space. To counter this, it can help to encourage visitors to remember how they initially felt when they began the tour. It is also productive to connect the topic to an analogous experience in visitors' own lives, such as their first time in Times Square or on a crowded rush hour subway train. This seems to help visitors discern the difference between their current feelings and the ones they had initially empathized with.

CONCLUSION

Our goal in this chapter was to introduce the museum community to some of the rich psychological research on empathy and perspective taking and to consider ways in which museums like the Tenement Museum may use this research in their efforts to promote empathy and perspective taking. Granted, much of this research has been conducted inside university psychology labs and not "real-world" environments, and museum professionals may find that these research findings apply only in certain circumstances or in certain ways. For instance, perhaps they will find that explicitly discussing the fundamental attribution error with visitors sets them up to be more empathic, or perhaps they will find that vivid instructions to empathize are most effectively sprinkled throughout an exhibit instead of just at the beginning. Furthermore, additional research is needed to explore the relationship between empathy with specific individuals and empathy with a broader group: How might it be different to encourage empathy with an individual, such as Anne Frank, versus empathy with a broader group, such as Jews during the Holocaust? In addition, if museum professionals hope to foster empathy in visitors, it is necessary to examine how a single museum visit can impact how a person empathizes. While assessments have been made of longer-term empathy-related curricula in classrooms, museum professionals would be wise to consider the extent to which empathy, if sparked in a single visit, endures after a visitor leaves. Longitudinal studies would be most useful here. We invite museum professionals to build creative new means of promoting empathy using these research findings, to conduct their own studies in their own institutions, and to report on their own findings.

While we have focused on empathy and perspective taking in the context of a history museum, we argue that these research findings may apply readily to other kinds of museums. Educators at natural science museums, for instance, may examine how visitors may be subject to hindsight bias when they evaluate past scientists' work based on what we know today, or how visitors empathize with animals or even broader ideas like an anthropomorphized Earth. Art museum professionals may find that visitors are desensitized by engaging with a large number of graphic and disturbing artworks. At the very least, this chapter helps us use psychological research to illuminate nuances of empathy and perspective taking that we may have observed before but not had a shared vocabulary on which to base discussions. We encourage museum professionals to use tools such as Google Scholar to search for and read the latest articles that come out in this burgeoning field of research. Doing so will help museum professionals to think smarter about these complex mental acts that may have wide-ranging benefits for visitors.

ACKNOWLEDGMENTS

This chapter builds on a presentation at the American Alliance of Museums' 2015 annual conference entitled *Exploring Empathy: Research on a Hot (but Tricky) Topic*, given by the authors and Rebecca Shulman Herz.

NOTES

1. Leslie Bedford, *The Art of Museum Exhibitions: How Story and Imagination Create Aesthetic Experiences* (Walnut Creek, CA: Left Coast Press, 2014); Mihalyi

Csikszentmihalyi and Kim Hermanson, "Intrinsic Motivation in Museums: Why Does One Want to Learn?" in *Public Institutions for Personal Learning*, ed. John H. Falk and Lynn D. Dierking (Washington, DC: American Association of Museums, 1994), 65.

2. Nancy Eisenberg, Richard A. Fabes, and Tracy L. Spinrad, "Prosocial Development," in *Social, Emotional, and Personality Development*, ed. Nancy Eisenberg, vol. 3 of *Handbook of Child Psychology*, 6th ed., ed. William Damon and Richard M. Lerner (Hoboken, NJ: Wiley, 2006), 646.

3. Adam D. Galinsky and Gordon B. Moskowitz, "Perspective-Taking: Decreasing Stereotype Expression, Stereotype Accessibility, and In-Group Favoritism," *Journal of Personality and Social Psychology* 78, no. 4 (2000): 708.

4. Ruth J. Abram, "Harnessing the Power of History," in *Museums, Society, and Inequality*, ed. Richard Sandell (New York: Routledge, 2002), 125.

5. Eisenberg, Fabes, and Spinrad, "Prosocial Development," 646.

6. Adam P. Nilsen, "Navigating Windows into Past Human Minds: A Framework of Shifting Selves in Historical Perspective Taking," *Journal of the Learning Sciences*, forthcoming.

7. Nicholas Epley, Boaz Keysar, Leaf Van Boven, and Thomas Gilovich, "Perspective Taking as Egocentric Anchoring and Adjustment," *Journal of Personality and Social Psychology* 87, no. 3 (2004): 327.

8. A. P. Nilsen, "Museum Visitor Encounters with Real People of the Past" (in preparation).

9. Lawrence J. Sanna, Norbert Schwarz, and Eulena M. Small, "Accessibility Experiences and the Hindsight Bias: I Knew It All Along Versus It Could Never Have Happened," *Memory and Cognition* 30 (2002): 1288.

10. Ronaldo J. Mendoza, "Emotional Versus Situational Inductions of Empathy: Effects on Interpersonal Understanding and Punitiveness" (PhD diss., Stanford University, 1997).

11. Steven J. Stroessner, Laurie Susser Beckerman, and Alexis Whittaker, "All The World's a Stage? Consequences of a Role-Playing Pedagogy on Psychological Factors and Writing and Rhetorical Skills on College Undergraduates," *Journal of Educational Psychology* 101, no. 3 (2009): 605.

12. Anthony Jackson and Jenny Kidd, *Performance, Learning, and Heritage* (Manchester, UK: Center for Applied Theater Research, 2008).

13. Adam D. Galinsky, "Perspective Taking: Debiasing Social Thought" (PhD diss., Princeton University, 1999).

14. Nilsen, *Journal of the Learning Sciences*.

15. Leaf Van Boven and George Loewenstein, "Empathy Gaps in Emotional Perspective Taking," in *Other Minds: How Humans Bridge the Divide Between Self and Others*, ed. Bertram F. Malle and Sara D. Hodges (New York: Guilford Press, 2005), 284.

16. Loran F. Nordgren, Mary-Hunter Morris McDonnell, and George Loewenstein, "What Constitutes Torture? Psychological Impediments to an Objective Evaluation of Enhanced Interrogation Tactics," *Psychological Science* 20, no. 10 (2011): 1.

17. Troy Campbell, Ed O'Brien, Leaf Van Boven, Norbert Schwarz, and Peter Ubel, "Too Much Experience: A Desensitization Bias in Emotional Perspective Taking," *Journal of Personality and Social Psychology* 106, no. 2 (2014): 272.

altruism→cognitive→compassionate→emotional→empathy

8

Finding Inspiration Inside

Engaging Empathy to Empower Everyone

Dina Bailey

What does it mean to have empathy? Why do we need to be empathetic? As we increasingly become global citizens, human beings come in ever closer contact with those who are seemingly different from themselves. Fostering empathy has become an essential component of not only international relations, but everyday interactions. As our schools, neighborhoods, and workplaces become more diverse, individuals are asked to find within themselves the capacity to understand and feel for those who are "the other." Empathy asks a person to place him- or herself in another's position; to experience, feel, and understand from another person's perspective. Conversely, a lack of empathy has contributed to an increase in violence, hate crimes, and intolerance of "the other" due to manipulating the acknowledgment of differences in ethnicity, gender, age, orientation, and social/economic status. That said, empathy is still a shared human value.

We all want to be accepted on both intellectual and emotional levels. It stands to reason that if we want to be understood in this way, then we must also strive to understand and accept others on these levels. Sometimes this is easier said than done. Attributes that ultimately come together to shape empathy include the awareness that, as individuals, we need to be more self-aware, more culturally aware, and more sensitive in order to be more accepting and more inclusive of those we deem to be different from ourselves. As cultural institutions, museums are often looked upon as safe places in which individuals can immerse themselves in dialogues, experiences, and knowledge attainment in order to learn more about a world that is becoming increasingly smaller and more complex for everyone.

The National Center for Civil and Human Rights (the Center) is just such a place. The Center has consciously worked to establish itself as a space that is grounded in institutional empathy, that utilizes empathy as a tool for more deeply engaging audiences, and that provides opportunities for empathy to be recognized as an outcome of the Center's various experiences. This chapter will use the knowledge gained from the first eighteen months of the Center's opening as a case study that will highlight a focus on empathy from conceptualization, to current status, to potential paths for the Center's future. Having opened in June 2014 in the heart of Atlanta, this cultural institution utilizes the lessons of the past in order to better understand what is happening in the present. Guests are not only immersed in experiences of the past, but also in human rights movements that are happening today. Throughout the exhibitions is a thread that emphasizes the power that individuals have to make a difference. In drawing such visible connections between the struggles and triumphs of the past to those of the present, guests are more amenable to taking positive action in the present in order to build a better future for all people. How does the Center strategically engage in fostering empathy? And why is this seen as an institutional responsibility?

As cultural institutions have done for centuries, the Center began with the spark of an idea and an intention. The spark came from civil rights legends Evelyn Lowery, Juanita Abernathy, and Andrew Young. In a meeting with the mayor at the time, Shirley Franklin, they spoke with passion about the need for a new institution in Atlanta, a concept that would eventually lead to the creation of one of the few places globally that strategically works to increase guest awareness about the bridge between the American Civil Rights Movement and contemporary human rights movements around the world. The intention of the Center is to create a safe space for guests to explore the fundamental rights of all human beings so that they leave inspired and empowered to join ongoing human rights movements. Simply put, the Center's purpose is to educate, inspire, and empower individuals to be positive change agents for the protection of everyone's human rights today. It is admittedly a tall order, and empathy is at the heart of this original intention and overall purpose.

The Center engages with empathy on a number of levels and it all began with seeing a need and making a commitment—a mission and vision that intend to positively change hearts and minds. As stated on the Center's website (www.civilandhumanrights.org), the mission of the Center is to "empower people to take the protection of every human's rights personally." Through sharing stories of courage and struggles from around the world, the Center encourages guests to gain a deeper understanding of the role they play in helping to protect the rights of all people. This is accomplished by harnessing Atlanta's legacy of civil rights in order to strengthen worldwide movements for human rights. Those who conceptualized the Center recognized that Atlanta played a unique leadership role in the

American Civil Rights Movement and that the legacy of this may be used to galvanize individuals to reflect on the past, transform the present, and inspire a better future.

Established in 2007, and having opened its doors in 2014, the Center has consistently been supported by civil rights icons, contemporary human rights leaders, and others whose influence from within governmental, educational, and faith-based organizations promoted inclusivity and empathy from the first focus group to the opening of the Center's doors and beyond. In addition to inclusivity and empathy being natural values placed at the heart of all strategic discussions, the Center developed a cadre of additional values that have since been converted into tried and true techniques and critical frameworks. This foundation, upon which the Center has been built, is a solid base from which the Center will be able to expand its efforts as a relevant, impactful institution.

The founding principles of the Center have been a strong part of the development of a space where individual empowerment is paramount, where knowledge is gained through individual inspiration, and where a focus on the future and future generations is vital to measurements of successful impact. Those who are familiar with the Center see these threads throughout its exhibitions, programs, and institutional statements. The exhibitions highlight individual experiences that are woven together to culminate in a complex tapestry that utilizes the highlights and lowlights of people's triumphs and struggles in order to bring empathy, hope, and empowerment to those guests who witness the power of the exhibitions. Similarly, the Center's programs are intentionally shaped to bring together a variety of perspectives that highlight connections between the past and present, local and national/international priorities, and generational memories. The programs emphasize personal storytelling, interpersonal dialogues, broadening audience awareness, and encouraging individual actions. And as the Center makes statements on a number of platforms (utilizing both traditional and innovative methods), institutional statements promote the protection of every person's human rights, not just those whose values are similar to the current leadership team's.

What makes the Center distinctive? Part of what sets the Center apart from others is that empathy has been at the heart of the institution since its inception. Another aspect is that the Center is currently one of the newest cultural institutions in the United States. And in just starting out, it has the benefit of being able to shape itself within the context of contemporary stakeholder expectations such as relevance, present-day emphasis, and social action. While many museums are attempting to adapt and update their missions and institutional interpretations, the Center is starting from a place of fostering soft skills that will aid individuals in adapting to the world as it continues to "shrink." As countries, communities, and neighborhoods are being impacted by what other countries, communities, and neighborhoods are doing, the Center is in a position to dynamically support understanding, empathy, and positive action.

This institution is still in an exploratory phase with its exhibitions, programs, and overall institutional strategies. In the first several years of the Center being open, its leadership team will continue to define its identity as stakeholders are influenced by global politics, economics, and social/cultural emphases. Acknowledging this from its inception, the Center will continue to develop processes that will allow for increasingly faster reaction times and even proactive statements based on valuing legacies and lessons of the past that are impacting current issues. Because of this, the Center is developing in a space and time where it will be able to dynamically impact the fostering of empathy and social change through multiple generations. It has the potential to truly be at the heart of its community, and its community is inclusive of conversations happening at the local, state, regional, national, and international levels in the realms of both civil and human rights.

To be clear, civil rights fall under the umbrella of human rights. Civil rights protect individuals' civil and political freedoms in order to ensure that people are able to contribute civically within a specific society. Examples of civil rights include freedom of speech, freedom of the press, and the right to vote. Human rights are inherent to all human beings regardless of any specific attribute or status (like gender, religion, ethnicity, etc.). Examples of human rights include the fact that all human beings have the right to be born into freedom, that human beings should be recognized as human beings in the eyes of the law, and that human beings have the right to times of rest. All of these examples were taken from the United Nations' Universal Declaration of Human Rights, which will be discussed in more detail later in the chapter.

Dialogues about individual and collective civil and human rights are continuously swirling in and around the Center. Within the physical space, parents and grandparents are having conversations with their children and grandchildren that they've never had before. Students are asking their fellow classmates about their cultural traditions, heroes, and histories. People from different ethnicities, genders, and faiths are respectfully listening to others' opinions as facilitators moderate dialogues on topics as diverse as immigration, school to prison pipelines, and environmental justice. And conversations are being had digitally about how individuals are responding to both global threats and global victories. There is often a direct connection between these contemporary, global events and the past events that draw the focus of the Center's civil rights exhibition.

It is within *Rolls Down Like Water: The American Civil Rights Movement* that guests encounter acts of violence and resilience that look strikingly similar to what we see through our media outlets on a daily basis. Every inch of the exhibition space encourages guests to acknowledge the perspective of an individual, empathize with those who lived through the modern civil rights era, and reflect on what they would have done (or did do) during the American Civil Rights Movement. While there are numerous aspects of note within this exhibition, the most well-known interactive within *Rolls Down Like Water* is an immersive experience that focuses on the sit-ins that began at Woolworth's lunch counter in 1960. The interactive was developed with the latest technology. In sitting down at the counter, an individual may experience approximately ninety seconds of what it might have felt like to prepare oneself to be nonviolent at a sit-in. As short as the experience is, and while guests recognize that the interactive pales in comparison to actual events, those ninety or so seconds are enough to internalize what otherwise might have been merely glanced at in a more traditional museum setting. It is enough for some individuals to see their parents, grandparents, or mentors in a new light. It is enough for many to more deeply respect the courageous activists of the past and to ponder what actions they might be courageous enough to take today.

The civil rights exhibition is more chronological in nature than the Center's other exhibitions, and just like its title, *Rolls Down Like Water*, implies, the thread of empathy flows and builds throughout the exhibition until guests are completely and naturally embraced by a sense of understanding, sympathy, and compassion in the final room titled "Requiem." Here, in a place of personal and collective remembrance, individuals are given the space to come to terms with the internal changes that have taken place since they first stepped into *Rolls Down Like Water*.

A similar sense of serenity and emotional quietude may be found in the *Voice to the Voiceless: The Morehouse College Martin Luther King, Jr. Collection*. While this gallery is permanent, its exhibition consistently rotates archival documents and personal objects from the collection. The collection is owned by Morehouse College and is within the custody of the Robert W. Woodruff Library at Atlanta University Center. The Center has an agreement to publically display it. The distinctive aspect of this permanent exhibition space, in addition to the fact that the objects and themes consistently rotate, is that the focus is on Martin Luther King Jr. as a human being, a complex individual who had strengths and weaknesses just like every individual who views the rotation. Each time a rotation is introduced, guests see Dr. King from a new lens; while still unquestionably powerful, he becomes multifaceted rather than remaining the uncomplicated icon that it is often easier to accept him as being. Whether they are learning about the meaning of the Nobel Peace Prize or drawing inspiration from Dr. King's relationship with youth leaders, guests to the rotations see Dr. King as someone who they can relate to through intrinsic values that may be shared by all human beings.

Dr. King's capacity for empathy was one of his strongest character traits. And by spotlighting one of Atlanta's most recognized sons, guests are able to put a face to the value. Empathy, as well as other values shared by human beings, is visible within the Center's next (and final) permanent exhibition.

It is within the Center's human rights gallery, *Spark of Conviction: The Global Human Rights Movement*, that guests are introduced to the breadth of global threats and triumphs happening today. The United Nations' Universal Declaration of Human Rights (UDHR) is the foundation upon which examples of victories and challenges are spotlighted within the Center's exhibitions and programs; this is done in a way that intentionally encourages guests to take the impetus to delve deeper into issues that they personally find of interest. The introduction to the human rights exhibition begins with a recognition of the significance of the UDHR, which was a direct result of the global reaction to World War II. The UDHR was adopted by the United Nations in 1948 and is recognized as a milestone document in the history of human rights. This document declares that there are universal rights that people have simply because they are human beings; consisting of thirty articles, the UDHR promotes a collective respect for the inherent rights of human beings regardless of status or any other differentiator.

Within this gallery, guests are encouraged to explicitly make connections between the past and present. Beginning with images from the Holocaust, guests move forward into a brightly lit, open space in which they witness a "battleground" of human rights. To the left, guests see images of human rights offenders—Adolf Hitler and Idi Amin being just two examples. To the right, guests see images of human rights defenders—Mahatma Gandhi and Nelson Mandela being examples here. And in the middle of the room are images of real people who are fighting for human rights today. Many of these current freedom fighters have visited the Center since its opening.

It is also within the human rights gallery that guests are brought face to face with legacies of the American Civil Rights Movement; these are issues that those who live within the United States are still working through today, issues that are both a part of our civil rights history as well as a part of our civil rights present. In this space, panels delve into such subjects as abolition, civil rights, reparations, democracy, and rule of law. Additionally, guests are encouraged to measure their personal values against national and international focuses. Examples of these focus areas include economic rights, LGBT rights, women's rights, national security, education, voting rights, and racial discrimination. Nearing the end of the human rights exhibition, guests are asked to consider their own ethical footprints, their relationships with technology, and their understanding of political freedom as viewed on an international spectrum. As evidenced earlier, *The Spark of Conviction* includes a breadth of human rights focus; it is the intention (and the Center has found success here) that guests will be inspired by the breadth of knowledge and will hold themselves responsible for gaining more depth. Finally, it is within the interactive tables in this exhibition that guests are encouraged to consider what positive acts of social change they can take in sixty seconds, sixty minutes, and sixty days. The emphasis on action comes after guests have used the interactive (touchscreen) tables to learn about more subjects that were not otherwise covered within the physical constraints of human rights gallery. Many of these subject areas align with true stories that also take precedence within the interactive tables.

To conclude the visitor experience, guests are given the opportunity to view a video in the Center's *Move, Free, Act* gallery. This gallery encompasses a fast-paced, lively video that emphasizes the power individuals have to be positive change agents in the world. As with the *Spark of Conviction* exhibition, the video within this space is meant to embolden its viewers. Through both historically recognizable images (such as Tiananmen Square) and the bonding of broader experiences (such as voting), guests feel a connection to others physically sharing the experience with them as well as to those people from around the world whose life experiences helped to create the video. As guests exit this space, they may share their voices or their commitments through an image/video booth. Individuals are able to take a picture of themselves (and a video if they choose) and complete the following sentence: "I AM _____." These images are then displayed in an open gathering space on the mezzanine. They are enduring yet dynamic examples of how guests have been impacted by their time at the Center. And they continue to give opportunities for other guests to find connections and to empathize with others who shared the experience of the Center.

Valuing empathy is something that institutions like the Center know is essential to substantive success. As such, successful institutions consistently focus on how to ensure institutional empathy not just within the exhibitions and programs, but also within the operational and strategic life of the institution as well. For example, consciously focusing on building a diverse staff is something that institutions can and should do in order to develop a culture of empathy. It takes time and it takes consistent, long-term effort; however, there are people of all backgrounds who are inclined to work at museums and cultural institutions. Building a diverse workforce is not impossible in today's world. And diversity is writ large in this aspect—it includes diversity of thought, diversity of learning styles, and diversity of methodologies, to name a few that may not immediately come to mind.

Another aspect of building institutional empathy has to do with the speed by which an institution can respond to events happening at the local, national, and international levels. It should not only be institutions who have "national" in their titles who decisively react to what is happening globally. Everyone has the opportunity to do so because the response is a part of being relevant to the community and the community's needs. It is not always that an institution must have an opinion about each and every domestic or world event; it has more to do with encouraging an institution's audiences to look at myriad perspectives on any one topic and to support the growth of their capacity for empathy as they learn to see events from points of view that might be different from their own. For the Center, this may simply mean reminding its audiences that the Center stands for the protection of *every* human's rights, no matter what ethnicity, gender, orientation, faith, etc. The key is not just to inspire an individual to think more deeply, but that they then feel empowered to take action in a positive way.

The Center's staff has found that true change really comes when an individual is not only inspired, but also *empowered* to do something. That is why the Center focuses on building awareness, deepening knowledge, inspiring action, and empowering an individual to actually take steps toward positive action. The Center embraces its role in providing tools for empowerment through exhibitions, programs, and institutional messages that are consistently and strategically focused on providing takeaways and making widely evident lessons that guests have learned during experiential learning opportunities. The lessons that the Center's guests learn often align with the predetermined objectives set by staff members; however, time after time, we have found that the most important and sustainable lessons are the ones that guests discover on their own.

While many institutions are still interested in voicing a unilateral curatorial voice, the Center has opened itself up to multiple curatorial voices, voices that are all calling out at the same time. In this way, guests may return several times and hear different voices each time. The layering of the curatorial voices within the exhibitions provides yet another opportunity to engage empathy as a strategic tool. Guests witness the power of storytelling, utilize technology, and are moved by the sometimes simple outreach that the Center's staff and volunteers have been trained to provide. In layering the opportunities for empathy within the exhibitions, the odds are consistently in the Center's favor that guests will feel personally impacted by what they see, hear, touch, and feel.

An example of this lies in the transition to the human rights gallery. Guests enter a space where they see the image of a person in a mirror. While seeing this person, they also see a reflection of themselves. The use of this mirror (think of it as a computer touchscreen) immediately connects the two beings together. Next the guests have the ability to interactively choose a word that is also on the mirror that connects them to the image individual shown: Christian, woman, blogger, activist, etc. Once the guests have selected a word that they share in common with the image individual, they hear the authentic story of that individual. It is a true story that describes how the image individual in the mirror has been discriminated against based on the word that the guest and the image individual have in common. This use of sight, touch, and sound immediately provides an opportunity for guests to deepen their empathetic capacity before they move into the main human rights exhibition space.

In attempting to create opportunities for guests to broaden and deepen their empathetic capacity, institutions are making themselves more relevant and so more intellectually, emotionally, and socially impactful to their guests. The Center staff has made strategic efforts to provide these opportunities through stories of the past and present that dynamically connect to each other. More and more often, our stakeholders are becoming more adamant about seeing how our collective history connects to our present and to our future. Maintaining relevance has always been at the heart of our institutions; however, it is now, more than ever, a nonnegotiable expectation of our guests. The effort to make these connections may seem difficult to some at first, but institutions can build these opportunities by determining values that their institutions hold paramount and then connecting the past and present through those values. For example, the National Underground Railroad Freedom Center in Cincinnati, Ohio, utilizes courage, cooperation, and perseverance as the values that connect the era of the Underground Railroad to contemporary times. In this way, the Freedom Center staff can make numerous connections between historical American slavery and contemporary global slavery.

Making connections between the past and present ultimately leads to a broader and more complex collective memory. The concept of collective memory is the shared knowledge that is maintained through the collectively interpreted memories of a group. For example, those who were activists during the American Civil Rights Movement might have a collective memory about how the movement progressed. However, by providing opportunities to share stories and perspectives, this collective memory may deepen in ways that encourage empathy for all those who were affected by the American Civil Rights Movement, not just for those who were most visible or active during the movement. Creating dialogues around memories is another example of the ways in which the Center engages with diverse individuals who share varying degrees of perspectives about what happened in the past and how it influences the present.

Based on the techniques and values discussed earlier, institutions have the ability (and responsibility) to empower individuals through approaches that lead to a more empathetic outcome. When guests leave the Center, they should be more empathic than when they arrived—whether it is because of what they experienced in the exhibitions, what they witnessed and internalized during a program, or what they absorbed through the Center's institutional messaging. As institutions increasingly provide opportunities for guests to explore their own values and their own behaviors, guests become active participants in the interpretation of the exhibitions, the programs, and the institutional message. They come to have ownership and see themselves as stakeholders in the essential concepts of the institution. We at the Center believe that guests find themselves to be more self-aware as individual agents as well as in their understandings of their place in the larger context of current human rights movements when they become positive change agents through choosing to activate themselves.

In recognizing and embracing this, museums may truly become the trusted spaces in which this exploration may safely be done within their communities. Having concluded its first year, the Center has established itself as a space that is grounded in institutional empathy, that utilizes empathy as a tool for more deeply engaging audiences, and that provides opportunities for empathy to be recognized as an outcome of the Center's various experiences. Admittedly, the Center is brand new and will continue to shape itself during these formative years. However, it is on a path of great impact if it continues along this trajectory. How will it continue to grow its positive impact in a community that increasingly finds itself focused on international events, issues, and goals? The Center will do so by continuing to strengthen its relationships with its local, national, and global audiences. It will deepen its current relationships and foster new relationships that are beneficial to its audiences. And in this way, the Center's partners and stakeholders will be invested in its success and will provide a depth and breadth of civil and human rights connections and momentum that will keep the Center moving forward in an ever-changing, fast-paced environment.

The Center will also continue to develop its criteria of success through positive impact. Each new exhibition and program will be measured by how well it forwards the relevance of the institution, how well it advances the social value of the institution and the field, and how responsive it is to social events and global issues. Strategies to ensure these areas of success will include developing transdisciplinary partnerships, consistently providing opportunities to inspire positive change agents, and providing support and avenues for action once people feel that they are empowered to act. And throughout, a measure of success will be how well the Center provides a platform from which to amplify empathy across a wide variety of contemporary human rights movements.

The role of empathy in the future of the Center is directly connected to the impact that the institution has the potential to have on personal, institutional, and collective levels. As the Center provides opportunities to engage a more complex collective memory, it will make itself more relevant and more credible. If the Center holds true to its foundation, it will continue to impact social change. In order to hold true, the Center (just as any other institution) must truly hear, balance, and act on the expectations of the institution's staff, leadership team, board, and community stakeholders. It must adapt to the varied interests of its guests—those who are physically present as well as those who are digital. And it must continue to galvanize itself by consciously and strategically weaving empathy into the operational institutional plans, the programs and exhibitions, and the strategic messaging of the Center.

Empathy will further the Center's mission by providing a visible path for the Center's values, engagement tools, and desired outcomes. Each opportunity brings with it a checklist, a measurement tool, and a guidebook for success. For the Center, the same aspects that make it distinctive are also the aspects that may ultimately provide the largest barriers. Established institutions know who they are and their audiences generally accept this identity. The center is still establishing its own identity and this provides guests with undefined space in which they can create their own interpretation of what the Center should be; sometimes the Center will live up to these expectations and at other times it may not. Providing a clear identity while still being flexible is something that the Center can work toward in tandem with its community. As the Center continues to work on who it wants to be and where it wants to focus in terms of the many human rights movements simultaneously happening around the world and the continued influences of legacies from the American past, it will remain true that the key to the Center's future, and the key to the future of museums, lies in how and to what level we are all willing to engage with empathy.

connections → empathy history → new perspectives → internalize → unpacking

9

Interpreting Arapaho Chief Niwot

Complex Pasts in Contemporary Community

Seth Frankel

> When people see Boulder Valley, they will stay, and their staying will ruin the beauty.
>
> —A legend known as "Niwot's Curse," apocryphally credited to Arapaho chief Niwot and often recited by contemporary residents of Boulder, Colorado, to portray the impact of "settlement" on this former Native American region

Drive down the streets of Boulder, Colorado, and its surrounding communities and the veiled legacy of historical conflict reads like billboards. Once home to the Arapaho and Cheyenne Native American tribes, the area scarcely preserves visible remains of their presence. Yet reminders of their former residence, and of the people who removed them from this place (or failed to protect them), are plainly visible. Streets, nearby towns, and mountain communities are named after tribal leaders. Tribal names adorn a dormitory at the University of Colorado in the heart of the city. A European-sounding name identifies a nearby mountain peak, commemorating an early settler's contribution to progress. Yet the honoring ignores the brutalities the settler committed in the name of that progress.

A serene creek courses through this town, now largely populated by wealthy newcomers and university students. Alongside the creek meanders a bike path, and next to this path stands a sandstone sculpture—more caricature than realistic portrait—of Chief Niwot, a peace-seeking Arapaho leader of the Civil War era. (Niwot is also known as Left Hand, the English equivalent of his name.) In the chief's larger-than-life hand is a real flower, placed there by a kind-hearted soul as if honoring the dead at a cemetery.

Well intentioned as this gesture might have been, it was most likely made with little knowledge of Chief Niwot's story and that of his people.

Hundreds of miles away, the descendants of Chief Niwot (and the many other Native American peoples now missing from Boulder) live on reservations in Wyoming, Oklahoma, and other states. Barely a handful of them call Boulder home.

In this highly educated university town and high-tech community, with nearly one hundred thousand residents (including forty thousand students), place names and monuments become disassociated from their historical meaning and their intent. All that remains are indicators of place: a handy way to give directions or tell the location of a trendy coffee shop. Yet most residents, and even visitors, sense that this area, like most communities in the United States, has a history that is both painful and relevant to community dynamics today. The superficial relationship with place begins and ends with names for commonly shared landmarks—but a deeper understanding of their meanings is possible.

WALKING ON STREETS SHADOWED BY MASSACRE

Chief Niwot was a leader of the Southern Arapaho. Their wintering grounds were in the mountains that form Boulder's western boundary. During summer, the tribe moved south and east to live among the buffaloes—a range of hundreds of miles.

In the middle of the nineteenth century, the Arapaho and members of the Cheyenne tribe found themselves in a continuously shifting relationship with their newly arrived and rapidly proliferating White neighbors. When the Civil War took hold of the nation, the Colorado Territory aligned itself with the Union and pinned its future on the North's victory. Statehood was the eventual goal. As the war progressed, the relationship between the territory's White leaders and Native Americans evolved from tolerance to fear, and then to intolerance, manifested first as containment and finally as elimination and removal. At a critical moment of conflict, on November 29, 1864, volunteer troops from Boulder and other nearby areas ambushed a group of several hundred Native Americans who were peacefully encamped for their own protection under the Union army's thirty-five-star American flag. Nearly 175 of them, mostly women, children, and elderly, were killed and mutilated, their body parts turned into trophies. While a handful of the soldiers themselves were appalled by the brutality, they came home to a victory parade, with Indian body parts in hand. After an eventual congressional investigation, these actions—now known as the Sand Creek Massacre—were met with both national and international condemnation.[1]

Some of the instigators of and participants in the massacre went on to lead lives of distinction. One of them helped establish the University of

Colorado. Over the following century, as the community grew, local places and streets needed names. Some were named after the people responsible for the Sand Creek Massacre.

By the 1960s, however, White Americans were opening their eyes to injustices past and present. The appropriateness of honoring men who carried out the Sand Creek Massacre came into question. For example, a 1987 University of Colorado report recommended changing the name of a campus dormitory, finding that the original name was "a terrible gesture of inhospitality to Indian students. To celebrate Sand Creek . . . would be tasteless, a dreadful way of saying 'Our people killed your people, and we're still glad they did.'"[2] Amid public controversy, the building was renamed after the tribes murdered at Sand Creek.[3]

Although Boulder's bloody past comes into focus occasionally, the city's shifting population remains largely unaware. Ironically, Boulder residents are politically liberal for the most part, concerned with issues of race, wealth, and inequity. Cultural arts leaders, including museums, performing arts companies, city government, and educational institutions, have recognized the gap between good intentions and understanding, and have sought ways to engage constituents with the area's complex past. This has proved to be no easy task. Cultural leaders have struggled to find effective ways to engage current residents and to inspire them to consider their responsibilities as the inheritors of both the land and the history that gave them title to it.

WRESTLING WITH PAIN—A MULTIFACETED COMMUNITY CONVERSATION

In 2012, as part of *One Action—One Boulder* (a community-wide, arts-inspired collaboration and community action project), the Boulder History Museum launched a temporary exhibition titled *Chief Niwot—Legend and Legacy*. Set in the museum's historic mansion, the exhibit occupied two connecting rooms with a total area of less than 600 square feet. The exhibit sought to:

> Highlight the inspirational figure in Boulder's history, Southern Arapaho Chief Niwot, whose story is wrapped up in the violent history of the Sand Creek Massacre. However, by turning away from this painful local history, we have also turned away from the people we should be honoring. Thus, the Museum's goal with this exhibit is to provide an understanding and acceptance of our community's history, no matter the reality: to stand both within the parts worth celebrating and within the more painful moments; to resist defensiveness and guilt, replacing them with strength and courage as we make inequities visible for reflection, engagement and education; to ask profound questions of ourselves, our communities and our nation, examining our worst moments, so we might avoid repeating them in the future.[4]

Aware of the complexity of the subject, with its mingled past and present storyline, the museum recognized that it would need to proceed carefully through the exhibition development process. As gripping as the facts were, the historical narrative needed to be shaped with sensitivity to the emotions it would arouse and to the curatorial voice. This understanding guided the museum in its selection of the curatorial team, which expanded from a largely academic core to a diverse group that reflected as many perspectives as feasible on both the historical and the contemporary aspects of the subject.

The team choice paid off. The developers designed the exhibits in a way that created personal connections between story and viewer. The history became less bookish because it was interpreted through the reflections of living Native Americans. Preliminary ideas about what content would be included were superseded by a broader vision, embracing aspects of the history that might have otherwise been lost.

The *One Action—One Boulder* project began as the brainchild of Kirsten Wilson, a local activist/theater artist and the executive director of the Motus Theater Company. Several years earlier, Wilson had been moved by the powerful historical account *Chief Left Hand* by novelist and local author Margaret Coel.[5] This 1981 book provided a thoroughly researched history of Chief Niwot, an Arapaho chief generally regarded as a highly intelligent, English-speaking peace activist and leader. Niwot, with others, represented his people in negotiations with White territorial leaders and struggled to maintain the Arapaho culture and homeland during the complex Civil War period. That difficult period culminated in the Sand Creek Massacre, during which Chief Niwot was mortally wounded. Others murdered included both Arapaho and Cheyenne; about two-thirds were women, children, the elderly, and the infirm.[6]

In 2009, Wilson's theater company produced and performed a highly successful multimedia performance, *Rocks, Karma, Arrows*, which brought the community's history into focus, acting as a mirror to its audiences and reflecting issues of immigration, hate crime, home value, public land, and Boulder's woefully deficient cultural diversity (figure 9.1). The artist used Chief Niwot and other historical figures to make connections with issues Boulder faces today. The performance wove its narrative with media, images, diverse actors, and participatory dialogue.[7] Wilson intends her theater productions to serve as tools of change through the analysis of history. At one moment in the performance, a speaker stated, "Chief Niwot aimed his life in the direction of peace. His arrow is still on the move in Boulder, Colorado."

Seeing strong community interest in the Niwot/Boulder story, Wilson sought to broaden the reach of her production and its audience.[8]

Figure 9.1. The set of *Rocks, Karma, Arrows* used a montage of powerful historical imagery along a 180-degree backdrop, and a diverse cast that directly engaged the audience. *Source*: Motus Theater/Michael Ensminger.

THE ONE ACTION—ONE BOULDER MOVEMENT

While *Rocks, Karma, Arrows* demonstrated theater's potential for building audience interest in human rights issues both historical and contemporary—and empathy for those who have suffered—theater audiences represented only a small segment of the broader Boulder community. Wilson looked to other institutions for possible ways to adapt the content of her performance and to expand it into a broader community dialogue. She called her project *One Action—One Boulder*.

Wilson gained support from a wide range of organizations for a second run of *Rocks, Karma, Arrows*, but she wanted to increase its impact and duration and engage more of the community. To expand her audience, she reached out to Boulder Public Library and the Boulder History Museum, each of which has its own constituency.

In earlier years, Boulder Public Library's *One Book, One Boulder* program brought community members together around a single book for discussion. The library expressed interest in using Coel's *Chief Left Hand* for the program, to complement a second run of *Rocks, Karma, Arrows*. Although the book had been nominated for community reads, the library had not used it in the past, but exploring the Niwot story in the context of Wilson's broader movement offered a perfect synergy.[9]

Wilson also approached the Boulder History Museum, a small institution embedded within a historical residence near the University of Colorado campus. The museum had wanted to create an exhibition about Native Americans in the Boulder area for quite some time, but had not formulated a specific direction. When approached by Wilson about using the museum as a centerpiece for community dialogue about the Niwot story and contemporary Native American issues, museum director Nancy Geyer emphatically gave her support.[10] Geyer stated, "It's not a story that has really been told before. There are so many places in this area named for Arapahos, Niwot and Lefthand. It's such an important local story."[11] The museum agreed to participate—albeit with a compressed ten-month timeline from kickoff to public opening, a modest budget, and no artifacts to support either a historical or contemporary storyline.[12] These limitations would challenge an exhibit team yet to be defined.

CRAFTING THE APPROACH AND NARRATIVE FOR *CHIEF NIWOT—LEGEND AND LEGACY*

Mostly visited by local adults and school groups, along with a few out-of-town visitors, the museum has historically had an audience nearly devoid of Native Americans and their descendants. This reflects the area's demographics: the majority of Boulder residents tend to be White, educated, and financially stable.[13]

The museum saw in the stories of Chief Niwot and the Arapaho a chance to reach beyond its traditional audiences. The topic offered a meaningful opportunity to consider complex content that it had long hoped to explore. By collaborating with both a theatrical company and area public library, the museum saw a chance to capitalize on its own and its partners' collective strengths. The theater company was more of a fringe institution, with a younger, creative audience, but it lacked larger community support and exposure.[14] The library's *One Book, One Boulder* audience mostly consisted of older participants. The museum, meanwhile, had the respect of Boulder's establishment, but it struggled to have impact on the broader community. For the most part, the people of Boulder simply ignored it if they knew of it at all.

Using its in-house team, as well guest curators and a development/design consultant, the museum arrived at the opinion that even without compelling artifacts it could mount an exhibit built on solid historical research that would connect the community to its shameful past and promote a forward-looking and productive dialogue. The museum and *One Action—One Boulder* leadership saw the importance of bringing together a working team much broader than the museum typically engaged in exhibit development. This team, which included scholars, historians, Arapaho tribal members, and exhibit development professionals, was charged with developing the exhibit approach based on input from diverse sources.[15]

Source Material

Approached first by Kirsten Wilson and then the Boulder History Museum, *Chief Left Hand* author Margaret Coel agreed to support the exhibit development team by crafting historical storylines based on her book. She saw the exhibition format as a way to take her work beyond the page and possibly to connect the story more directly with contemporary issues. Her stated goals express the ideal of creating empathy in a museum audience:

> I wanted [the audience] to have an understanding of our common history. To have empathy for [the Arapaho]. To see them for what they were . . . people. I wanted the audience to imagine what it would have been like for this to happen to themselves and their families.[16]

The book, by then thirty years old, served as the spine of the historical narrative. Since its publication, however, further research had added clarifying details and raised some new questions about the life of Chief Niwot and the Sand Creek Massacre. To bring the historical understanding up to date, additional researchers were engaged to provide content review, including historian and former museum director Tom Meier. Local filmmaker, cultural researcher, and Southern Arapaho tribal member Ava Hamilton also agreed, somewhat reluctantly, to join the exhibit's development team. Her hesitation stemmed from distrust based on past experiences of superficial inclusion or tokenism in projects including nonnative participants.[17] An exhibition development and design firm, Studio Tectonic, was engaged to lead the process and help focus the storyline into an exhibitable format, as well as to provide exhibit design and fabrication.

As the team worked, additional project influencers—including Arapaho tribal members and an Arapaho linguistics scholar—became important in shaping the exhibition and providing photography, media, and objects.

Working with Limited Objects

While immediately drawn to crafting an exhibition about the life of Niwot and the Sand Creek Massacre, the museum's staff recognized that their usual artifact-rich exhibition strategies would be challenged. The museum's collection lacked Arapaho objects and images of any kind. Objects in nearby university collections and the state archives/museum were also thin and unconnected to Niwot or his immediate contemporaries. Complicating matters further, there has been a steady debate among tribal members and historians regarding the existence of any authentic Niwot photographs. While many of his contemporaries have clearly verifiable photographic records, no universally accepted photographic image of Niwot exists.

Rather than turning to Civil War military artifacts, the team gathered a collection of period trade goods to help demonstrate the early, close, and productive relationship between the Arapaho and incoming Whites. These artifacts became a counterpoint to the story of this relationship's evolving hostility. While military actions played an important role, a display of arms and uniforms might have distracted from the exhibit's focus on the changing relationship between Native Americans and Whites.

In light of these limitations, the museum had to shed its tried and true object-based approach and wade into unfamiliar waters.

Embracing Process to Shape the Exhibition

While Coel's book served as the backbone of the historical record, several new directions came into focus as the team worked together—particularly through the insightful eyes of its South Arapaho member Ava Hamilton. First, it became clear that a strict chronology of the historical narrative would not provide the contemporary lens the team wanted. Second, the exhibit would need to focus significantly on both the contemporary legacy of the Arapaho and Boulder's continuing struggle to "live right" within its history.

Coel's narrative began during Niwot's lifetime and ended with the immediate aftermath of the massacre. As powerful as the story was, it included neither the history that lay behind White/Indian relations of Niwot's time nor the legacy of the massacre.

An impassioned Hamilton engaged the story through her lens, one less familiar to audiences and to her collaborators. An approach crystalized. Rather than tell the history as something separate from our time, the exhibit narrative wove in contemporary Arapaho voices, which provided an interpretive layer. For example, as other Native American chiefs of Niwot's time were introduced, Virginia Sutter (a living descendent of the last reigning chief of the Northern Arapaho) provided a personal statement regarding the role of chiefs in Arapaho culture. By mingling history and interpretation, the exhibit brought visitors up to date on current thought and helped dispel ignorance about Native American culture. These contemporary Arapaho voices in the historical sections also foreshadowed the gallery's second half, which focused on the present.

The exhibition development process also forced the team to consider the question of where to begin the narrative. Niwot was born in 1825. The first treaty directly connected to the story, the Treaty of Fort Laramie, was signed in 1851. However, the relationship between Whites and Indians, which formed the foundation for Niwot's story, began much earlier. Team member Ava Hamilton brought forth a 1823 US Supreme Court decision that unanimously codified for the United States a fifteenth-century Catholic doctrine stating that all lands not inhabited by Christians was open to be "discovered." (Incidentally, this court decision still stands today.) This provided the legal basis for westward expansion and the United States' claims on Indian lands.[18] Hamilton presented it as follows:

> Understanding what happened to not only my people—the Arapaho—but to all the Indigenous Peoples in the western hemisphere requires an intense scrutiny of what came to be American history and the laws of the land. It very much requires a discussion of The Doctrine of Christian Discovery and the power of interpretation of words.[19]

The exhibition team discussed Hamilton's point and decided to make this piece of history (along with contemporary Native American commentary) the central entry point to the exhibit. Here as well, the exhibit presented historical documentation in parallel with interpretation by a Native American whose life has been shaped by the history (figure 9.2).

EXPLORING CONTEMPORARY ARAPAHO LIFE AND BOULDER

Niwot's life, and the exhibit's nineteenth-century historical narrative, ended just after the Sand Creek Massacre. The exhibit team expected that the audience would be left with a strong emotional response at this point. As the story of the Arapaho people did not end here, neither did the exhibition.

Figure 9.2.   A video with leading quotes and historic photographs serves as an entryway into the introductory exhibit element, which looks at the larger historic context of the conflict. *Source*: The author.

In a second gallery, the exhibit shifted direction and explored recent area history, presenting a broad view of contemporary Arapaho life.

Modern Arapaho Life

Today's Arapaho are recognized as two distinct tribal units: the Southern Arapaho (mostly near Oklahoma City) and the Northern Arapaho (mostly on the Wind River Reservation, a Wyoming location shared with their traditional enemy tribe, the Shoshone). As is true for all Native American tribes, the Arapahos' tumultuous past has left a difficult legacy. Yet life endures, and the exhibit presents this in several ways. A photographic essay by Sarah Wiles looks at modern life at the Wind River Reservation, blending a series of powerful black and white photographs with a series of small, uninterpreted, personal Arapaho snapshots (figure 9.3). Together, the pictures help capture the similarities between contemporary Arapaho life and the lives of non-Native Americans. A mixture of video, personal quotes, interpretive panels, and images express the balance Arapahos have struggled to achieve between living in a state of modernity and preserving tradition. From the exhibition:

Figure 9.3. Contemporary Arapaho life is expressed in a photo essay with media and quotes from ordinary Arapaho people. At the end is a call to action for the US government to honor its obligations to Native Americans; beneath this, a comment book has been highly utilized. *Source*: Studio Tectonic/Seth Frankel.

One person said that we were so busy being White that we forgot who we are. We lost part of our values, culture and respect trying to be like the Whiteman. Now we're trying to restore that. It's a tough battle, but we can do it.

—Harold Moss, 1988

We've come a long ways from the moccasins, from the horses, from the buffalo, to modern technology. And Arapahos living through the generations, the emotions, the loving, the livelihood, have all changed in time, with that.

—Elizabeth Lone Bear, 2005

Exhibit Element—Meaning of Words

During the development team's conversations, certain words used in the exhibit came into question. "Reservation," "civilized," "settler," and other words became the subject of intense discussion because they seemed to mean different things (or suggested different intents) to different speakers and listeners. The same issues became visible in many of the historical documents.

If the exhibit team struggled, would the public as well? Perhaps not because the simple, traditional meanings of these words would have no counterpoint unless the exhibition created one. Not as a point of political correctness, but rather as a means to help audiences feel what others may feel or to identify commonly held misinterpretations, the team crafted an exhibit element that called attention to these differences in meaning. Audio interviews were conducted with Native Americans in which they were asked to give *their* definitions of certain words. An audio interactive was developed at which visitors could play a short interpretation of one of six words' impact as personally felt by the recorded speaker. The public response to this interactive was powerful, as observed by the museum and documented in the exhibition's heavily used, emotion-filled comment book.[20]

From the audio interactive: "*Discovery* is a political word to American Indians today. It is not a good word for us, because we had been living here thousands of years. . . . The indigenous people consider themselves to be from this world. We didn't come from anywhere else. We have always been here. This is where we came from and we're still here."

Place Names

The history of Whites naming locations that reflect Native American individuals and culture is long. During the 1914 bid to establish nearby Rocky Mountain National Park, a team of park supporters engaged several

Arapaho elders from the Wyoming Wind River Indian Reservation. Over several weeks, they hiked mountains and trails well known to the Indian guides. Many of the traditional names referenced by visiting Arapaho elders directly influenced the area's contemporary names. A digital interactive area in the Niwot exhibition enabled visitors to explore these names, their meanings, and how they came to be. This area also presented actual street and building signs that bore the names of the Sand Creek Massacre's White leaders—signs preserved by local historical groups and the University of Colorado. The signs, along with photographs, documentation, quotes, and narrative, tell the story of more than twenty years of struggle by community activists to have such names removed.

Designed to Create Connection and Complexity, Not Guilt

In liberal, mostly homogenous Caucasian Boulder, Colorado, White guilt is a likely, even expected, psychosocial outcome of a community dialogue focused on the past treatment of Native Americans.

The museum felt a strong sense of responsibility to interpret this history not as a story of bad guys and victims, but rather to engage visitors in learning about the actions and complex motivations of history's players. Though widely known as the main leader of the Sand Creek Massacre, Colonel John Chivington also served as a clergyman and staunch abolitionist. Other White leaders defied the push to exterminate the Indians and took action to live civilly with them or protect them against attack. Among the Arapaho as well, leadership and public opinion were divided as to how to deal with the White Man. As political as any community, Arapaho disagreed about the usefulness of peace negotiations or violent resistance.

In order to preempt a simplistic public response—White Man = evil, Indian = innocent victim—the team made these complexities central elements in the exhibit's story. In both the exhibit text and the visuals, developers sought to humanize the central characters and prevent audiences from automatically categorizing them as heroes or villains (figure 9.4).

SUPPORTING OUTCOMES THROUGH ADULT PROGRAMS

Seeing limitations in both exhibit space and format, the museum developed a series of eight lecture programs. These included a wide range of voices, from historians to individuals directly engaged with Indian concerns in the community. Rather than hosting lectures at its usual locations, the museum partnered with the Native American Rights Fund (NARF), a nationally focused nonprofit based in Boulder that provides legal assistance to Indian tribes. NARF also houses the National Indian Law Library. The nonprofit is

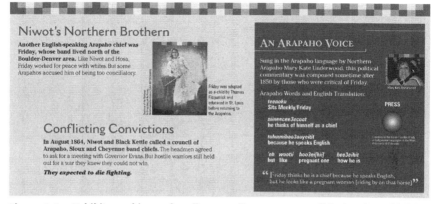

Figure 9.4. Exhibit graphics and audio recordings capture political satire criticizing peace-seeking Arapaho chiefs for favoring negotiation over battle. *Source*: The author.

located less than half a mile from the museum on one of the city's main thoroughfares, yet remains largely invisible to Boulder's public.[21]

The museum had not collaborated with NARF in any significant way before. NARF's executive director John Echohawk saw partnership as an opportunity to amplify his organization's educational outreach:

> [A] major issue that our people face is the lack of knowledge and understanding about us. . . . [Contemporary Indian leaders] have got to do "Indian 101" with just about everyone we meet. It makes it difficult to talk to people about what needs to be done because they don't have any context. . . . The Niwot exhibit was an opportunity to help educate [the people here in Boulder]. Most of them don't have any idea about this history. They may have some general idea that there used to be Indians here, but they didn't have any of the particulars.[22]

NARF's intimate, living room–like space became home to the lectures and discussions comprising the series. Each event filled the space to capacity, again demonstrating a high level of interest in the connection between the exhibit content and current Native American issues.[23]

In the years following the six-month Niwot exhibition, Boulder History Museum and NARF have produced the Chief Niwot Forum, an annual program of presentations and community dialogue concerning ongoing Native American issues.

ADAPTING HORRIFIC HISTORY TO SCHOOL-AGE AUDIENCES

During the development of the exhibition, the museum expressed fear that the content would be too gruesome and too complex for schoolchildren—or that schools would not want their students to learn about the massacre. The museum's school educator Emily Zinn stated:

> We had an assumption that school groups would not want to come and have the Sand Creek Massacre as part of what they do. And we were wrong. . . . Before any school has come we've asked them if they want to explore the massacre and they all have said, "Yes." It really opened our eyes to their desire for this sort of empathic experience within a museum context.[24]

Visiting middle school groups worked through a series of panels from the exhibition and then roamed in pairs through the exhibit. Prior to these explorations, students were briefed about the story and instructed to use a handout "journal," which directed them to look for answers to specific questions about one of the historical characters. They were prompted to find the person in the exhibit and to gather facts about the person's role in the story. Students were also encouraged to develop a sense of the motivation and worldview that influenced the person, and to write about how he or she may have understood his or her role. Questions included:

> What was my job?
> What am I known/remembered for?
> In your opinion, does history remember me in a positive or negative light? Why?
> How do you think I felt about Manifest Destiny?

Through this guided dialogue, students came to a much more complex understanding of character than they might have without prompting. For example, one respondent team studied the role of John Evans, the territorial governor and founder of the school that eventually became the University of Denver; one of Colorado's most prominent mountains was named in his honor. When asked how history remembers him, a team responded, "Both positively and negatively." Through the dialogues and exhibit exploration, students swiftly saw how an overly simplistic "good/bad" interpretation of the past fails to do justice to history.

The students struggled, though, when it came to internalizing the circumstances, motivations, and decision-making process of the massacre's most influential leaders—factors including community pressure and fear, professional ambitions, and other, more subtle elements. The museum's educator said, "It is very challenging to present it in a way [the kids] can understand where [the historical figures] were coming from. It's a really big story."[25]

Students also encountered an object-based lesson focusing on three artifacts: an "Indian Fighter" recruitment army poster, a thirty-five-star American flag of the period, and a contemporary buffalo hide painting by a Native American depicting the Sand Creek Massacre (figure 9.5). Lesson

Figure 9.5. Student workbooks were used by the museum's educators to tease out tensions within the historical narrative. The workbooks included period quotes showing contrasting viewpoints. *Source*: Boulder History Museum.

plan materials compared the American flag to the same flag painted in the center of the hide. Just prior to the massacre, the Indians were told that they were "encamped under the direction of our officers and believed themselves to be under the protection of the flag."[26] This quote from the congressional inquiry into the event became central to the discussion about what protection means and how flying the flag was literally intended as a security measure—and how the flag's trampling at Sand Creek shows that collapse of commitment and honor occurred on the part of soldiers representing the US government.

With elementary school groups (typically fourth graders because Colorado history is a focus for that grade level), the museum began with an exploration of the various treaties signed by Indians and Colorado Territory leaders. A child from the class was asked to read an agreement (treaty) out loud, but the text was in Italian, a language likely to be unknown to the students. Then the child was asked to sign it. Because most children at this age are only loosely aware of how a signature becomes a commitment, both this and the foreign language helped students envision how the Arapahos signing treaties may have experienced their negotiations. The children were told that the agreement signed by *one* of the children represented a commitment on all their parts, only to learn that the document handed over their personal beds and from then on they'd have to sleep outside. The children naturally felt victimized—with an appropriate mixture of seriousness and levity—and that the commitments were completely unjust. This reaction was then directly related to nineteenth-century treaties handing over Indian rights and land to White negotiators.

Through these programs, the museum overcame its initial concerns about how to develop appropriate and powerful connections between schoolchildren and the *Chief Niwot—Legend and Legacy* exhibit.

CONCLUSION

Combining the community book read, the museum exhibition, and the theater performance created greater visitation and deeper engagement than any of the participating institutions had ever received from similar individual efforts. Visitors came out of interest and also a sense of community obligation. The museum saw a nearly 30 percent increase in membership and more visitors than to any past exhibit.[27] The director stated, "The reaction from the community was astounding. Comments reflected the fact that people were extremely moved by this story. It is gratifying to discover that this deep historical exploration is so meaningful to the local community."[28]

Visitor comments expressed both appreciation for the powerful content and a strong sense of guilt, sorrow, and even shame. This was not one of the exhibition team's desired outcomes. Visitors were clearly wrestling with this new information and with what it should mean to them. Indeed, the exhibition did not aim to elicit specific reactions; rather, the primary goal was to create awareness and a connection to the historical content, as well as an appreciation for the Arapaho as a contemporary people. Understandably, though, some visitors' inner voices expressed this newfound empathy with the question, "What I do in response to this new information and feeling of responsibility?" The exhibit's goal was not specifically to inspire activism; however, that response may have been inevitable.

(This raises an interesting question for museum exhibition developers: When the goal is to educate visitors to tragic events with contemporary ramifications and to create empathy, is there also a responsibility to offer possible paths of activist response? Many museums will conclude that it should be left up to individuals to act on their new awareness and seek out opportunities to address current problems; but others may opt to include, integrated within exhibitions, a range of options for those who strongly want to take action.)

Although the exhibition proved to be a great success, *Chief Niwot—Legend and Legacy* initially felt like a risk to the museum for many reasons. Would the content be too complex or too disturbing? Could an exhibition so thin on supporting artifacts meet the expectation of an audience accustomed to object-based historical interpretation? Was the content too controversial and would it alienate audiences? Would the audience be able to see itself in this history, and would this awareness inform them about contemporary issues facing Boulder and Native Americans?

A note from the comment book, left by a twenty-year-old visitor, conveys the deep empathy the exhibit inspired:

> I was [born] and raised in Boulder and never learned its history until [now]. [The exhibit is] changing the way that I think about the land, the people, my education, race & class issues in Boulder. I am in deep gratitude to all of the brave souls who came together to actualize the exhibit. This story needs to be told, if we living are going to continue to work for social justice in Boulder. I have a lot of anger and grief that I grew up in a land of lies and I send my prayers and blessings to all the Arapaho, Sioux, Cheyenne, Ute and other Native Coloradans who suffered such atrocities and who live on to carry on their story, language, traditions and culture.[29]

Because of public reactions like this one, the exhibition has been recognized as a success both inside and outside the Boulder community. The State of Colorado's historical society granted the exhibit the Josephine H. Miles Award for its "major contribution to the advancement of Colorado history" and the Mountain Plains Museum Association also recognized *Chief Niwot—Legend and Legacy* through its Leadership and Innovation Award for the exhibit's "excellent example of community involvement and creating relevance between a historical topic and modern day."[30]

Further gratifying evidence of the exhibition's success: it was extended by about two years and will be relocated and enlarged as a permanent exhibit when the museum moves to its new home in Boulder's downtown area.

NOTES

1. *Joint Committee on the Conduct of the War, Massacre of the Cheyenne Indians,* 38th Congress, Second Session, Washington, 1865; Report of the Secretary of War, 39th Congress, Second Session, Senate Executive Documents No. 26, Washington, 1867.

2. Patricia Nelson Limerick, *What's in a Name? Nichol Hall: A Report* (Boulder: University of Colorado, 1987).

3. Melanie O. Massengale, "Cheyenne Arapaho Residence Hall Renaming Marks 20 Years," *Inside CU* (February 10, 2009), http://www.colorado.edu/insidecu/editions/2009/2-10/story3.html (accessed November 22, 2015).

4. Boulder History Museum, *Exhibition Press Release* (Boulder, Colorado, 2012).

5. Kirsten Wilson (executive director, Motus Theater), interview by the author, September 15, 2015.

6. Margaret Coel, *Chief Left Hand* (Norman: University of Oklahoma Press, 1981), 276.

7. Author's direct observation of *Rocks, Karma, Arrows,* 2012.

8. Wilson interview.

9. Cindy Sutter, "Chief Niwot, Peacemaker: Exhibit Details Life of Arapaho Chief of Boulder Valley," *Boulder Daily Camera*, May 19, 2012, http://www.dailycamera.com/ci_20646249/chief-niwot-peacemaker-exhibit-details-life-arapaho-chief (accessed November 21, 2015).

10. Nancy Geyer (executive director, Boulder History Museum), interview by the author, September 25, 2015.

11. Sutter, "Chief Niwot."

12. Geyer interview.

13. *Demographic Profile Boulder, Colorado* (Boulder Economic Council, 2011).

14. Wilson interview.

15. Geyer interview; author's direct experience as project development/design consultant, 2011–2012.

16. Margaret Coel, interview by the author, September 15, 2015.

17. As observed by the author, 2011.

18. "The Doctrine of Discovery, 1493: A Primary Source by Pope Alexander VI," *The Gilder Lehrman Institute of American History*, https://www.gilderlehrman.org/history-by-era/imperial-rivalries/resources/doctrine-discovery-1493 (accessed November 23, 2015).

19. Ava Hamilton (guest content expert to the Boulder History Museum), from *Chief Niwot—Legend and Legacy* exhibition panel, 2012.

20. Geyer interview.

21. John Echohawk (executive director, Native American Rights Fund), interview by the author, October 7, 2015.

22. Echohawk interview.

23. Carol Taylor (curator of public programs and research, Boulder History Museum), interview by the author, October 2, 2015.

24. Emily Zinn (curator of youth programs, Boulder History Museum), interview by the author, October 2, 2015.

25. Zinn interview.

26. *Joint Committee*, 1867.

27. Boulder History Museum, *Annual Report* (2012).

28. Geyer interview.

29. Exhibit comment book, Boulder History Museum, October 25, 2012.

30. Joe Rubino, "Boulder History Museum's Chief Niwot Exhibit Wins State Award, Now Open Through January," *Boulder Daily Camera*, November 11, 2012, http://www.dailycamera.com/news/boulder/ci_21971702/boulder-history-museums-chief-niwot-exhibit-wins-state (accessed November 22, 2015); Press release, Mountain Plains Museum Association, August 14, 2012.

10

Designing a Story-Based Exhibition

A Case Study from the Freer and Sackler Galleries

Thomas Wide

In early 2015, the Freer and Sackler Galleries (Freer|Sackler), the Smithsonian's museums of Asian art, announced a forthcoming exhibition, *Turquoise Mountain: Artists Transforming Afghanistan*. The exhibition was to be a partnership with a British arts charity, Turquoise Mountain, which had been working in Afghanistan since 2006. The idea of the exhibition was to tell a story of transformation: how the historic eighteenth-century district of Murad Khani in Kabul was transformed over a ten-year period from a war-torn derelict slum into a flourishing center for the revival of Afghan arts and culture.

The exhibition was a new direction for the Freer|Sackler in several ways. The museum had not partnered with a charitable organization on an exhibition before. It had also never created an exhibition on contemporary Afghanistan. The exhibition was to be held in the "International Galleries," a ninety-foot-long rectangular space that the Freer|Sackler had not used for exhibitions for many years. Most importantly, the show was not focused on objects in the permanent collection of the museum; indeed, the show wasn't focused primarily on objects at all. Rather, it was to be a show that focused on the story of one historic district of Kabul and the stories of the artists and residents there who had led its regeneration. In other words, this was to be a "story-based" rather than an "object-based" show.

In conceiving of this exhibition and its basic design approach, the exhibition team was—unwittingly at first—engaging with several questions that are at the heart of this volume. While we (the exhibition team) at the Freer|Sackler did not at first view our approach as "empathetic," nor our method as "harnessing empathy," nor our goal as "generating empathy," we became increasingly conscious as the exhibition developed that this is what we were doing.[1] This chapter thus explores the ways "empathy" came to inform the exhibition's philosophy, goals, and method. This account can inevitably only be a partial one: the exhibition is still in the design stages at the time of writing and does not open until March 2016. Still, even in the initial period of exhibition concept, curation, and design, I believe there is sufficient material for useful study. I argue that while I have reservations about what Steven Pinker has called the "empathy craze,"[2] I do believe that the term *empathy*—if carefully parsed, defined, and delimited—can be a really useful concept for museum professionals looking to create exhibitions that are memorable, delightful, and valuable in terms of social utility.

DEFINING EMPATHY

In the month that I'm writing this (September 2015), the word *empathy* has been Googled more times than it has ever been Googled before. The use of the term in books has been steadily increasing over the last fifty years, sharply rising over the last ten.[3] Despite the great interest in the term, our understanding of what it means remains surprisingly fuzzy. We need clear definitions, otherwise we will end up talking past each other. For the purposes of this chapter, I want to focus on two different but related meanings of the term *empathy*. First is the idea of *perspective taking*: the imagining of what someone else is feeling, thinking, and seeing. This does not imply that we are always accurate in our imaginings, just that we do engage in such imaginative exercises. This meaning—which psychologist Jamil Zaki calls "mentalizing"—is the one truest to the original meaning to the term, as introduced by Edward Tichener (as a translation of aesthetic philosopher Theodor Lipps's term *Einfühlung*) in the early twentieth century.[4] The second meaning I want to focus on is what we might call simply compassion or *empathic concern*. This is an emotional reaction we feel when we perceive someone, which is based on our understanding of what that someone is thinking or feeling, but is not necessarily the same emotion (in kind or intensity) as the emotion of that person.

These two meanings of empathy seem the most relevant for the purposes of this volume and are the two meanings that I think are implied in the common phrase of "putting yourself in someone else's shoes." They suggest a combination of understanding and emotional engagement, which is potentially very attractive and useful to those working in museums. However, before I go any further, it is worth sounding a note of caution regarding these two phenomena. It is not the case that either of them are *necessarily* a good thing. In the case of *empathy-as-perspective-taking*, psychologist Nicholas Epley has illustrated how inherently *inaccurate* humans are: how poorly we imagine what other people think or feel.[5] Even with people very close to us, like our children or spouses, we consistently overestimate our ability to "get inside" another's head. In the place of perspective taking, Epley usefully introduces the term *perspective getting;* better to *actually ask* someone what they think, rather than indulge in some kind of empathetic telepathy (empathepathy perhaps?). Asking people directly and noting down what they say is far more accurate than empathetic imagining; it offers a better way to understand and help other people than empathy-as-perspective-taking. As for empathy as *empathic concern:* we know how easily humans can be swayed by cuteness; whether it is the panda at the zoo or the photograph of the little girl on the charity poster, we cannot help but have our emotions triggered.[6] But this leaves us vulnerable to being manipulated; our emotions can lead us to support wrong-headed causes because we are attracted by a cute photo, or to ignore the most needy or vulnerable because they do not trigger our emotions in the same way. Empathy-as-empathic-concern is thus a tool that can be used for ill as well as for good.[7]

Does this brief discussion imply that empathy in the two ways that I have defined it is either too flawed an activity or too manipulable an emotional experience to be useful for museum professionals? I don't think so. We just need to clearly explain how we use the concepts in our practice and be aware of the limitations. With the common meaning of empathy-as-perspective-taking, I have revised the term as *empathy-as-perspective-getting,* which I believe is a much more useful activity. With regard to empathy-as-empathic-concern, one must remain alive to the fact that this empathic concern can be manipulated and is not an unalloyed good in itself. But one also has to trust that museum professionals are aiming at the social good. Those of us who create exhibitions are not attempting to manipulate visitors through empathy in order to gain personal advantage or to promote some dangerous ideology (I hope). We are not advertisers, conmen, or—heaven forbid—politicians, aiming at selling a product, fleecing people of their savings, or persuading people of the rightness of some bankrupt ideology. Rather, museum professionals want to foster empathy-as-empathic-concern toward worthy objects, such as other humans and cultures that are in need, are misunderstood, or are persecuted. Empathy is a tool, which in responsible hands, I believe can do much good.

ONCE MORE WITH FEELING

I now want to discuss empathy in the context of the Freer|Sackler as an institution. Where has this interest in empathy at the Freer|Sackler come from? Let me give a brief anecdote: I recently asked Julian Raby, the director of the Freer|Sackler, what he thought about "empathy" as we sat in a taxi in a traffic jam somewhere between Georgetown and Independence Avenue.

His simple answer was: "Well, 'empathy' is like the term 'understanding,' but with emotion added." It was a throwaway comment, but I think it gets to the heart of the museum's interest in empathy. A few months later, I was able to sit down with Julian and ask him in more detail about the subject. In answer to my questioning, Julian noted that he had long been concerned about the "arid" nature of many contemporary galleries and museums—of how these institutions often seemed caught in "the thrall of dispassion." He stated that "we have created a myth—a myth of the cool, anonymous museum environment." Such a myth was perhaps most visible in the way museums wrote labels and text panels:

> We have created a myth that the 3rd person voice is somehow closer to objectivity. But we are really lying to ourselves. Every piece of writing involves choices being made, and we should be explicit about those choices. Once we do that, we have the potential for dialogue with the visitor.

In place of the museum as a "dispassionate storehouse of objects," Julian argues for the museum as an "emotional storehouse." For this to take place, he wants to see a "movement away from didacticism to theatre, from anonymity to voice." Such a movement requires the injection of emotion, a more human-centric approach, and an increased "social role" for museums. These ideas have been exercising Julian, and many others working in museums, for years. And in the concept of "empathy," he—like many others—has found a useful catch-all term for these ideas. The impact of "empathy" is clear in the Freer|Sackler's new statement of purpose, which describes the museum's goal as "generating empathy across cultures." This move reflects a feeling that *understanding*—a term previously used in the Freer|Sackler's institutional statements—is too desiccated a term to cover what the museum is trying to achieve, suggesting a dryly intellectual pursuit rather than a richly human one. *Empathy* as a term has helped the Freer|Sackler recalibrate its goals: the museum is still aiming at "understanding," but now it seeks "understanding with feeling."

VALUING EMPATHY

If "empathy" has become an important *goal* for the Freer|Sackler, it is also shaping the museum's *values*, that is, what the museum judges to be important. The very fact that the museum decided to create a show about contemporary Afghan artisans is testament to the museum's desire to focus on human stories and to generate empathic concern regarding issues of social and global significance. In the case of the *Turquoise Mountain* exhibition, this empathic concern had to do with the destruction and imperiled status of cultural heritage sites around the world. The idea for the exhibition was significantly inspired by, and developed against the backdrop of, the destruction of sites of global cultural significance in the Middle East during 2014 and 2015. Such events as the destruction of the Northwest Palace at Nimrud in Iraq and the Baalshamin Temple at Palmyra in Syria were very much in the minds of the exhibition team as we planned an exhibition on cultural heritage preservation in Afghanistan. Moreover, the exhibition from the beginning saw itself as engaging with a country that had been at the center of US foreign policy concerns for over a decade; with the declaration of the "end of combat operations" in Afghanistan in 2014, the Freer|Sackler wanted to show the human face of a country largely perceived and understood by a US audience through the lens of foreign policy and military intervention. Such an approach was "human-centric" in that the Freer|Sackler wanted to focus on the human element—the human response, the human value, and the potential human cost—of endangered cultural heritage sites. Our exhibition team was clear that "cultural heritage" should not mean just buildings, archaeological sites, and objects, but *people*. For us, the intangible cultural heritage of traditional skills, oral culture, and the cultural practices of residents of historic areas were as important as the tangible heritage of plasterwork and wood paneling.

Such human-centric values extended to our exhibition goals. Our two primary goals as we initially conceived them (indeed, I pull these goals directly from my first Power Point "concept note" I made in early 2014) were "to disrupt stereotypes about Afghanistan" and "to make connections between Afghans and U.S. visitors." These two goals are instructive: the aim of disrupting stereotypes signposts a desire on our part to engage with current politics and social norms, that is, to challenge negative perceptions of Afghan culture among US audiences who have been fed a steady drip of stories about the corruption, "tribalism," and "warlike" nature of Afghans. The second goal of "making connections" is testament to the human-centric aim of bringing together peoples across cultures and of establishing a shared sense of humanity. Such phrases as "shared sense of humanity" can become pat, lazy labels for what we rather airily assume we should all be doing with cross-cultural projects at museums. But there is a serious aim behind it worth spelling out: scientific research suggests that perception-getting exercises, such as hearing other people's stories, can produce empathic concern and that empathic concern can lead to changed views of groups of people, and even to altruistic action.[8] For an exhibition like ours, our dream goal is such change in views and actions. We seek a change of norms: in our case, a change of norms in terms of the general societal perception of, and accepted behavior toward, Afghan, Muslim, and Asian cultures. Now museums have to be careful not to exaggerate their potential impact: exhibitions rarely directly lead to a change of norms or policies. But exhibitions can create opportunities for experiences of perception getting and empathic concern, which can in turn lead to such change. It is a long chain of things that need to happen, but museums have a part to play in certain key middle links in that chain. For that reason, we do not put the goal of our exhibition as "changed norms and policies." That would be unrealistic. But "making emotional, intellectual, and physical connections between Afghans and U.S. visitors" is realistic, and clearly involves empathy-as-perspective-getting and empathy-as-empathic-concern.

EMPATHY AS EXHIBITION APPROACH

If empathy informed the goals and values of the *Turquoise Mountain* exhibition, it also informed the approach to exhibition planning. This is most particularly true of the role of empathy-as-perspective-getting. Most basically, the exhibition was itself a partnership between the Freer|Sackler and a charity, Turquoise Mountain. Such a partnership was an extraordinary act of "putting oneself in someone else's shoes": the Freer|Sackler worked with Turquoise Mountain to realize Turquoise Mountain's vision of what an exhibition about Murad Khani should look and feel like. As Turquoise Mountain's representative, I worked for several months at the Freer|Sackler with a team of three Freer|Sackler staff. I watched as they attempted to understand my viewpoint and those of my colleagues in Kabul, and I in turn learned to see the perspective of Freer|Sackler staff. Beyond the partnership between our two organizations, the whole approach for the curation of the exhibition was consciously led by the notion of perspective getting. Our basic idea from the beginning was that this should not be a conventionally curated show. In keeping with the exhibition's experimental "story-based" approach, we wanted the exhibition's story of Murad Khani and the revival of Afghan traditional arts to be dictated by the people who lived or worked there. We thus instituted a collaborative process by which I acted as a mediator between Afghan artists in Afghanistan and the exhibition team in Washington, DC. I clocked up more air miles than was good for my conscience, but this travel did allow for the incorporation of a rich range of voices and perspectives.

To give one an insight into how this worked in practice, let me give an example of the woodwork section of the exhibition. My interlocutor in Kabul for this section was Ustad Nasser Mansouri, Afghanistan's preeminent woodworker and furniture designer, who runs his own woodwork business in western Kabul. Ustad Nasser and I started with a long walk around the historic buildings of Murad Khani and Asheqan-o-Arefan in central Kabul, discussing what ideas he wanted to get across from his section of the exhibition, and seeking inspiration in these old buildings for the pieces that he would make. We then sat down for interviews in Kabul, which were recorded. Ustad Nasser also made sketches of potential designs (figure 10.1). I then traveled back to Washington, DC, where I discussed the feasibility of his ideas with the exhibition team and the design company

Figure 10.1. Ustad Nasser Mansouri, one of the featured artisans in the *Turquoise Mountain* exhibition.

(ROTO, based in Columbus, Ohio) who would help realize his vision. Ustad Nasser had three main points he wanted to get across: first, the practical skill needed in carving traditional *jali* latticework paneling by hand; second, the social function of such *jali* latticework in dividing up public spaces; and third, the aesthetic purpose of the pieces in creating beauty and harmony through geometric design. After discussions with the exhibition and design teams, I went back to Kabul, where I talked Ustad Nasser through the proposed design ideas and we made modifications. Ustad Nasser and I later both traveled to Washington, DC, where he was able to see the finalization of designs and have face-to-face discussions at the Freer|Sackler. This approach was mirrored to varying degrees in the calligraphy, jewelry, ceramics, and carpet sections. Long-winded as it was in many ways, working this way forced all of us to take part in significant perspective-taking and perspective-getting exercises. Ustad Nasser was forced to imagine what a US visitor would want to see and learn from an exhibition of Afghan artwork, and we at the Freer|Sackler, in turn, were made to imagine what kind of exhibition design would be true to the visions of the Afghan artists. We then tried these ideas out on each other, with the US-based team responding to the Afghan team's design ideas, and vice versa. Perspective taking as

Figure 10.2. Ustad Abdul Matin Malekzadah and curator Thomas Wide discuss exhibition design in Kabul.

an imaginative exercise was thus paired with perspective getting as an open exchange of perspectives. One illuminating example of such perspective taking on the part of the Afghan artists was ceramicist Abdul Matin Malekzada, who lives in the pottery village of Istalif north of Kabul (figure 10.2). In collaborating on an informational text panel on Istalif, Abdul Matin and I discussed what we should include. Abdul Matin wanted to have a section on the traditional layout of Istalifi potters' houses, all of which have a ceramics workshop built onto the side of the house. Abdul Matin thought it would be helpful for a US audience to note that such pottery workshops incorporated into their houses was similar to the way that US houses "all have garages for their cars." I think he was right.

IPOP AS EMPATHETIC APPROACH?

Another important element of perspective getting in exhibition design was our approach to the exhibition's proposed visitors. Exhibitions are traditionally curated based on some combination of what a curator believes visitors should see and what a curator believes visitors want to see. The second part of this clearly involves empathy-as-perspective-taking: the curator imagines him- or herself "in the visitor's shoes" and makes a show that he or she believes will satisfy that imagined visitor. However, as I've described earlier with the distinction between perspective taking and perspective getting, it turns out we're not very good at imagining what other people want. If we can't even imagine accurately what our spouse is experiencing, how can hope to imagine the experiences of a museum visitor? Fortunately for us, recent academic research into visitors' preferences, led by Andrew Pekarik and James Schreiber, has done the hard work of not just imagining what visitors want, but actually going out and asking them. The product of this quantitative and qualitative research, carried out by the Smithsonian's Office of Policy and Analysis over several years, is a "theory of visitor preference," IPOP.[9] IPOP offers a typology of experience preferences as:

> *Ideas*—an attraction to concepts, abstractions, linear thought, facts and reasons; *People*—an attraction to human connection, affective experience, stories, and social interactions; *Objects*—an attraction to things, aesthetics, craftsmanship, ownership, and visual language; and *Physical*—an attraction to somatic sensations, including movement, touch, sound, taste, light, and smell.[10]

As the authors note, we are obviously still drawn to all four of these experiences in some degree. But it does seem that most of us have one preference that is dominant. This IPOP theory suggests that to create the most meaningful, enjoyable, and significant exhibition for the largest numbers of visitors requires creating an exhibition that combines these four ideas, that is, stimulating ideas, strong human stories, beautiful objects, and rich varieties of somatic experience.

IPOP theory also has important insights for curatorial teams during the design stage. By highlighting curators' own preferences, it brings to light some of our own ingrained biases. I, for example, have taken the simple survey on which one's preferences are analyzed, and happen to have an almost equal preference for ideas and people (perceptive readers may notice that this chapter reflects my preferences, divided as it is into a predominantly "ideas-centric" first half and a predominantly "people-centric" second half). With my preference for ideas and people, it is not surprising that I gravitate toward elements of the exhibition in which ideas and people are at the forefront. Fortunately, however, other members of our exhibition team have different preferences. To overcome my own biases, I can seek their perspective and incorporate such perspectives into the show. Through so doing I have been forced to carry out "perspective-getting" exercises that have enriched my understanding of our visitors and made, hopefully, an exhibition that will resonate with more visitors than if I had been left to my own devices. In the case of the *Turquoise Mountain* exhibit, this "empathetic" approach has, unfortunately, been relatively unsystematic: a product of the exigencies of time and budget. However, Andrew Pekarik and his team have developed more systematized IPOP-based exhibition design materials that can be used during the exhibition process by exhibition staff to get a greater range of perspectives on the exhibition as it develops. At the Freer|Sackler, many staff members have been trained in IPOP theory techniques, and it is being used as a useful tool in several of the Freer|Sackler's exhibitions currently in design.

IPOP theory offers useful insights for "empathy" as an approach and as a goal for museums. As an approach to exhibition design, IPOP research strengthens the case that *perspective getting* is more important than *perspective taking*. We can "imagine" all we like what we think visitors will feel about an exhibition, but IPOP research illustrates that visitors' experiences of exhibitions are incorrigibly plural. However, through perspective getting based on serious research in which we ask questions and listen to visitors' answers, we can start to build up a much better idea of what visitors look for in their museum visits. No one is claiming that IPOP offers a fully developed psychological model—there are many years of further research, much larger datasets, more case studies needed. It is also clearly a work in progress (the "physical" typology in particular seems underdeveloped at present). However, it is a very useful tool for (1) realizing the biases within all of us (including curators) and (2) going some way to correcting them. IPOP's recommendations—that exhibition teams are made up of different people with different preferences—also illustrates that personal empathy is not the answer to good exhibition design; rather, it is creating a kind of "empathetic group" in which different perspectives are incorporated. We are not claiming that we can all accurately "feel as another feels" or "walk in another's shoes," but by putting together a team of people with different preferences, we can create an exhibition that is fully "human-centric," in the sense of being tailored to the broadest range of people possible.

Perhaps more fundamentally, IPOP theory has suggestive insight for "empathy" as a goal of exhibitions as well. It would be interesting to see what percentage of those interested in the issue of "empathy" in museums are themselves very empathetic. I would hazard a guess that, like myself, an interest in empathy in museums is particularly pronounced in those who are "people" people, in IPOP's typology. We must recognize that some people are significantly more interested in feeling empathy and are more oriented toward "people" in their preferences than others. To design exhibitions that focus heavily on "people"—which is a seemingly inevitable technique when aiming to "foster empathy"—risks marginalizing the majority of visitors for whom "people" are not the main or even minor reason for visiting an exhibition.

BRINGING *TURQUOISE MOUNTAIN* TO LIFE

Having discussed "empathy" in the context of institutional values, goals, and curatorial approach, it is now time to turn to the *Turquoise Mountain* exhibition itself: How are the values, goals, and approach translated into an exhibition? The final section of this chapter offers a detailed description of the evolution of the exhibition design.

In line with IPOP principles, the exhibition team aimed to create an exhibition that combined stimulating ideas, powerful human stories and interactions, beautiful objects, and rich somatic sensations in fruitful counterpoint with one another. A few examples of how this works in practice may elucidate the method. I will return to the woodwork section and to Ustad Nasser Mansouri. Once we had worked out the messages, which Ustad Nasser wished to achieve with his woodwork installations, we began putting together other elements that would interact with the beautiful objects he created. First was the setting for his *jali* woodwork creations. Ustad Nasser had the idea of recreating the feel of Murad Khani by creating a carved set of arches, exact replicas of a nineteenth-century caravanserai in Murad Khani. These arches would be part of the exhibition build, architectural elements framing the artwork. To achieve this we commissioned a team of fifteen woodworkers in Kabul to work for several months to create these arches; Ustad Nasser oversaw the carving and polishing. These arches were made of Himalayan cedar wood and weighed several tons—it was no easy task to ship them from Kabul all the way to Washington, DC (figure 10.3)!

Figure 10.3. Turquoise Mountain woodworkers practice installing.

These arches helped create the feel of a small wood workshop in Kabul. We then populated the area with a range of video, text, photograph, and woodwork objects. For the video, we hired a filmmaker, who lived in Kabul with Turquoise Mountain for several months. The filmmaker spent many hours with Ustad Nasser, filming his workshop and the process of creation, as well as interviewing him in various formal and informal settings. Ustad Nasser then was recorded speaking about his life, and this recording was used as a voiceover for the film. In it, he described his early life as a refugee in Iran, his return to Afghanistan, and his finding inspiration for his artistic work in the historic district of Murad Khani in Kabul. Next to the video, we placed a text board; but rather than text written by a Western curator or art historian, the text was written by Ustad Nasser in Dari, which I then translated. This meant that the whole space became a holistic reflection of Ustad Nasser's life and work: text that he had written, the sound of his voice, his images on the screen, and work made by his hand, including the arches in which the very installation was housed.

Such an installation was pure IPOP. In terms of "ideas," we had set up various questions (What is the social purpose of *jali* screens? What role does geometry serve in Islamic art?) and facts (a *jali* panel takes one woodworker two weeks to make; *jali* panels are made by hand without any nails) that people could read about; for "people," we introduced one strong character and created the whole section in his voice, through video, text, and photographs; in terms of "objects," we had beautiful handcrafted woodwork that people could admire and even touch; in terms of "physical" experiences, one could run one's hands over the arches, enjoy the play of light and dark as strong lights passed through *jali* panels, and feel immersed in the atmosphere of a Murad Khani house by stepping through the recreated arches. Such an approach continued through the whole exhibition space. There were six main sections, matched to five artists and one engineer, who each wrote text for their section and were the subjects of film and photographs. We ensured that these artisans had a range of backgrounds, talents, and stories. This variety was based on the basic insight that humans are most likely to feel an emotional connection with those who are "like" themselves in some way, whether it be background, gender, age, profession, or circumstance.[11] Thus we had a middle-aged male potter named Abdul Matin Malekzada, who came from a village in the foothills of the Hindu Kush; a young female artist named Sughra Hussainy, who lived in the suburbs of western Kabul and studied calligraphy and miniature painting at the Turquoise Mountain Institute; a sixty-something engineer named Hedayat Ahmadzai, who oversaw much of the restoration of buildings in Murad Khani; and a young deaf jeweler named Saeeda Etebari, who had spent her early years in a refugee camp in Pakistan.

Alongside these Afghan voices we also created sections on Western designers and artists who were involved in the Turquoise Mountain project. This was based on the knowledge that some people are more "empathetic" than others and differ in their ability to find common ground across distances of background, character, culture, etc. These Western voices thus acted as bridging characters: cross-cultural figures who could help "take" visitors to Afghanistan, rather in the way a US television presenter is able to guide a US audience through a foreign subject that might otherwise be too alien for many to engage with. Thus the exhibition included sections of text and video on English jeweler Pippa Small, who has worked with Turquoise Mountain for eight years and who collaborated with Saeeda Etebari on a spectacular emerald necklace for the exhibition. We also had a section created by Turkish-American carpet designer Erbil Tezcan, who wrote movingly about the challenges for a foreigner of traveling and working in Afghanistan and the satisfaction he had in producing beautiful carpets made by Afghan weavers. Such text was paired with a specially commissioned rug, designed by Erbil Tezcan, in which twenty-three Afghan design motifs were interwoven in a single carpet (figure 10.4).

Figure 10.4.   Carpet designer Erbil Tezcan works on the designs for his exhibition carpet.

MAKING PHYSICAL CONNECTIONS ACROSS CONTINENTS

Many of the elements in the exhibition space thus relied on making emotional and intellectual connections between a US visitor and the Afghans who were the subjects of the show. The text and video encouraged people to take the perspective of the Afghan artists and helped them not just imagine, but concretely experience, the artists' worldview by having all the text in the artists' own words. But we were also more ambitious about how we made connections between peoples and wanted to move beyond just imagined connections to actual *physical* connections. We decided to do this by arranging for Afghan artisans to visit Washington, DC, during the lifespan of the exhibition. We received funding for eighteen artisans to each spend two weeks in Washington, DC, during which time they would carry out displays in the exhibition space, meet visitors, and carry out crafts workshops. This would provide a wonderful opportunity for visitors to meet face to face with the Afghans who had created the exhibition and to share experiences and ideas. And in turn, it would be a powerful learning experience for the Afghan artisans to meet US visitors. This is an important point; despite the fourteen years in which the United States has been "on the ground" in Afghanistan, many Afghans have very little contact with Americans, and their view of the United States is largely filtered through their understanding of US political and military action in the country. Their experiences in the United States would thus allow them to gain a much more nuanced understanding of the United States than could be garnered from life in Kabul.

Such artisan trips to the United States would also ensure that the exhibition had a social impact outside of the museum, stretching all the way to Afghanistan. These artisans were also going to visit many of the great museums of the United States and meet US artisans working in Washington, DC, and the area. They would return to Afghanistan, it was hoped, full of ideas and inspiration for their own artistic practices there.

CONCLUSION

If this chapter's primary purpose has been a case study of a single exhibition at a single institution, the chapter has also inevitably had to engage with larger theoretical concerns regarding the definition of *empathy* in a museum context, its import for an institution's goals and values, its use in exhibition design, and the question of IPOP experience preference theory as an "empathetic approach" to exhibition design. If the chapter has been, at times, a touch skeptical of empathy's value for museum professionals, this has been merely to sound a note of caution to those who would see empathy as the panacea for every current concern in museology and curatorial studies. A term loses its analytic grip when it is used too often to describe too many disparate phenomena. This chapter has, nevertheless, made a case for empathy-as-perspective-getting and empathy-as-empathic-concern as valuable goals for museums to pursue, in their ability to promote action and societal change. The chapter has also illustrated how such empathetic approaches can be a useful tool in exhibition design. However, we would be wise here to take note of what Mark Twain (allegedly) said of tools: "For the man with a hammer, everything looks like a nail." For the *Turquoise Mountain* exhibition, we treated empathy as one tool, among others, in our curatorial toolbox. Whether the exhibition succeeds or not—and how much "empathy" will have played a role in that success—is a question whose answer will have to wait until after the exhibition.

NOTES

1. The core exhibition team was made up of myself, Julian Raby, Cheryl Sobas, Katelynn Averyt (later Elizabeth Dion), and Flore de Taisne.

2. Steven Pinker, *The Better Angels of Our Nature* (New York: Viking, 2011), 695.

3. Google Trends (the data for which stretches back to January 2004). While the word *empathy* has increased roughly fivefold, according to Google Ngram, in books published in the forty-eight-year period between 1960 and 2008, it has more than tripled in terms of the amount of online word searches in the last eleven years.

4. A succinct introduction to Zaki's work can be found in Jamil Zaki, "Choosing Empathy: A Conversation With Jamil Zaki," *Edge*, https://edge.org/conversation/jamil_zaki-choosing-empathy (accessed October 20, 2015), 2.

5. See Nicholas Epley, *Mindwise* (New York: Knopf, 2014).

6. I do not have the space here to discuss Jamil Zaki's interesting discussion of the role of "choice" (see his article referenced in note 4) in empathy, other than to note that while we clearly often have a choice of putting ourselves in situations where we will feel empathy, or of avoiding them, this is not always the case. Charity posters we see while waiting for a bus or images that flash up on our TV screens are clear examples: we cannot *choose* to look or not, they catch us unawares. Advertisers know this better than anyone!

7. The most eloquent proponent of the "empathy is overrated" school is psychologist Paul Bloom. For an introduction to his arguments, see his response to Jamil Zaki in "Choosing Empathy."

8. The most research on this topic has been carried out by C. D. Batson and colleagues over several decades of work on the topic of empathy. For one example of the relation of perspective taking and empathic concern, see C. D. Batson, J. L. Dyck, R. B. Brandt, J. G. Batson, A. L. Powell, M. R. McMaster, and C. Griffitt, "Five Studies Testing Two New Egoistic Alternatives to the Empathy-Altruism Hypothesis," *Journal of Personality and Social Psychology* 55, no. 1: 52–77.

9. The clearest articulation of the theory is Andrew J. Pekarik, James B. Schreiber, Nadine Hanemann, Kelly Richmond, and Barbara Mogel, "IPOP: A Theory of Experience Preference," *Curator: The Museum Journal* 57, no. 1 (2014): 5–27.

10. Ibid., 6.

11. Such commonsense assumptions are backed up by psychological studies. See, for example, C. D. Batson, C. L. Turk, L. L Shaw, and T. R. Klein, "Information Function of Empathic Emotion: Learning That We Value the Other's Welfare," *Journal of Personality and Social Psychology* 68, no. 2 (1995): 300–313.

curiosity
empathy
engagement
sensitivity
understanding

11

Invoking Biography in Museum Presentations of Islamic Art

Successes and Challenges

Amy S. Landau

Biography can serve as a powerful way to approach works of art. Museum visitors are profoundly drawn to the personal stories of others, even of people far removed in time and place; human emotions, including envy, love, and fear—as well as life experiences such as the birth of a daughter, the death of a brother, and victory or defeat over a competitor—all traverse centuries and geographies. As a curator of Islamic and South Asian art with collections inscribed in languages only a minority of American visitors can read and from parts of the world few have visited, I have looked to the object, as one looks to literature, to relate stories about people and the times in which they lived. In this chapter, I describe successes and challenges of featuring biographical narratives as a means to engage American audiences with Islamic art in the temporary exhibition *Pearls on a String: Artists, Patrons, and Poets at the Great Islamic Courts*. This international loan exhibition was organized by the Walters Art Museum in partnership with the Asian Art Museum. It opened at the Walters in Baltimore on November 8, 2015, and ran through January 31, 2016, and then traveled to the Asian Art Museum, San Francisco (February 26 to May 8, 2016).

As organizing curator, my point of departure was that works of art are vestiges of the values, intentions, and actions of authors, artists, patrons, and their communities. The major challenge with a biographical approach was writing label texts that would give visitors enough information to lure them into the worlds of the featured protagonists without overwhelming them. Not only was there the need to offer engaging human-centric stories, but also to explain locations, cultural traditions, and religions of the Middle East and South Asia, many of which are unfamiliar to American museum goers. After much discussion, the *Pearls* exhibition team at the Walters decided to experiment with longer than average texts for this particular exhibition.[1] Not only were there wall texts and object labels, but additional reading materials were also provided in the exhibition spaces. On the basis of visitor comments, timing and tracking evaluations, and press reviews, it is clear that the additional textual layers enhanced the exhibition experience. In the words of Lee Lawrence of the *Wall Street Journal*, "Throughout the show, the Walters bucks the current trend of paring explanations to a minimum—thankfully, for the many wall texts, labels and laminated cards are so readable and engaging that they bring out nuance without overshadowing the objects or proving taxing."[2] I believe the exhibition's success was due to good storytelling and exhibition design that put people and human experience at the center of both, as I illustrate in this chapter.[3]

WHY BIOGRAPHY?

In museum contexts, histories of Islamic art often assume an autonomous development without the mediation of historical events or culture, or, indeed, even people: patrons, artists, architects, or craftsmen. Anonymous presentations of Islamic art have given rise to the unfortunate impression of Islam as a cultural and artistic monolith. Cultural critic and author Edward Said (1935–2003) and other like-minded thinkers have rightly criticized such presentations as vestiges of Eurocentric and Orientalizing retellings of Islamic history whereby rich diversities of cultural experience of Muslims are reduced to a few timeless adages. As American society is plagued by a polarizing discourse around Islam, supported by media that constantly presents Muslims and Islam in the context of violence,[4] I believe museums can offer counter-narratives to negative portrayals of Islam by moving away from anonymity and didacticism to human-centric stories and to voice. As a curator over the last decade, I have learned that visitor interests tend to circle around *human* exploration, *human* experience, and *human* beliefs (i.e., faith), and that these frames support intimate engagements with works of art: they can transform dead histories into living histories. Drawing upon biographical narratives, we can explore the differences in experience, thought, and belief of individuals in historic Islamic communities, while also observing commonalities among all human beings, including the need to express and preserve a sense of identity and communal belonging through various modes of private and public expression.

At the start of the exhibition *Pearls on a String*, the visitor encountered a text panel that communicated why a biographical lens was chosen for the show. It explained that Islamic traditions maintain that people may be known through their words, drawings, and painted images. The notion that art is imprinted with human "traces" (*asar*, which also translates as "footprints," "vestiges," or "relics") is embedded in the words of sixteenth-century Persian artist and writer Dust Muhammad: *Our works point to us, so gaze after us at our works.*[5] The text panel continued by noting that biographical narratives are often absent from presentations of Islamic art. Yet from the inception of Islam in the seventh century, representations of the past have relied heavily on accounts about individuals, their innovations, and their social connections.

Indeed, my desire to invoke the genre of biography in an exhibition dedicated to the arts of Islamic societies was to apply historiographical approaches common to the writing of Islamic history to presentations of Islamic art. Biography characterizes writing in all branches of the humanities, from narratives of the traditions attributed to the Prophet Muhammad (*hadith*), to the genre of *risala* or technical treatises, to the *tadhkira* ("aide mémoire") containing notices of exemplary cultural figures, including poets, calligraphers, and painters. Within such genres, there are repeated references to relationships between artist and patron, master and pupil, and rival calligraphers and painters, creating chains of transmission from one person to the next referred to as *isnad* (lit. "leaning against") or *silsila* (lit. "chain"). There is also a particularly strong tradition of attributing "firsts" (*awa'il*), or innovations, to specific people, resulting in numerous foundation stories built up around persons linked to particular artistic and cultural developments.[6]

Admittedly there are challenges when applying a biographical lens to Islamic art. Artistic production before the late fifteenth century rarely offers signatures and, although painters' names abound on works of art and in texts post ca. 1500, the field of Islamic art struggles with issues of authorship as the appearance of a name on an artwork does not necessarily connote individual authorship. Further, there are undeniable gaps in the textual sources as to the lives of artists, as well as patrons and poets. Nevertheless, one may collect evidence from a range of textual and physical materials to understand the outlines, if not the details, of an individual's life in Islamic societies. Although biographical discussions in Islamic vernaculars do not by their nature yield details about a person's private and public life, as one finds in the other biographical traditions, an individual's agency and personal circumstances can be retrieved to varying degrees. Biographical information can be culled from different textual genres: histories, prefaces, technical treatises, and biographies. These sources typically communicate individuals' agency through the ways in which they contributed to the continuity and advancement of scholarly, artistic, poetic, or political lineages. That is to say that the emphasis is on social collectives, whether they be groups comprising court officials, religious scholars, poets, calligraphers, or painters.

My aim was to replicate historiographical approaches not only by introducing the genre of biography to presentations of Islamic art, but also by focusing on constellations of individuals. The project's title was inspired by the Islamicate metaphor "like pearls on a string," which refers to collections of particulars, whether they be individual letters strung together or a poet's words or works of calligraphy and paintings compiled in an album (*muraqqa'*), that when experienced together create a fully formulated composite whole. Focusing on constellations of people allowed the project to shift the weight of emphasis from the person of the king (caliph, shah, sultan) to the men and women who surrounded him and composed the service elite. These individuals—courtiers, women of the harem, noblemen, and slaves—actively participated in the shaping of Islamic court culture. This gave voice not only to ruler, as has been the paradigm in previous exhibitions, but also gave agency to makers and consumers and women of the harem. Weaving stories about individuals within their social collectives seemed to reverberate with our visitors. As Lawrence writes, "like a chemical reaction, individuals' characteristics in combination with a set of circumstances and a web of relationships produced cultural and artistic explosions. What we see are not so much personal portraits as they are biographies of phenomena."[7]

CURATORIAL AMBITION WITH A SPLASH OF FOLLY

My initial plan was to present an overview of Islamic art in seven stories or "vignettes," spanning the early centuries of Islam up to the early modern period. I was fully convinced of the importance of biography for presentations of Islamic art, and being tasked by my former director Gary Vikan to organize a "major" Islamic art exhibition, I conceived of a "blockbuster." The original set of seven vignettes covered from tenth-century Spain to eighteenth-century Istanbul, across Persian-, Arabic-, and Turkish-speaking court contexts informed by Shi'i, Sunni, and Sufi intellectual currents. These independent sections would allow for different voices and perspectives to emerge, enabling the visitor to see that Islamic societies are not monolithic but made up of a tapestry of individuals with distinct and varying views. Reaching across communities and geographies, the selected vignettes (or snapshots of time and place) of *Pearls on a String* would present multiple Islamic perspectives for the visitor to encounter.

Every section would be framed by a captivating story from historical sources about specific people that underscored the centrality of human relationships in creating great works of art. Each story was linked to a nexus of charismatic objects, which were selected for their aesthetic quality and richly documented histories. Works of art with signatures, inscriptions, ownership stamps, and heraldic images would be used to illustrate that outside the genre of portraiture, one may encounter ("see") the various individuals associated with a work of art.

Historical architectural pieces, archival photography, and video documentation of Islamic architecture were chosen to anchor the visitor in the place and period of each vignette. These visual aids would also provide the context for the displayed utilitarian objects, including candlesticks, mosque lamps, carpets, and large-scale oil paintings. Such visual references were inspired by the new galleries at the Victoria and Albert Museum (Islamic Middle East: The Jameel Gallery) and the Metropolitan Museum of Art (Art of the Arab Lands, Turkey, Iran, Central Asia, and Later South Asia). In the Walters's exhibition, not only would the historical architectural pieces and documentation situate the visitor in time and place as he or she journeyed through the rooms, but they would also underscore the central issue of patronage: each of the exhibition's patron-protagonists was linked to an architectural complex they commissioned.

From its inception, the exhibition's strategies paralleled research by the Smithsonian's Office of Policy and Analysis in their evaluations of what visitors wish to experience in a museum: although I was unaware of it at the time, the winning combination of "IPOP" characterized the concept and interpretive strategies of *Pearls on a String*.[8] As Thomas Wide discusses in the previous chapter, IPOP defines four types of experiences to which visitors gravitate. IPOP is as follows: "ideas," "people," "objects," and "physical, as in a sensory experience defined by placement of architectural details or streaming sound, for example.[9] The *Pearls* team wished to create an immersive aesthetic and intellectual experience for the visitor.

Many on the academic committee for *Pearls on a String* warned me of the dangers of having too many stories, too many vignettes. Chief among them were Julian Raby and Massumeh Farhad, who expressed their deep concern that I would overwhelm the visitor with information and objects. My colleagues at the exhibition's second venue, Dr. Qamar Adamjee, curator of Islamic and South Asian Art at the Asian Art Museum in San Francisco, and Dr. Pedro Carvalho, who was then deputy director of that museum, eventually forced my hand to abbreviate the exhibition experience into three vignettes. Together we agreed upon the three that were close in time and geography. The new focus of the exhibition became individuals at the Mughal, Safavid, and Ottoman courts, which flourished from the sixteenth to the eighteenth century in India, Iran, and Ottoman Turkey, respectively. The three individuals were sixteenth-century writer Abu'l Fazl in Fatehpur Sikri, seventeenth-century painter Muhammad Zaman in Isfahan, and eighteenth-century patron Sultan Mahmud I in Istanbul.

In the process of reducing the vignettes, the possibility of addressing thriving Arabic-speaking cultures, such as Umayyad Spain and Mamluk Egypt, were lost, as were some powerful human stories that involved relationships between a father and daughter, as well as rivals and lovers. These episodes were however captured in the publication: a multi-author book in which the chapters were co-written.[10] For this publication, I partnered people from different disciplines with different language skills with a view to replicating

the diverse skill sets and areas of expertise the historic individuals pos-
sessed. The end result was that the accompanying publication of "Pearls on
a String" covered the initial seven vignettes, while the exhibition itself was
a "three-vignette solution." I am deeply appreciative of my colleagues, in
particular Julian Raby, Massumeh Farhad, and Qamar Adamjee, who saved
me from my overly ambitious seven-vignette exhibition scenario.

THE ART OF STORYTELLING

Artful storytelling was key to inspire the visitor to "walk in the footsteps" of
our protagonists. Their life stories revealed a deep curiosity about a world
that was quickly changing in the early modern period through the global
movement of people, ideas, and technologies. One of the strategies to differentiate the visitor's experience in each vignette was to highlight agency
(i.e., the writer, the painter, and the patron) and the specific medium toward
which they gravitated. By the written word, the painted image, or the ingeniously engineered object, each protagonist endeavored to understand new
ideas and perspectives. Writer Abu'l Fazl in Fathepur Sikri, painter Muhammad Zaman in Isfahan, and eigtheenth-century patron Sultan Mahmud I
in Istanbul each embodied the spirit of his time. Through human imagination and collaboration, these men had a dramatic impact on the arts.
While all were "gifted" in their own way, they could not have achieved their
ambitions without the help of a community of people surrounding them.
This was an important point I wished to underscore.

    All the protagonists were deeply rooted in their communities. Painter
Muhammad Zaman ibn Haji Yusuf (active 1670–1700), for example, who
changed the course of seventeenth-century Persian painting at the Safavid
court of Shah Sulayman (r. 1666–1694) in Isfahan, was so successful as the
champion of *farangi-sazi* (European style), which blended Persian artistic
traditions with European iconography and techniques, that he was able
to interpret European art in ways that were exciting and meaningful to his
community. While his patrons were reliant on his skills, he himself was
reliant on their agreement that his innovations accurately represented their
hopes, ambitions and desires.

    I aimed to highlight human struggles when the historical sources allowed
me. I wanted our visitors to see the human ways the historical figures dealt
with challenges. For instance, in the first vignette dedicated to Abu'l Fazl,
the introductory text noted that the celebrated sixteenth-century writer and
historian had had both friends and foes at Akbar's court and that he suffered
from perfectionism and had a very argumentative nature (see figure 11.1).
I included biographical information that touched upon very palpable
human experiences, such as death and mourning. The label text for Abu'l

THE WRITER | *ABU'L FAZL AT THE MUGHAL COURT*

The writer and historian Abu'l Fazl ibn Mubarak (1551–1602) witnessed both intimate and momentous events at the court of Emperor Akbar in 16th-century Mughal India (present-day India and Pakistan). Abu'l Fazl constructed an image of Akbar's court as a multicultural community engaged with different religious, artistic, and intellectual traditions. His words preserve for us the cultural achievements of his time.

Sensitive, awkward, and sometimes argumentative, Abu'l Fazl had friends and foes. He was a person of extraordinary education with a passionate sense of right and wrong. Abu'l Fazl's intellectual vigor, humanitarian values, and liberal religious sentiments resonated with Akbar. The emperor appointed him as his chief secretary, and the two became trusted friends.

Abu'l Fazl's major achievement was a biography of Akbar, the *Akbarnama* (History of Akbar). Artists translated this account of Akbar's life into some of the most beautiful manuscript paintings of Mughal India. Abu'l Fazl's *Akbarnama* and other illustrated works composed by Abu'l Fazl's peers, on view in these galleries, express the intent to define an emerging empire with assimilated non-Muslim populations. They show how Akbar and the court historian Abu'l Fazl, as well as other poets, artists, and intimates of the court, sought to understand the visual, ritual, and ethnographic landscape of South Asia.

Figure 11.1.   Section 1 introductory text, *Pearls on a String* labels, Baltimore.

Illuminated Frontispiece, from the *Akbarnama* (Book of Akbar)

Mughal India, ca. 1600–1603

Abu'l Fazl began his biography of Akbar in 1590 and obsessively wrote and rewrote the text until his death in 1602. He entrusted parts of the *Akbarnama* to his brother, Fayzi, the celebrated court poet, to render his words more elegantly. Abu'l Fazl read sections of the biography aloud to Akbar for final approval.

The *Akbarnama* is written in Persian, the official language of the Mughal court, and is divided into three volumes. The first two volumes describe Akbar's genealogy and record royal

events. The third volume contains geographic and ethnographic descriptions of India as well as a wealth of information on such subjects as the Mughal government, the royal workshops, and Hindu philosophy.

Abu'l Fazl also reveals personal information in the chronicle. In the most moving disclosure, he speaks of his grief over the death of his beloved brother, Fayzi; he felt the loss so deeply that he was unable to work on the *Akbarnama* for an entire year.

Opaque watercolor, ink, and gold on paper
IL 2015.13.5, Trustees of the Chester Beatty Library, Dublin (In 03.1b–2a)

Figure 11.2.   Case 1.2 object text, *Pearls on a String* labels, Baltimore.

Fazl's magnum opus the *Akbarnama* describes how Abu'l Fazl suffered over the death of his beloved brother Fayzi and how he could not write for an entire year (figure 11.2). Despite the fact that Mahmud I was a sultan, he too had a great many hurdles to overcome. His greatest challenge was a physical deformity: a severe abnormal curvature of the spine. Rarely are individuals with physical or mental difficulties represented in museum contexts; featuring Mahmud we were able to be more inclusive in our representation. The introductory text to his vignette discussed how he was able to overcome his physical challenges and a less than perfect home life to become one of Istanbul's great eigtheenth-century rulers (figure 11.3).

FROM ANONYMITY TO VOICE

Good storytelling involves building up the personality of the protagonists: a difficult task keeping to the word count prescribed by museum labels (averaging between 60 and 250 words; *Pearls* labels averaged between 90 and 350). Where possible and within limits, words said by or about the featured individuals at the time in which they lived (i.e., the sixteenth through the eighteenth century) were included in the didactics. Because Abu'l Fazl was a writer and historian and authored many pages, quotes appeared most frequently in his section (figure 11.4). Quotes built up a story around Mahmud's predilection for ingeniously crafted objects (figure 11.5), while Armenian sources were cited in the second vignette dedicated to Muhammad Zaman at Isfahan to illustrate the painter's patron's interest in images of the pre-Islamic prophets (figure 11.6). The inclusion of primary sources in a variety of languages (e.g., Persian, Ottoman Turkish, Arabic, Sanskrit, Armenian, and French) not only brought the general visitor closer to the protagonists, but also gave academic audiences versed in Islamic history access to new English translations.

THE PATRON | *SULTAN MAHMUD AT THE OTTOMAN COURT*

Sultan Mahmud I (r. 1730–54) was celebrated in his own day as a sponsor of the arts and as a ruler who brought peace to the Ottoman Empire. The next galleries explore collaborations between Mahmud, his artisans, and merchants to define a cosmopolitan court poised at the crossroads of Asia and Europe in the empire's capital of Istanbul.

Lacking experience in imperial affairs and born with a severe curvature of the spine, Mahmud had challenges to overcome upon gaining the throne. In 1703 as a boy, Mahmud witnessed his father's humiliating removal from office by his uncle Ahmed III (r. 1703–30). In 1730 a revolt broke out against Ahmed, and Mahmud was made ruler of a vast and unstable empire. Those who elevated him to the throne thought they could control him; Mahmud proved them wrong. He calmed public unrest and initiated military reforms.

Mahmud used art and architectural patronage to stress his royal lineage and to communicate his vision of a technologi-cally advanced empire engaged with Europe. Those who knew Mahmud observed his personal involvement in commissions and his taste for cleverly engineered objects of rare materials. There were even rumors that the sultan himself drafted architectural plans, crafted objects in gold with jewels, and carved "toothpicks of ebony and ivory." The works displayed here reveal Mahmud's intimate knowledge of art, architecture, history, and music.

Figure 11.3.   Section 3 introductory text, *Pearls on a String* labels, Baltimore.

Interviews and Archives

> *I began to exert myself to the utmost to gather narratives*
> *and accounts of the events of His Majesty's life, and I*
> *spent a long time questioning members of the court and*
> *intimates of this illustrious family.*
> —Abu'l Fazl, *Akbarnama*

"The place of history was in ruins," lamented Abu'l Fazl, appalled by his contemporaries' reliance on long-standing and sometimes flawed chronicles. Abu'l Fazl set out to write a different type of account that, while recording the past, emphasized the present and highlighted the people who surrounded him as worthy subjects of biography.

Abu'l Fazl's approach, comprising archival research and oral interviews, was strikingly contemporary. To compose biographies of Akbar's father, Humayun (r. 1530–56), and grandfather, Babur (r. 1526–30), Abu'l Fazl consulted dynastic histories like the *Baburnama*, seen to your far left, and interviewed women of the harem and Muslim and Hindu court officials.

Abu'l Fazl asked Akbar, "whose memory is perfect," to resolve discrepancies among the reports. "Over the course of many sessions I ascertained the truth, and I scratched out doubts with the penknife of certainty."

Figure 11.4.   Section text 1.3, *Pearls on a String* labels, Baltimore.

Royal Treasures: An Ottoman Inheritance

They were brought to him on a table at the back of a large room in which was spread all that was most precious in every genre of the choicest productions of nature or art. . . . Each jeweled object was put out on the day when it was needed, and each had its place. It would be taken back there exactly when His Majesty had stopped examining it.
—Jean-Claude Flachat, chief merchant to Mahmud I, *Observations on Trade and the Arts in Part of Europe, Asia, and Africa, and Even the Eastern Indies* (1766)

The French merchant Jean-Claude Flachat, who procured luxury wares for Mahmud I and the Ottoman elite, describes the vast number and variety of precious objects in the sultan's treasury. Mahmud's inheritance from the royal line included extraordinarily crafted objects in jade, jewels, and gold, as well as rarities imported from abroad.

Mahmud's interest in jeweled objects was noteworthy even by royal standards. Flachat writes, "[Mahmud] would spend several hours with his favorites examining everything one after the other, without tiring of admiring them. . . . In choosing [these items], there was no less regard for the perfection of the work than for the richness of the materials that had been employed."

Figure 11.5.   Case 3.8 object text, *Pearls on a String* labels, Baltimore.

Images of the Biblical Prophets at Isfahan

> *Occasionally, Shah Sulayman, with a great entourage, would visit the splendid monastery of All Savior's Cathedral. Sulayman asked many questions about the gilded and colored images that were painted in the house of the Lord our God, about the divinity of Christ and the nature of the Trinity. He inquired: "Why do you paint images in houses of prayer where it is not appropriate?"*
> —Khatchatur Julayetsi, *History of the Persians*

Muhammad Zaman's patron, Shah Sulayman, was apprehensive about the images of pre-Islamic prophets in churches in Isfahan and its suburb of New Julfa built by Armenian Christians and Catholic missionaries during the 17th century. The Muslim faith prohibits figural imagery in places of worship and in the sacred text of the Qur'an, and it shares with Judaism and Christianity the abhorrence of idolatry. Shah Sulayman and his peers nonetheless commissioned small-scale paintings of biblical subjects, which they enjoyed in albums and manuscripts.

Between the 1670s and 1680s, Muhammad Zaman painted Old and New Testament scenes for the Muslim political elite, responding to his peers' avid interest in stories about the prophets. Biblical narratives are recounted in the Qur'an and in a literary genre dedicated to the subject, called Qisas al-anbiya, or "stories of the prophets." As the art in this room demonstrates, Isfahan was awash with images of biblical prophets.

Figure 11.6. Section text 2.2, *Pearls on a String* labels, Baltimore.

In the process of referencing quotes by early modern contemporaries in different languages, the plurality of Islamic societies came to the fore. As Phil Kennicott wrote in his review of the show in the *Washington Post*, "The underlying theme throughout is an attitude toward diversity and culture that goes beyond the usual bromides of mere tolerance."[11] On the basis of evaluations and visitor comments we can confirm that the theme of Islamic cultural and religious pluralism engaged people. This makes sense, as pluralism is such an important issue in our own day. A thread that ran through the exhibition is that the art object bears testimony to human interaction and exchange. This engagement within Islamic communities involved Muslims and non-Muslims. Islamic societies were mosaics of religious, ethnic, and linguistic groups. Today, this pluralistic tradition is being challenged by portrayals of Islam as exclusive and intolerant of cultural diversity. Within the frame of biography, I wanted to demonstrate that there is a rich tradition of religious and cultural pluralism at Islamic courts. The *Harper Collins Dictionary of Religion* defines "religious pluralism" as "the problem and opportunity of the simultaneous presence of different religious traditions within a single society." Religious pluralism does not connote peace, love, and harmony; nor is it merely tolerance. Instead, religious pluralism is an active engagement across lines of difference. Attitudes of pluralism are empathetic stances. In each vignette of *Pearls on a String*, these attitudes were apparent.

VISUAL AND AURAL SURROUNDS

Another strategy to bring the visitor closer to the featured individuals and the time in which they lived was to reference key architectural monuments

Figure 11.7.   Scrim of the Hasht Bihist Palace, Isfahan, *Pearls on a String: Artists, Patrons, and Poets at the Great Islamic Courts*, Baltimore, November 8, 2015–January 31, 2016.
Source: Photograph by Susan Tobin, copyright Walters Art Museum.

and music. Large-scale architectural scrims of buildings constructed during the lifetimes of our exhibition protagonists anchored the visitor in the specific place and period of each section. We produced sheer scrims with images of Fathepur Sikri, Hasht Bihist (figure 11.7), and Tophane palace.

The team debated whether or not we should give the scrims a textual layer of interpretation. In the end we did decide to offer label texts. The scrim for the second vignette dedicated to the painter Muhammad Zaman was the Hasht Bihist palace. It is likely that Muhammad was commissioned for the building's paintings and as a favorite court artist he would have been invited to royal audiences in the building. We also projected large-scale images to simulate the experience Muhammad Zaman and his peers looking at painted images of prophets in the Christian sacred spaces built in and around Isfahan (figures 11.8–11.10).

In the first vignette we displayed Hindu, Jain, and Christian works of art that were of the type that Abu'l Fazl wrote about in this *Akbarnama* and in the third vignette we installed luxury European wares that Mahmud and his harem collected in Istanbul. The latter text panel allowed us to reference the

Figure 11.8. **Projected images of All Savior's Cathedral, New Julfa, Iran 1655–1664 (all photos: Hrair Hawk Khatcherian, 2011),** *Pearls on a String: Artists, Patrons, and Poets at the Great Islamic Courts,* **Baltimore, November 8, 2015–January 31, 2016.** *Source:* Photo by Amy Landau, copyright Walters Art Museum.

Hasht Bihisht Palace

Shah Sulayman built the Hasht Bihisht (Eight Paradises) in
AH 1080 (1669/70 CE) in Isfahan's palace precinct. This two-story
pavilion has a central domed hall and four octagonal chambers on
each floor, making eight rooms or "eight paradises" (*hasht bihisht*).

    The German doctor Engelbert Kämpfer, traveling in Iran
in the 1680s, describes the Hasht Bihisht as being decorated
with paintings: "Underneath Venetian glass there are paintings
by famous artists and among those the image of a shah of
the 17th century as well as some queens of the 16th century."
Muhammad Zaman would have been one of the imperial painters
commissioned for these murals.

    Praising the building, Sulayman's leading court poet wrote the
following verses:

> *How glorious! The royal palace, may the entire world be in its*
>   *shadow.*
> *It is a beautiful, mirthful and elated bride, who has in her*
>   *hand a mirror made of its glass*
> *The moon is consumed by the desire, to be its slave at the gate*
> *For its celebrated paintings and portraits, they brought soot*
>   *from the eyes of the angel.*
> *Because of the skill of the painters' flower-decoration, dew*
>   *appears on the face of the flower.*

    —Muhammad Tahir Nasrabadi, *Tazkira* (Biographical Notices)

(Photo: iStock/nmessana, 2015)

Figure 11.9. Scrim text, *Pearls on a String* labels, Baltimore.

agency of women, which is something infrequently done in exhibitions on
Islamic art (figure 11.11). And finally, we used music that the featured individuals would have heard, played, or commissioned. In the first vignette,
we had listening stations of Tansen, who was a renowned musician at the
Mughal court, about whom Abu'l Fazl wrote. Songs attributed to Tansen
involve a variety of subjects, including the praise of Hindu deities such as
Sarasvati and Krishna, sculptures of which were in the galleries. The panel
text for the listening station explained that Tansen was best known for writing and performing in a style of Hindustani classical music called *dhrupad*

All Savior's Cathedral, New Julfa, Iran
1655–64

> The Muslims come to this church [All Savior's
> Cathedral] as if to a theater, to amuse themselves by
> looking at the paintings; it is necessary to open the door
> for them at all hours.
> —Jean Chardin, *The Travels of Sir Jean Chardin in Persia and
> Other Places of the Orient*

The French merchant Jean Chardin, who traveled in Iran
during the 1660s and 1670s, observed the interest among
Isfahan's Muslim population in the religious paintings at All

Savior's Cathedral, the seat
of the Armenian Apostolic
Church's bishop. The interior
of the cathedral is decorated
from floor to ceiling with
European-style murals of
episodes from the Old and
New Testaments painted by
Armenian artists. Muhammad
Zaman probably knew some
of these artists, who, like him,
benefited from the patronage
of the Persian court. Some of
the paintings in All Savior's
Cathedral are projected on
the wall.

Facing the Apse

(All photos: Hrair Hawk Khatcherian, 2011)

Figure 11.10.   Label for projected images, All Savior's Cathedral, New Julfa. *Pearls on a String* labels, Baltimore.

Furnishing the Palaces with European Luxury Goods

Mahmud, his courtiers, and royal women amassed large quantities of European luxury wares, similar in date, style, and workmanship to those displayed here. To procure these goods, they relied on European and Ottoman merchants.

The French merchant Jean-Claude Flachat, who served the Ottoman court for 15 years, became Mahmud's chief merchant. In this capacity, Flachat forged direct relationships with the sultan, his chief eunuch of the harem Morali Bashir Agha (tenure 1746–52), and a number of courtiers, supplying them with mechanical clocks, jewelry, fine porcelain, and furniture.

An important part of Flachat's activities was supplying women of the imperial harem with European novelties and luxury goods. These business transactions were mediated through Morali Bashir Agha. Flachat reported that the harem women were especially fond of mechanical devices and observed that the public areas of Mahmud's Beshiktash Palace and other 18th-century palaces were filled with European luxury items, some of which were sent as gifts. When Mahmud's ambassador to France, Mehmed Sa'id Pasha, traveled to the court of the French king Louis XV in 1742, he returned with a wealth of items, ranging from palatial furnishings to gold snuffboxes and watches.

"View of Beshiktash Palace," from *Tableau général de l'empire othoman*, vol. 3, pl. 169 (Paris, 1788–1824), by Ignatius Mouradgea d'Ohsson (Ottoman Armenian, 1740–1807) (Photo: Ott 137.2, Houghton Library, Harvard University)

Figure 11.11. Section text 3.5, *Pearls on a String* labels, Baltimore.

and explained that musical form. In the third vignette, we piped in music that would have been heard by Mahmud in his palace with labels that explained that no less than thirty-seven musical compositions are attributed to the Sultan Mahmud himself. This allowed us to introduce a musical instrument as an object. The ambient music was "Segah peshrev" by Hizir Agha, performed by Lalezar on their 2001 album *Music of the Sultans, Sufis & Seraglio. Volume IV, Ottoman Suite* (Producer: Traditional Crossroads).

HUMAN-CENTRIC EXHIBITION DESIGN

As a team, we were sensitive to the amount of material we were asking our visitors to read. We wanted to make the exhibition experience both educational and enjoyable. Of course we knew that certain visitors would not engage with all the texts. For those who did read every text and for those who did not, we wanted to offer comfortable spaces to linger in the exhibition. We also hoped for repeated visitations to the exhibition, as it was free of charge. We therefore offered comfortable seating throughout the exhibition where visitors could read additional reading materials provided in the pockets.

We encouraged visitors to sit and relax as they engaged with works of art, enjoyed period music, and read the additional reading materials provided. The *Pearls* team produced in-house textile designs for the seating

Figure 11.12.   Seating and reading materials, *Pearls on a String: Artists, Patrons, and Poets at the Great Islamic Courts*, Baltimore, November 8, 2015–January 31, 2016.
Source: Installation photo by Amy Landau, copyright Walters Art Museum.

inspired by interpretations of three historic textiles dating to the time of the protagonists, evoking the interior settings and objects in the exhibition: a sixteenth-century Mughal animal carpet (vignette 1); a seventeenth-century Safavid bird and flower cloak (or cope) (vignette 2) (figure 11.12); and an eighteenth-century Ottoman voided velvet (vignette 3).

CONCLUSIONS

The international loan exhibition *Pearls on a String: Artists, Patrons, and Poets at the Great Islamic Courts* taught me that biography can be a useful tool to introduce American audiences to art produced by Islamic societies of the past. Museum visitors responded very positively to the exhibition and we have gathered evidence of repeat visits. As the curator who defined the approach, I benefitted from a team of individuals who thought through with me ways we could inspire understanding with feeling, that is, a way to understand Islamic art through an empathetic lens. A recent *New York Times* op-ed titled "The Return of History" written by Aatish Taseer quotes a present-day ideologue in Karachi, claiming that there are two kinds of history: living and dead: "Dead history is something on a shelf or in a museum, [while] living history is part of your consciousness, something in your blood that inspires you."[12] Extremist groups selectively change historical narratives to suit present-day ideologies in order to motivate violence, especially in the Middle East and North Africa, where modern states have been grafted onto ancient, medieval, and early modern cultures marked by cultural and religious pluralism. Art produced by these cultures, displayed in European and American museums, attests to engagements among religious communities. In the twenty-first century, as histories of pluralistic societies are being denied and attacked, how are these objects displayed and discussed in the museum? *Are our presented histories of these objects "dead histories"?* Do our labels inspire thought, reflection, or social participation?

By taking a biographical lens, we were able to show the diversity of views and the plurality of Islamic societies. Rather than diachronic and teleological histories of Islamic art, I believe fragmented histories, like the vignettes in *Pearls on a String* in which a specific period is approached from different viewpoints, corresponds better with the ways our visitors process information. These different points of view can incorporate the art produced by the Muslim, Armenian, and European communities that resided within Islamic empires. The past is indeed alive as never before. Those of us versed in Islamic textual and visual sources are custodians of histories. The irretrievable loss of cultural heritage and human lives in the Middle East and North Africa and decreasing religious literacy in the United States coupled with Islamophobia suggests that we no longer have the luxury to speak solely of linear art histories within the walls of the museum.

ACKNOWLEDGMENTS

Pearls on a String was generously supported by the National Endowment for the Humanities: Celebrating Fifty Years of Excellence; the Institute of Museum and Library Services; the National Endowment for the Arts; the Gary Vikan Exhibition Endowment Fund; Ellen and Edward Bernard; Douglas and Tsognie Hamilton; the Herb Silverman Fund; and anonymous donors.

The author also wishes to acknowledge Julian Raby, Massumeh Farhad, Charles Dibble, Avinoam Shalem, and David Roxburgh for advice and support during the planning of *Pearls on a String*.

NOTES

1. Here I wish to thank members of the *Pearls* exhibition team who reviewed and provided feedback on the didactics: Amanda Kodeck, director of education; Brittany Powell, manager of school programs; Robert Mintz, chief curator and curator of Asian Art; and Ellie Hughes, director of art and programs. Special thanks are due to Charles Dibble, manager and editor of publications, Katherine Kasdorf, Mellon Fellow, and Melissa Forstrom Al kadhi, who all dedicated their time and expertise to the label texts.

2. Lee Lawrence, 'Pearls on a String: Artists, Patrons, and Poets at the Great Islamic Courts," Review, *Wall Street Journal*, January 4, 2016, http://www.wsj.com/articles/pearls-on-a-string-artists-patrons-and-poets-at-the-great-islamic-courts-review-1451948541 (accessed January 10, 2016).

3. I especially wish to thank Ashley Boycher (exhibition designer) and Johanna Biehler (senior designer) for the design of *Pearls on a String*.

4. Alison Kysia and Homayra Ziad, "Baltimore Speaker Promotes Fear of Islam," *Baltimore Sun*, February 13, 2016, http://www.baltimoresun.com/news/opinion/oped/bs-ed-hirsi-ali-20160125-story.html (accessed February 15, 2016).

5. See this quoted and discussed in David J. Roxburgh, *Prefacing the Image: The Writing of Art History in Sixteenth-Century Iran* (Leiden: Brill, 2001), 57 and 114–15.

6. Ibid.

7. Lawrence, "Pearls on a String."

8. See Andrew J. Pekarik, James B. Schreiber, Nadine Hanemann, Kelly Richmond, and Barbara Mogel, "IPOP: A Theory of Experience Preference," *Curator: The Museum Journal* 57, no. 1 (2014): 5–27, and the discussion of this theory in the chapter by Thomas Wide in this volume.

9. This is discussed in the previous chapter by Thomas Wide.

10. Amy S. Landau, ed., *Pearls on a String: Artists, Patrons, and Poets at the Great Islamic Courts* (Seattle: University of Washington Press and Walters Art Museum, 2015).

11. Phillip Kennicott, Review of "Pearls on a String," *Washington Post*, November 14, 2015, https://www.washingtonpost.com/goingoutguide/museums/art-review-pearls-on-a-string-artists-patrons-and-poets-at-the-great-islamic-courts/2015/11/12/f3465a20-8895-11e5-9a07-453018f9a0ec_story.html.

12. Aatish Taseer, "The Return of History," December 11, 2015, http://www.nytimes.com/2015/12/11/opinion/the-return-of-history.html?_r=00 (accessed January 20, 2015).

12

Adopting Empathy

Why Empathy Should Be a Required Core Value for All Museums—Period

Jon Carfagno and Adam Reed Rozan

Most museums have a mission. Most museums also have a vision statement. These two tools help them understand who they are and where they would like to go in the future. However, this chapter examines core values, another foundational element, which is often missing from the museum's organizational identity. This chapter is in direct response to the void of core values statements found in museums today. Its writing follows a research phase and a survey of the field, where a questionnaire was sent out to museum colleagues leveraging the contacts of major professional organizations, including the Association of Art Museum Directors, the Museum-Ed Listserv, as well as the authors' own personal networks of peers in the field. Based on the email and social media distribution channels that were utilized, the amount of people who had an opportunity to respond numbers safely in the thousands. The survey results were low, however, as few were able to provide responses to our questions. While this and countless web queries on the subject indicate a paucity of core values in museums, many wrote with gratitude and encouraging remarks about the significance of the topic and potential impact of the project. As a result, this chapter looks to the business world for the role that core values have played in building successful companies whose brands have become synonymous with their ideologies. The paragraphs that follow can be considered a call to action as they explore why museums should have core values, what it means to truly live by those core values, and why every institution should adopt empathy as one of them, particularly at this point in our social history. Along the way, thought leaders from the corporate innovation community, museum field, and the global empathy movement have contributed their voice to supplement this assertion by way of quotes that reflect their unique perspective.

The conclusion presents a vision for the transformative power of brand loyalty that can be fostered when all of these pieces are put together.

THE IMPORTANCE OF HAVING A VALUE STATEMENT

In the case of core values, it is instructive for museums to examine how other industries have tackled this foundational aspect of organizational dynamics. In their seminal book *Built to Last*, Jim Collins and Jerry Porras define core values as "an organization's essential and enduring tenets—the values it would hold even if they became a competitive disadvantage."[1] Like the US Constitution or the Ten Commandments, core values are statements that answer the question "should we or shouldn't we?" Core values are discovered over time, they are enduring, and they are the defining elements of an organization's culture.[2] Collins and Porras undertook an extensive six-year research process that studied the founding, growth, and development of exceptional companies that have sustained enduring success. By examining businesses that continue to prosper in the long term, such as 3M, Nordstrom, and Proctor and Gamble, they uncovered fundamentals that enabled their ability to thrive. Of the companies surveyed, a recurring characteristic was that these visionary enterprises were all guided by values and a sense of purpose beyond just making money. In his book, Collins asserts that "a deeply held core ideology gives a company both a strong sense of identity and a thread that holds the organization together in the face of change."[3] Like many industries, museums currently face seismic shifts that will transform nearly every aspect of their business model. From the ascendance of audience participation and authorship fueled by the social media revolution, to crowdfunding and the impact-orientation of a next generation of donors, driven more by a passion for supporting causes rather than institutions, the earth is shifting under their feet. Museums must adjust to this changing landscape that is evolving as rapidly as the ubiquitous smartphones that their guests carry in their pockets.

In this period of enormous, rapid, and ever-present change, museums will benefit from looking at the cultures of organizations that are flourishing in today's marketplace. For instance, in a ten-year period beginning in 1999, the shoe seller Zappos scaled from a small upstart online retailer to a billion-dollar enterprise.[4] Its growth continues as demonstrated by a nearly 80 percent increase in operating profit for 2015, which will be up from their $54.5 million figure in 2014. Visionary chief executive officer Tony Hsieh notes that the driver of the company's success engine is its commitment to core values, asserting that "our number one priority is company culture. Our belief is that once you get the culture right, most of the other stuff like delivering great customer service or building a long-term enduring brand will just happen on its own."[5] The company's formal values statement, which serves as the foundation of its storied enterprise culture, speaks to the significance of an unwavering commitment to core beliefs:

> With so many new employees joining Zappos as we grow, we want to make sure that everyone is on the same page and acting consistently with what we want our companies to be all about. . . . Ideally, we want all 10 core values to be reflected in everything we do, including how we interact with each other, how we interact with our customers, and how we interact with our vendors and business partners. . . . As we grow, our processes and strategies may change, but we want our values to always remain the same. Our core values should always be the framework from which we make all of our decisions.[6]

The well-documented challenges facing nonprofits today mandate that museums adopt similar core ideologies, which will enable them to reconcile cross-departmental turf wars or any other competing values that are especially detrimental in today's turbulent climate. In his strategic planning textbook for nonprofit organizations, expert John Bryson underscores this need for institutions like museums to invest the time in developing core values in order to enable their most catalytic effectiveness. "Unfortunately," Bryson writes, "because organizations rarely discuss their philosophies, values, and culture, they often adopt strategies that are doomed to failure. Clarity about philosophy and values in advance of strategy development is one way to avoid this error."[7] Both Collins and Hsieh agree that the definition of core values is a crucial first step toward creating alignment and correcting the misalignments that prevent organizations from living out their guiding ideologies, executing their strategic initiatives, and doing their best work over long periods of time.[8]

Consider the museum that commits to embracing guest-centered museum practices as an aspect of its strategic planning. Across the institution, staff members at all levels agree that they want visitors to experience exemplary levels of customer service and experience design that will inspire audiences to return and bring a friend. However, in the implementation stage, the initiative falters in the absence of an institutional core value that helps new hires understand the significance of this commitment and a redesigned organizational chart that empowers the operation to deliver on the promise. What does structural alignment look like in a museum that asserts empathy as a core value? Who is the arbiter on decisions that impact the audience's experience across digital, onsite, in-gallery, and person to person touchpoints? What interventions can the museum make from an operating standpoint to ensure that these filters stand at the center of customer-facing interactions? The adherence to a core value provides a lighthouse to help the organization find its way to the answers for these difficult questions.

WHAT IS EMPATHY AND WHY IS IT IMPORTANT?

Philosopher and founder of the first Empathy Museum in the United Kingdom, Roman Krznaric has recently emerged as a prevailing voice in the discussion about empathy being one of contemporary society's most important issues. He defines empathy as "the art of stepping imaginatively into the shoes of another person, understanding their feelings and perspectives, and using that understanding to guide your actions."[9] Krznaric contextualizes his definition against the backdrop of a distressing empathy gap in recent history. He uses the example of President Obama, who built part of his 2008 election platform around the theme, and stated:

> There's a lot of talk in this country about the federal deficit. But I think we should talk more about our empathy deficit—our ability to put ourselves in someone else's shoes, to see the world through the eyes of those who are different from us—the child who's hungry, the laid-off steelworker, the immigrant cleaning your dorm room. . . . We live in a culture that discourages empathy, a culture that too often tells us that our principal goal in life is to be rich, thin, young, famous, safe, and entertained.[10]

Krznaric cites a study at the University of Michigan to demonstrate a dramatic decline in empathy levels among young Americans between 1980 and today to bolster his case for the need to proactively teach about empathy. The root causes of the trend are manifold, ranging from the fracturing of communities by urbanization, free market ideologies, deepening individualism, more people living alone, and the omnipresence of technology and devices that support isolated engagement in an abundance of information.[11] In an age where religious fundamentalism continues to create violent divides among people, and a time when two-thirds of developed countries have a wider gap between rich and poor than in 1980, we cannot help but question how adopting empathy as a core value could enhance the impact and efficacy of museums as drivers of community and shared understanding.

Empathy goes to the heart of reinventing public culture in the 21st century. Whether it's museums, theatre or in other realms of cultural life, creating space where people are able to step into the shoes of others and see the world through their eyes is a way of forging new kinds of social connection, overcoming cultural divides, and challenging the hyper-individualism that pervades modern society. Empathy is a wellspring for forging common values, asking us to redefine the old Cartesian view "I think, therefore I am," with a more inclusive vision of "You are, therefore I am."
—Roman Krznaric, author of *Empathy: Why It Matters and How to Get It* and founder of the Empathy Museum

MUSEUMS, EMPATHY, AND SOCIAL IMPACT

Now more than ever before in our society there is a need for places like museums. Not our historical ancestor, but a modern visitor-facing cultural and social institution. The role for these modern museums will continue to grow, transitioning from being the destination of the infrequent and isolated field trip to being the public's new communal living room. Today's communities' museums will become the room in the house where everyone is welcomed. At the same time, museums will adjust to the new needs, wants, and demands from the public while facilitating new and important civic, social, health, and educational services. This is all in consideration to reimagining how these modern institutions will utilize existing collections to engage these modern visitors and connect with their institutions' modern mission.

In light of this shift, museums can play a role in building an empathetic citizenry. They become open and accessible spaces where civil society can grow and evolve. As urban planner Larry Beasley proposes, the empathy-driven museum becomes:

> The agora of the city—the place where people come together to learn about issues, debate the future, consider new propositions, and evaluate the various development moves that are changing the cityscape each day. Again, the idea is that the museum barriers come tumbling down and the physical plant of the museum becomes not just a repository but also a safe and respectful gathering place.[12]

In this new museum, people matter, as their experiences, histories, and dreams provide us with the interconnections of our shared history. This understanding helps us see where we have been and helps us better understand where we are going. When people come together they form communities. The formation of communities is as much a part of us as is our DNA. People are programmed to form communities, help one another, care for, bond, protect, feed, mate, and, above all, *belong*. Because communities are so important, so essential to the human experience, space or the idea of areas to come together to congregate, discuss, learn, pray, meditate, and live is life's true nucleus.

The empathy-driven museum becomes the stage for the enactment of these connections. Here the institution creates important social capital by its ability to bring people together through bonding and bridging. Bonding is when people in a homogenous group come together to support one another. For vulnerable people in particular (indigenous peoples, youth, new immigrants, etc.), becoming a member of these groups can be an important form of empowerment. Bridging, on the other hand, refers to networking and interweaving among socially mixed groups. Groups that bridge share and exchange information and ideas and can build consensus among people of different backgrounds.[13] Consider for a minute the power of a bridged group consisting of recent immigrants and local business owners who have coincidentally encountered one another on a tour of a museum. A docent facilitates a conversation about a work of art, such as James Drake's *Juarez El Paso Boxcar*. Through inquiry and dialogue, the group explores the experience of eighteen illegal aliens who perished by suffocation in 1987 when attempting to cross the border in a sealed railroad boxcar.[14] Encountering the work of art provides an opportunity for these museum visitors to understand the feelings and perspectives of those who participate in the conversation. When a museum stands at the center of these experiences, empathy is expanded at a time when it has never been more needed.

THE EMPATHY IMPERATIVE FOR
MUSEUMS IN TIMES OF TRANSITION

Empathy is a popular topic, but don't be fooled, this is not merely an Internet meme but rather a concept that is here to stay. In 2015, when journalist Marilynne Robinson interviewed President Barack Obama for the *New York Review of Books*, empathy remained a subject of his consideration. He said:

> It has to do with empathy. It has to do with being comfortable with the notion that the world is complicated and full of grays, but there's still truth there to be found, and that you have to strive for that and work for that. And the notion that it's possible to connect with some[one] else even though they're very different from you.[15]

The president is not alone in expressing the importance of empathy. Philosopher Krznaric has also observed a surge in empathic thinking across the globe driven by political activists, self-help advice columnists, and religious leaders. Protesters during the Occupy movement in Britain and the United States erected Empathy Tents and ran workshops on empathic activism. In an effort to prevent a revival of ethnic violence, a radio soap opera in Rwanda, heard by 90 percent of the country's population every week, inserts empathic messaging into its storyline about Hutus and Tutsis living in neighboring villages. A German social entrepreneur named Andreas Heinecke—who is also a contributor to this volume—has established a worldwide network of museums where blind guides have taken more than seven million visitors around exhibits that are in total darkness to give them the experience of being visually impaired.[16] The empathy wave is even now being ridden by male comedians, musicians, and professional athletes, who have banded together to launch #strongerthanstigma to raise awareness about the unique challenges that men face when discussing mental health. This group seeks to encourage open dialogue and to promote help-seeking behaviors. Each of the prominent spokespeople, including pop culture staple Wayne Brady and Edmonton Oilers goalie Ben Scrivens, either lives with a mental health diagnosis or has chosen to serve as an empathetic advocate, and shares his story to encourage men to start the conversation and end the stigma.[17]

> In today's over-crowded marketplace with numerous products, services, and businesses, and a complex world of fierce competition and varying levels of customer expectations, creating desirable and viable solutions gets more challenging. Empathy—a methodology to uncover true customer pains and their unspoken needs and wants—by asking, observing and engaging users can become a valuable tool for innovating human centered solutions that create new value propositions and true differentiation.
> —Sudhakar Lahade, education lead and senior consultant
> for Applied Research and Consulting, Steelcase

More than a progressive social movement, empathy has transformed the world of business. For instance, the Lean Startup method for launching new enterprises embeds empathic understanding of customers at nearly every stage of the entrepreneurial process. The use of this process for business model design begins with the product developer "getting out of their building" or office to ask potential users, purchasers, and partners for feedback on all elements of their business plan, including product features, pricing, distribution channels, and affordable customer acquisition strategies. Where older methods of product development emphasized five-year planning and thorough implementation, now the focus is on nimbleness and speed. The entrepreneur rapidly assembles minimum viable products in order to immediately elicit customer feedback about the product. Then, using customers' input to revise assumptions, the entrepreneur starts the cycle over again, testing redesigned offerings and making further small adjustments or more substantive ones to ideas that aren't working. Lean Startups also practice something called "agile development," which originated in the software industry. Unlike typical product development cycles that presupposed a manufacturer's knowledge of customers' problems and product needs and taking longer times to bring products to market, agile development eliminates wasted time by developing the product iteratively based on the consumer empathy derived from user testing.[18]

The IMA has implemented a holistic approach to how we welcome
our visitors. It is not something that starts when you enter the gallery,
but from the moment you arrive on campus. How we greet, guide and
encourage interaction with our visitors is all connected. At the IMA we
have written this approach into our mission, to create unique experiences
through art and nature which engage our visitors in meaningful and relevant dialog. It is not a one-way interaction, nor a predetermined outcome, but rather an ongoing conversation in which our audience shapes
what and how we curate content. To achieve this goal, the IMA includes
our visitors in the process from the very outset of a concept all the way
through post visit evaluation. This runs counter to traditional museum
practice and can be scary (for some) due to the inherent uncertainty
and relinquishing of curatorial control. But the change is transformative
as long as the process is embraced with intentionality and consistency
across the entire institution.
              —Scott Stulen, curator of audience experiences and performance
                                    at the Indianapolis Museum of Art

The empathy imperative that stands at the heart of these practices is
potentially transformative for how museums do their work. A parallel
process can be seen now in exhibition development, historically a curator-
driven enterprise where a finished product is brought to market following
a three-year research and design cycle without any consumer input or concept testing. Already forward thinking institutions such as the Indianapolis
Museum of Art are using a visitor-centered approach to involve current and
potential visitors in the various steps of the exhibition development process
to guarantee that the final "product" is accessible, engaging, and easy to use.
In these cases, feedback is collected from visitors and sometimes nonvisitors to test the initial concept for the exhibition and refine the "big idea"
and learning outcomes, as well as to gauge people's preference for brand-
ing, titles, and marketing material. Concepts for hands-on activities are
also tested, as are computer and mobile phone app prototypes, wireframes,
and designs to guarantee that the final product is intuitive and easy to
use.[19] Imagine the possibilities for application of empathy-driven customer
engagement across the institution. From membership programs that actually deliver on the consumer's motivation to connect with the museum to
curriculum initiatives that help students with areas of their academic and
interpersonal growth, the opportunities for greater impact are endless.
    Positioning empathic thinking at the core of museum work means spend-
ing time with audiences and allowing that contact to shape decisions. With
empathy it's not a space race, but an opportunity for museums to slow their
roll and attempt to actually meet and understand the needs of the people

they are trying to serve. In a response to a survey conducted prior to writing this chapter, a staff member from Vizcaya Museum and Gardens in Miami, Florida, remarked that their first core value "is about people of diverse backgrounds and needs." She went on to say, "We make room for people to be different and to want different, if there was no empathy inherent in that statement, then everything that we did would reflect only our personal interests, or knowledge, or needs. We would be serving ourselves under the guise of serving others." This statement incisively summarizes the disruptive subversion of conventional museum practices that empathetic thinking as a core value initiates. This change to empathetic thinking necessarily takes into consideration the external factors that museums operate within, such as competition for visitors' time and attention, financial support and cultural philanthropy, graying audiences, and, above all, changes in demographics. Examining only the idea of language within the broad topic of population, you can begin to ponder the challenges at hand. Historically for museums in the United States, English was the only language spoken and used for interpretative and supporting materials. Now, as the percentage of nonnative English speakers rises in many communities, museums find their audiences speaking dozens of languages. Therefore the institutions are forced to change if they are to survive. If you work at a museum and you are not in survival mode, you should be. Empathy across your institution is the connective lifeline to guide customer-facing and internal interactions within this shifting landscape.

My experience has been that empathy is a game changer. It starts first with your end user. Most companies and organizations (for-profit and non-profit alike) say they know their customers and end-users, but in reality they typically have many assumptions and have not taken the time to put themselves in the shoes of the customer. When leaders and key influencers in the organization take the opportunity to interact in a meaningful way with customers, really trying to understand the realities of being a customer, eyes get opened and behavior of the organization changes. The next step is to realize that as a leader of a department or business unit, I not only need to understand my end customer, but I need to understand my internal customers and have empathy for them. So often we get an organization to think about its customers but departments have no empathy for other departments in their own organization—marketing has no empathy for sales and vice versa—then they both wonder why the experience isn't delivering. It turns out to deliver a succinct and meaningful experience, the organization and all departments need to work together. When marketing has no empathy for sales

(continued)

for example, the customer sees this in their experience as marketing messages that are not fully supported or maybe even contradicted by the actual sales engagement. I have spent many engagements where building empathy within the organization is the first step before we talk about anything else. It is the root of collaboration, it lays the ground work for trust building.

—Seth Starner, president of New North Center

LIVING WITH EMPATHY AS A CORE VALUE

What steps must a museum take to inculcate empathy a core value? Legendary CEO Hatim Tyabji, who led Verifone from a $30 million to a $600 million company, provides a short answer to this key question. Reflecting on his company's strong, values-driven culture, he quipped, "I essentially spent the last six years repeating myself."[20] When built out further, there are several often-documented vehicles that organizations with strong cultures have utilized to ensure the primacy of their values across all aspects of their operations.

First and foremost, authenticity is key to articulating empathy as a core value. Where many companies strive for a level of polish that rivals the writing of their strongest marketing materials, the best value statements resonate because they are memorable, bold, or aggressive.[21] For instance, Zappos values individuality, creativity, and joy in the workplace. As a result, it has expressed these qualities in their core value statement that reads: "Create Fun And A Little Weirdness."[22] Atomic Object, a very successful West Michigan software firm that specializes in complex custom software solutions for high-end clients, places great emphasis on the dedication of their employees to do whatever it takes to be effective. This is reflected in their core value statement that simply reads: "Give A Shit."[23] How could these examples influence a museum that is serious about placing empathy at the center of their internal and customer-facing interactions? The institution can create a value statement that exhorts employees to "Walk a Mile in Their Shoes," or "Experience Their Head and Heart." Perhaps a stronger admonishment such as "Don't Think Like Yourself" would resonate more deeply and convey the importance of getting into the minds and hearts of coworkers, volunteers, and visitors before rendering a judgment or making a decision.

After determining how to express empathy as a core value, the other 99 percent of the museum's effort is to keep empathetic thinking alive in employees by consistently adhering to it even in the face of great challenges. Museum leadership must go beyond merely posting the values on the wall and handing out laminated cards, although these interventions are an acceptable first step. The imperative is to find both consistent and creative ways to imbue the prevalence of empathy throughout the organization.[24] Nordstrom department store utilizes storytelling to advance its commitment to the core value of excellent customer service. During new hire orientation, instead of receiving a detailed handbook describing how to deliver great customer service to customers, new employees hear elaborate stories of how their coworkers have gone above and beyond the ordinary to impress their customers. These company tales include the customer service representative who, with no questions asked, accepted a return on a blouse that had been purchased two years earlier. During nonshopping hours, managers read customer comments, both positive and negative, over their stores public address systems so that employees can hear how they are performing.[25] For an empathic museum, the parallels are readily imagined. For example, upon hiring, new employees hear about the communications manager who was five minutes late for a radio interview because she stopped to walk a confused visitor to the nearest restroom or, during closed-door installations of the galleries, the preparators listen to comments from the visitor comment log while they build the next exhibition.

However, what will disciplined enactment of empathy as a core value for museums look like when the stakes are higher? Business theorist Patrick Lencioni asserts that "if they're going to really take hold in your organization, your core values need to be integrated into every employee-related process—hiring methods, performance management systems, criteria for promotions and rewards, and even dismissal policies."[26] Through this all-encompassing filter, many orthodoxies about museum employee roles, responsibilities, and job descriptions can be called into question. Tony Hsieh comments that his company has not hired "a lot of smart, talented people that we know could make an immediate impact on our top or bottom line . . . if they're not good for our culture then we won't hire them for that reason alone."[27] Through these lenses, the leading candidate for a museum's chief curator opening could shift from the person with the strongest publications or acquisitions history to a less experienced curator who had previously worked in the marketing or education departments at another museum because the latter candidate would command a higher qualification in understanding audiences and how to meet their needs. Or perhaps even more dramatically, the development director, who charms donors but is dismissive and rude to her colleagues, is terminated because of the inconsistency that her presence on the leadership team presents to lower level staff members. This is both the mandate of action and responsibility of living with empathy as a core value.

IS YOUR MUSEUM READY FOR EMPATHY AS A CORE VALUE?

"Whole Foods doesn't have a pricing problem—it has an identity crisis,"[28] writes Shelly Banjo in one of many similar comments published after the company's pricing scandal. Beyond the fines that were imposed and the fall of its once-robust stock price, the worst was still to come. For Whole Foods, the most deleterious aspect of this corporate failing is the erosion of public trust in the company. The company proudly continues to display its core values in supermarket branches across the country by way of fancy promotional signage spelling out what the brand is supposed to stand for, like the locker rooms of college and professional sports teams, encouraging athletes with inspirational messages. However, Whole Foods now champions its core values to a suspicious audience that questions the store's integrity because of its actions.

As children, we are taught the differences between right and wrong. We learn through life that the hard way is usually the right way. Ethical shortcuts, just like most other shortcuts, do not save us time, but instead create subsequent problems. Cheating not only leads to the principal's office, but will also always diminish trust. Living and working with core values is hard work. They serve not only as an organization's litmus test, but also as its foundation.

All organizations must first ask themselves if they are ready for core values. If the answer is no, that is not necessarily a bad thing—it is worse to have them and not live by them than to not have them at all. As *Harvard Business Review* writer Patrick Lencioni writes in a 2002 article:

> Coming up with strong values—and sticking to them—requires real guts. Indeed, an organization considering a values initiative must first come to terms with the fact that, when properly practiced, values inflict pain. They make some employees feel like outcasts. They limit an organization's strategic and operational freedom and constrain the behavior of its people. They leave executives open to heavy criticism for even minor violations. And they demand constant vigilance.[29]

Lencioni goes on to say:

> Most values statements are bland, toothless, or just plain dishonest. And far from being harmless, as some executives assume, they're often highly destructive. Empty values statements create cynical and dispirited employees, alienate customers, and undermine managerial credibility.[30]

Whole Foods erred when its core values served only as props for in-store decorations and not as the company's guiding ideology. Whole Foods is not alone in recent scandal. Car manufacturer Volkswagen proudly proclaims its core values of "responsibility and sustainability." The company elaborates on this by saying, "Volkswagen is more than an employer. We are responsible for people, the economy, society and the environment. Employees at Volkswagen take on responsibility by becoming involved in voluntary work. Sustainable, collaborative and responsible thinking underlies everything we do."[31] Yet despite such loftily stated standards, Volkswagen's recent failures of emissions control violations and false reporting are of a different kind. This is when the press and public refer to an event as a "scandal" or apply the suffix "-gate" as a marker of the misdeed. This is when it goes wrong, terribly wrong.

There is a similar potential for missteps if an art museum is not ready for the commitment that empathy as a core value demands. For instance, curators already vie with coworkers in their own department for the limited gallery spaces that their institutions can make available for exhibitions. But what happens when a strategic initiative to increase family visit attendance is thrown into the mix? Now more of the museum's footprint must be allocated to learning environments that support intergenerational learning and resources must be directed toward in-gallery activities for parents and children. Is the museum ready to think about things as though standing in the shoes of a parent with two children and redesign its public experience accordingly? Can coworkers with competing interests come to the table and try to understand one another? If not, the time is not right for your institution to claim empathy as a core value.

CONCLUSION: THE POWER OF PUTTING THE PIECES TOGETHER

There is a different story, however, that underpins the Southwest Airlines folklore recounted by Collins in *Good to Great*. For the last forty years, the brand's commitment to customer service has allowed it to continue to flourish in an incredibly challenging industry where its competitors frequently file for bankruptcy. Similarly, business writers and MBA programs turn to Apple CEO Steve Jobs as an exemplar due to his passion for enabling people who desired to make the world better by using his company's products. The results are manifested in tales of consumers waiting overnight, sometimes even for days, in anticipation of a new product hitting the stores: to be the first customer, the first of a thousand customers in line to purchase the latest iPhone. This is the story of the awesome power of brand loyalty that is ignited when core values are authentically employed. The memory of waiting at your local bookstore for J. K. Rowling's *Harry Potter*; the opportunity to not only own the new book, but also to participate with other brand enthusiasts.

IMPACTS has measured the relationship an organization's financial health and its reputation for years. The data is unassailable. How well the public perceives that an organization "walks its talk" in terms of delivering its mission has a strong correlation with its financial success. Being perceived as an organization that summons trust and credibility is critical for an organization's solvency. The data reliably indicate that being good at your mission is good business.
                              —Colleen Dilenschneider, chief market engagement
                                    officer at IMPACTS Research and Development

With an impetus for risk-taking and experimentation, we consciously created a values-driven culture that embraces and encourages innovation. Positive attitudes, an engaged staff, and energy around our mission are integral for our team and institution as we continuously evolve to meet the needs and aspirations of future generations.
                              —Karleen Gardner, director of learning and innovation
                                    at the Minneapolis Institute of Art

The corollary for the empathy-driven museum is the "super" member: the visitors that proudly display their membership cards in their wallets, the member who wears the museum t-shirt, hat, and scarf, or the member who brings each and every family member, neighbor, and business associate to the museum. Conducting business with empathy as a guiding principle allows your museum to understand its audience well enough to engender this degree of consumer loyalty. Empathy then becomes a bridge for sharing and understanding across departments that mitigates the stresses of competing interests and builds alignment to the core ideology, empowering the institution to create transformative experiences for its guests. When the museum provides these transformative experiences, the institution assumes new relevance and has greater community impact. When core values are the right values, they embody everyone. When empathy is a core value for museums, everyone wins.

NOTES

1. Jim Collins and Jerry Porras, "Building Your Company's Vision," *Harvard Business Review*, September 1996, https://hbr.org/1996/09/building-your-companys-vision/ar/1 (accessed February 7, 2016).

2. "Rockefeller Habits with Verne Harnish," http://www.catalystconsultantsllc.com/wp-content/uploads/rhw_two-day_0601.pdf (accessed February 7, 2016).

3. Jim Collins, "Building Companies to Last," http://www.jimcollins.com/article_topics/articles/building-companies.html (accessed February 7, 2016).

4. Jeremy Twithchell, "From Upstart to $1 Billion Behometh, Zappos Marks Ten Years," http://about.zappos.com/press-center/media-coverage/upstart-1-billion-behemoth-zappos-marks-10-years (accessed February 7, 2016).

5. Zach Bulgyo, Kissmetrics Blog, "Tony Hsieh, Zappos, and the Art of Great Company Culture," https://blog.kissmetrics.com/zappos-art-of-culture/ (accessed February 7, 2016).

6. "The Zappos Family Mission: To Live and Deliver Wow," https://s3.amazonaws.com/zidownloads/TheZapposFamilyCoreValues.pdf (accessed February 7, 2016).

7. John M. Bryson, *Strategic Planning for Public and Nonprofit Organizations* (Hoboken, NJ: Jossey-Bass, 2011), 141.

8. Jim Collins, "Aligning Action and Values," http://www.jimcollins.com/article_topics/articles/aligning-action.html (accessed February 7, 2016); Zach Bulgyo, Kissmetrics Blog, "Tony Hsieh, Zappos, and the Art of Great Company Culture," https://blog.kissmetrics.com/zappos-art-of-culture/ (accessed February 7, 2016).

9. Roman Krznaric, *Empathy: Why It Matters and How to Get It* (New York: Penguin, 2014), Kindle edition.

10. Ibid.

11. Ibid.

12. Gail Dexter Lord and Ngaire Blankenberg, *Cities, Museums, and Soft Power* (Washington, DC: AAM Press, 2015), 44.

13. Ibid.

14. "Sharp Edges of the Texas Border in Downtown Exhibit," http://articles.latimes.com/1989-02-03/entertainment/ca-2007_1_el-paso (accessed February 7, 2016).

15. "President Obama and Marilynne Robinson: A Conversation—II," http://www.nybooks.com/articles/archives/2015/nov/19/president-obama-marilynne-robinson-conversation-2/ (accessed February 7, 2016); "President Obama Says Novels Taught Him How to be a Citizen," http://www.theguardian.com/books/2015/oct/28/president-obama-says-novels-taught-him-citizen-marilynne-robinson (accessed February 7, 2016).

16. "Empathy Museum," http://www.empathymuseum.com (accessed February 7, 2016).

17. "Bring Change 2 Mind," http://bringchange2mind.org/programs/psas/ (accessed February 7, 2016).

18. Steve Blank, "Why the Lean Start Up Changes Everything," *Harvard Business Review*, May 2013, https://hbr.org/2013/05/why-the-lean-start-up-changes-everything (accessed February 7, 2016).

19. Shereen Dindar, "Silvia Filippini-Fantoni Q&A: How the Indianapolis Museum of Art Uses Visitor Feedback," http://www.quicktapsurvey.com/blog/2015/11/23/silvia-filippini-fantoni-qa-how-the-indianapolis-museum-of-art-uses-visitor-feedback/ (accessed February 7, 2016).

20. Verne Harnish, *Mastering the Rockefeller Habits: What You Must Do to Increase the Value of Your Growing Firm* (Ashburn, VA: Gazelles Inc., 2002), 44.

21. Patrick M. Lencioni, "Make Your Values Mean Something," *Harvard Business Review*, July 2002, https://hbr.org/2002/07/make-your-values-mean-something (accessed February 7, 2016).

22. "The Zappos Family Mission: To Live and Deliver Wow."

23. "Values," https://atomicobject.com/culture/values (accessed February 7, 2016).

24. Harnish, *Mastering the Rockefeller Habits*, 44.

25. Lencioni, "Make Your Values Mean Something."

26. Ibid.

27. Bulgyo, "Tony Hsieh, Zappos, and the Art of Great Company Culture."

28. Shelly Banjo, "Whole Foods and Low Prices Don't Mix," http://www.delaware-online.com/story/opinion/2015/11/09/whole-foods-low-prices-mix/75328512/ (accessed February 7, 2016).

29. Lencioni, "Make Your Values Mean Something."

30. Ibid.

31. "Our Values: Responsibility and Sustainability," http://www.volkswagen-karriere.de/en/what_we_stand_for/our_values.html (accessed February 7, 2016).

empathy
storytelling → listening → dialogue → questions

13

A Decade of Community Engagement through the Lens of Empathy

Emily Zimmern, Janeen Bryant, Kamille Bostick, and Tom Hanchett

> Here's what I think this team accomplished with *Changing Places: From Black and White to Technicolor*: This is not a presentation of cultures, it's a dialog with its community. . . . I was struck by the plethora of "talk back" boards with local voices, personal connections and experiences, emotional and intellectual outpourings. . . . It doesn't just "tell a story" about cultural change, it provides a platform for local residents, and for out-of-town visitors like myself, to put personal experience ahead of cultural stereotypes, and to expand our ability to communicate and empathize with people we don't know.[1]
>
> —Jeff Hayward, *Curator*, October 2010

Envisioned as the community's "front porch," the Levine Museum of the New South for more than a decade has served as a meeting place for people from different backgrounds to come together to talk about issues that matter to them and to share their stories. Through ongoing collaborations and partnerships with other groups and institutions, the museum has brought people together who do not normally meet and engaged many who traditionally have been absent from civic conversations. Using history to build community has been the guiding principle.

At the center of the Levine Museum's practice is dialogue. Since 2004 the museum has offered structured, facilitated dialogue sessions; it has also incorporated dialogic approaches in virtually all aspects of the museum's work, including board, staff, and community engagement. Dialogic approaches shape the development and design of exhibitions and programming in profound ways. Exhibits and programs are designed to be platforms for participation, interactive and responsive to community needs,

and catalysts for civic engagement and dialogue for individuals and organizations. The museum consistently uses dialogic elements—telling stories,
asking questions, and listening deeply. An important outcome of dialogue
and each of its components is an increased capacity for empathy, the ability
to understand and share the experiences and emotions of another person.
Why does the Levine Museum use dialogue? Why is empathy important
for individuals and communities, especially for the residents of Charlotte,
North Carolina, where the Levine Museum is located? How has the Levine
Museum employed dialogue to foster empathy?

BACKGROUND

The Levine Museum of the New South was founded in 1991 to interpret
post–Civil War southern history with a focus on Charlotte and the surrounding Carolina Piedmont. It serves a rapidly growing, increasingly
diverse metropolitan region of more than two million residents centered in
Charlotte and the surrounding Mecklenburg County. As a result of global-
ization, economic restructuring, migration and postmodern urbanization,
the Charlotte region is experiencing unprecedented social and economic
change.[2] In the past quarter century, as the southern economy has pros-
pered, Charlotte, like much of the South, has attracted newcomers from
across the country and around the globe. The population in Charlotte-
Mecklenburg has doubled since 1990. An emerging immigrant gateway, the
city has seen its foreign-born population grow from 3 percent of the population in 1990 to 15 percent in 2015. This is a seismic shift for a region long
known for its black and white racial landscape. In 2010, Charlotte became
a city with a majority of nonwhite residents for the first time in its history.
    During the past twenty-five years, the traditional manufacturing back-
bone for employment shrank dramatically and service jobs grew. Once a
regional textile town, Charlotte became the nation's second largest banking
center in the 1990s and, despite the major hit experienced by the financial services industry during the Great Recession of 2008–2009, economic
growth continues, particularly in the energy and health care sectors. At the
same time, the historically rural landscape is fast being consumed for housing and business.
    Charlotte celebrates its success at reinvention and ongoing growth and
prides itself on its "can-do" and welcoming spirit. Civic and business leaders were therefore surprised and alarmed at the results of the 2001 Social
Capital Benchmark Survey, conducted by famed Harvard political scientist
Robert Putnam. Putnam's survey of forty cities nationwide ranked Charlotte
highly in many community-minded activities, including volunteerism,
charitable giving, and faith-based engagement, but alarmingly low in trust

among different racial groups.[3] Community leaders were struggling with how to address this challenging issue. The Levine Museum board and staff wondered how the museum's programming could make a difference and what role the museum could play in building interracial trust. Based on recent reading about experiments in civic engagement at other museums and the provocative insight of a thought leader, the Levine Museum's president decided to pilot a new approach: using an exhibit as a catalyst for dialogue.

The call to action in the American Association of Museums' 2002 report *Mastering Civic Engagement* was one source of inspiration. The president agreed with its assessment that museums needed to do more to explore their civic role and become "places of dialogue, advocates for inclusion, places of values, and incubators of community."[4] This framework was a natural extension of the philosophy that had animated the thinking and practice of the Museum of the New South's leaders during the early years. John Kuo Wei Tchen's 1989 essay "Towards a Dialogic Museum" about the founding of the New York Chinatown History Project had been foundational:

> We want to bring together members from our various constituencies to talk, assess, and suggest. By so doing we hope to build a creative, convivial, and exciting educational space in which sustained cultural programming will facilitate the collaborative exploration of the memory and meaning of Chinatown's past. We want to fashion a learning environment in which personal memory and testimony inform and are informed by historical context and scholarship.[5]

Moved by Tchen's compelling vision, the founding executive director had worked with the board to incorporate similar elements into the mission of the fledgling Museum of the New South: to provide historical context to contemporary issues and to serve as a community forum for thoughtful discussion.

The second source of inspiration was Dr. Danielle Allen of the University of Chicago. In her keynote address at the 2003 annual meeting of the Foundation for the Carolinas, she made the following observation:

> The number one thing to remember about distrust is that it's historical. . . . When distrust comes as a surprise within a city, odds are that the different communities within it have developed pretty separate versions of history without anyone's noticing. When community memories get out of sync, it's important to go back and look at historical events and weave our narratives together.[6]

Inspired by Dr. Allen's insight and eager to test the potential of dialogue, the Levine Museum stepped forward to strengthen civic discourse about the complex issue of interracial trust. With support from the John S. and James L. Knight Foundation, in 2004, the Levine Museum mounted the exhibit *COURAGE: The Carolina Story that Changed America.* It traced the emotionally powerful story of the brave citizens of Clarendon County, South Carolina, who risked their livelihoods and lives to bring the first of the five lawsuits that would become the Supreme Court's landmark *Brown v. Board of Education* case ending racial segregation in public schools. The museum also announced that it would use dialogue about the Clarendon County story as a tool to build social capital and increase trust. In partnership with Charlotte's Community Building Initiative, it offered *Conversations on Courage,* designed to inform existing management teams from business, government, and community nonprofits about this important but little-known chapter of American history and to use the exhibit as a catalyst for dialogue. Participants viewed the exhibit and then engaged in professionally facilitated discussion about the legacy of the *Brown* decision and its lessons for contemporary issues of access, inclusion, and equity (figure 13.1).

The original target of 750 participants was surpassed in the first four months. By the end of the exhibition's six-and-a-half-month Charlotte run, *Conversations* had attracted 111 groups made up of more than 1,700 community leaders, 42 percent corporate, 47 percent education and nonprofit, and 11 percent government. From the evaluation report, 87 percent of participants called the dialogue "very" to "extremely" valuable. In

Figure 13.1.   A *Conversation on Courage.*

a post-*Conversation* survey, a majority mentioned a climate change in their organization as expressed by this comment: "There is a greater awareness and willingness to discuss race and other sensitive issues which I believe will help us move forward over time." Most participants also recognized that some forms of racism and segregation still exist, and that neither Charlotte nor the nation has achieved equal opportunity for all citizens. Most participants asked that further steps be taken to address these issues.[7]

Follow-up surveys and interviews with exhibit visitors and dialogue participants confirmed the exhibit's impact and demonstrated how it had sparked stories and insights that had not been shared before. Many whites expressed surprise at how unaware of inequality they and their parents were in the 1950s. One visitor wrote, "It's the same principle as Nazi Germany in that we don't see how damaging our values can be because they seem normal." Another recalled his mother forbidding him to use the newly integrated public swimming pool. "It's interesting to me in retrospect that she never tried to explain why. It's as if somehow she knew that whatever she said about race would not fit with what I was learning at Sunday school."[8]

African American visitors voiced different reactions. One remembered, "I was in 2nd grade when my mother explained that I'd be changing schools and referred to Dr. King and the role I'd be playing in his work. Then in high school, I was one of 7 black students in a school of 1100. It was tough." Another expressed appreciation: "I hold two MAs and an executive position due to the sacrifices made by those involved in Brown." A mother wrote, "My daughter who is African American and another girl in our group who is white had an 'aha' moment when they realized how difficult it would have been for them to be friends during segregation." A thirteen-year-old student said, "I thought it was cool to see that people who signed the petition were kids our age. And I thought, if that same situation happened now, would I have enough courage to stand up for what I was thinking?" The exhibit served as a reminder for many visitors that the nation has far to go to achieve social equity and justice. One visitor said, "We are headed back to segregation and many in our community do not mind, do not resist and in fact welcome this result. Many of these same people would never consider themselves to be racist."[9]

The project generated tremendous buzz among civic and business leaders and set in motion new initiatives. Six organizations, including the Police Department, Charlotte-Mecklenburg Schools, and the *Charlotte Observer*, were so moved by the experience that they asked for more and subsequently participated in a nine-month program entitled *Organizational Courage*. Its purpose was to dig more deeply into problems requiring courage today and find solutions that would benefit their firms and the community at large. The Knight Foundation's program director gave this overall assessment: "The *COURAGE* exhibit and conversations were overwhelmingly successful from Knight's perspective. What we've come to understand is that people both reference the exhibit and credit it for a renewed interest in social justice. That's what we'd hoped. This project effectively launched our on-going grant-making strategy to educate local leaders about the impact of race and racism in our community."[10]

For the Levine Museum of the New South, *COURAGE* proved transformative. The success of the project spurred the museum on to use dialogue with intention and focus and to be even bolder in tackling tough issues. A new strategic plan crystallized a dialogue-based approach and pointed the way to an expanded civic role. Active engagement in Charlotte's civic life has become the Levine Museum's hallmark. The museum stays alert to broader community research and civic initiatives to identify subjects that the community is grappling with and asks how history can add value to the discussion and deliberations. Subjects of exhibit projects since 2005 have included women's 1970s emergence on the public stage, LGBTQ issues, immigration, lynching, Charlotte's new religious diversity, demographic and cultural change, and the emergence of Latinos in the South. Facilitated dialogue is offered with every major exhibition. The museum's experience over the past decade has demonstrated that it can play a significant role in building community by telling the stories of those who have shaped the region's history and those who are continuously reinventing the South today. By offering multiple opportunities for people to connect and engage, the Levine Museum board and staff have come to believe ever more strongly that shared stories build community, everyone's history matters, and confronting the unvarnished truth about the past can set individuals and communities free to change and create a better future.

THE NEED FOR EMPATHY AND DIALOGUE

This inclusive vision focusing on connecting past to present and people to one another is vitally needed in a city where half the residents did not live in Charlotte twenty-five years ago, where longtime residents and newcomers alike grapple with a whirlwind of demographic, social, and economic change, and where the legacy of slavery and segregation continues to shape community life amid a new multicultural, multiethnic reality. Fostering and building "community" at neighborhood, city, and regional scales has been highlighted by UNC Charlotte's Urban Institute as a major challenge facing the Charlotte region.[11]

Increasingly, urban planners are pointing to empathy as a key element for successful cities in the twenty-first century. Creating a cohesive diverse community requires a shared capacity for empathy, the ability to understand and share the feelings of others. In the essay "The London Recipe:

How Systems and Empathy Make the City," British thought leader Charles Leadbeater writes:

> Creative cities depend on a kind of dark matter, something that must be there to make them work, but which cannot be observed directly. That dark matter is empathy, our capacity to connect with other people who are different from us, to find common ground and to engage in sharing and exchange. That is the basis for the collective genius of city life: collaboration, cooperation and civility.
>
> This capacity for empathy comes in two closely-related parts: it is one part cognitive—an ability to "read" what other people want to do—and one part emotional—caring enough to respond accordingly.[12]

Dialogue is a powerful tool in building the capacity for empathy. It brings people together to share reactions and stories, respond to questions and raise new ones, and listen receptively. Dialogue enables people to find meaning by learning with, from, and about one another. It invites people to bring all of themselves into the encounter: mind, body, spirit, emotion, and experience. Dialogue assumes that multiple perspectives can coexist.[13] Through dialogue, people hear one another's stories and come to know each other. Only by knowing each other can they come to trust each other. Only by trusting one another, they can help each other and thereby build something larger than themselves.

A DECADE OF DIALOGUE THROUGH THE LENS OF EMPATHY

Given the demonstrated need for a shared capacity for empathy among Charlotte residents and the demonstrated power of the *COURAGE* project to deepen understanding across difference, the Levine Museum has expanded its use of dialogue-based strategies during the past decade. To deepen conversation for those interested in digging more intensively, it has continued to offer facilitated dialogues, using the *COURAGE* model and piloting new ones, as well as extending the use of dialogue to teen groups. To broaden the conversation to include larger numbers of people, the museum has also consistently incorporated dialogic elements into exhibit development and design. A variety of approaches has been used to invite visitors to explore and talk about the ideas and issues that matter to them and afford multiple opportunities to encounter and interact with the views of others. All promote self-discovery as well as sharing and exchange, and reinforce the capacity for empathy, the ability to connect with people different from themselves. Reflecting on the experiences of the past ten years, the Levine Museum has come to understand the power of dialogue and its key elements—telling stories, asking questions, and listening—to build empathy. Below are reflections on what museum staff has learned and gives examples of approaches used.

TELLING STORIES

The Levine Museum's experience supports what social psychologists are finding in their research. Stories give context, touch people emotionally, open them up to accepting data, and help them organize new information. Putting a human face to nameless statistics can prompt individuals to think about an issue from a fresh perspective.[14] Visitor reaction at the museum underscores the views of master storyteller Andy Goodman and screenwriting coach Robert McKee: "If you can get a story in someone's brain, he will hear the data you present";[15] "To involve people at the deepest level, you need stories."[16]

To build connection in our diverse region and to foster empathy, the Levine Museum tells little-known stories and those that have never been told along with the well-known stories of the famous and powerful. Levine Museum exhibits present stories garnered from intellectual study and rigorous scholarship and first-person stories drawn from lived experience. In dialogue, "book knowledge" and "experiential knowledge" are both valued and welcome;[17] in Levine Museum exhibits they are frequently juxtaposed. Most Levine Museum exhibits feature interactives that invite visitors to add their own stories.

Community-Curated Exhibit

Conceived and developed by Mexican American artist Rosalia Torres Weiner, *El Papalote Magico/The Magic Kite* exhibit featured kites created by children affected by the deportation of a parent. The tail of each kite was made from a remnant of clothing left behind by the deported parent. Displayed next to the kites were statements by the children telling how the separation had affected them. The young people ranged from ages seven to seventeen. The emotional trauma revealed in the short narratives was heartbreaking. Some visitors were moved to tears. Many reported being surprised at how US immigration policy was tearing families apart. They expressed empathy for immigrant families and became aware of immigration issues beyond the headlines.

Story Kiosk

In the exhibition *Changing Places: From Black and White to Technicolor*, the Levine Museum used a video talkback booth for the first time. Visitors were invited to record their reactions to the exhibit and to Charlotte's changing cultures, then excerpts appeared on an adjacent touchscreen. Comments harvested from the booth were diverse, evocative, and thought provoking. Well over half of users were people of color ranging in age from teens to thirties. Something about the privacy of the booth encouraged people to open up, to be candid about their hopes and fears to a greater extent than museum staff had been able to capture in more formal video interviews. Some of the clips were used in a one-hour *Changing Places* documentary produced in partnership with local public television station WTVI, broadcast regionally every two months during the run of the exhibit. WTVI reedited the documentary each time it aired, incorporating fresh talkback.[18] In this way, the exhibit and documentary became part of an ongoing region-wide conversation, just the kind of sharing and exchange needed to build empathy in an increasingly diverse city. Hearing the stories, viewers came to see their community through someone else's eyes.

ASKING QUESTIONS

Questions are integral to all dialogue. Who? What? How? When? Why? They spark the conversation. Ask a question and the answer is the start of a story.[19] In almost all its exhibits, the Levine Museum asks visitors questions to spark self-reflection, as well as generate exchange with others. Empathy requires self-knowledge. "The more you understand your own humanity, the more you can appreciate the humanity of others."[20]

Without Sanctuary: Lynching Photography in America was the most challenging exhibit the Levine Museum ever presented. The exhibition's centerpiece was a collection of photographs, postcards, and memorabilia that were taken at lynching events in the United States in the early decades of the twentieth century. The images, many of which were made into postcards and sent through the mail, often depicted crowds of onlookers who appear to be celebrating the brutal spectacle. The Levine Museum staff and board spent more than a year preparing themselves for potentially volatile responses from visitors and the community and planning the framework for presentation of the exhibit in Charlotte. Staff members researched how other museums had framed their presentations, particularly the National Underground Railroad Freedom Center and the Chicago Historical Society. Different combinations of postcards were displayed in each city and each city tailored the exhibit according to their respective missions and community context. Levine Museum staff members sought community feedback through five listening sessions. Like the Freedom Center, the Levine Museum designed its framework with the hope that "visitors would be able to connect with the images to bring a sense of empathy to those who were without sanctuary in life or death."[21]

To guide guests through the graphic exhibit that stirred strong emotions, Levine Museum educators created an arc of dialogue that would assist visitors in processing their feelings and move toward an outcome that was constructive and meaningful, not harmful. Questions in large print were mounted on the wall in each section of the exhibit. Questions on Post-It boards asked for visitor feedback. Based on visitor response and the fact that they are still referenced in community conversation today, three years later, several questions in particular pricked the hearts and minds of visitors: "Where would you be in the picture?" was mounted on the wall in the gallery filled with postcards of lynching events. An interactive Post-It board asked visitors to leave their responses: Can you imagine yourself in the picture? As a bystander? As the victim? As a member of the mob? As the photographer? As someone who chose to stay home that day? Considering this series of options required visitors to place themselves in the image and see the picture through the lens of the essence of empathy. The final section of the exhibit asked: Who among us is without sanctuary today? It too required visitors to imagine the situations and feelings of a range of people, some alike and some different from themselves.

LISTENING

A crucial element of dialogue is listening. To pause and truly take in another person's response, to hear their story, and strive to see the story from the teller's point of view is affirming to the individual speaking and can shift the perspectives of both the teller and the listener. When a person or group of persons feels they are being heard, they begin to speak more openly and candidly. The listener begins to see that there can be multiple perspectives on reality. Listening can have a transformative power. It can create authentic connection and provide the foundation for a responsive relationship.[22]

Over the past decade, the Levine Museum has used listening sessions extensively to build authentic connection, start responsive relationships, and use what was heard and learned in the sessions to shape the design of exhibits and programs. Unlike a focus group in which participants answer questions and never engage with the results, listening sessions are designed to be the starting point of sustainable engagement. The Levine Museum communicates how participants' feedback is being used to shape a project; participants are asked how the museum can be helpful to them and their organization; and the museum responds accordingly, if resources permit. All are invited to see the exhibit and participate in programming. A culture of reciprocity begins to develop with dynamic give and take.[23]

The success of *Without Sanctuary* in Charlotte was directly related to the input the Levine Museum received from five listening sessions: two with African American men, one with white men, one with a group of men and women of diverse backgrounds and ages, and one with several artists. Each became a dialogue on issues of race, racism, and historical memory. Discussion was robust, emotional, and moving, rich in stories, questions, and listening. Key themes emerged:

- Make certain the history of lynching in Charlotte and North Carolina is included.
- Connect lynching to issues of social justice today.
- Figure out how you can help museum visitors pivot from the pain and trauma of lynching to something affirming, moving from the negativity of the past to a positive response preventing similar actions today.
- It will only be worthwhile if whites as well as African Americans come to see the exhibit.

The Levine Museum's staff historian drafted extensive exhibit text to contextualize the exhibit materials in ways that tailored the design to what had been heard and reflected North Carolina history. Key messages were synthesized and used in all public relations and marketing materials and in a gallery guide. Excerpts are below:

> In a spirit of reverence and remembrance, Levine Museum presents *Without Sanctuary: Lynching Photography in America*, a graphic exhibit that examines one of the most horrific chapters in American history and one that continues to influence society today. Our mission in bringing the exhibit to Charlotte is to recognize the humanity of those who were executed, educate visitors and acknowledge that these atrocities indeed took place, and to promote cross-cultural discussion that can bring healing and vigilance against future acts of bigotry and violence.

At the end of the exhibit, museum visitors encountered a piece of art—a rocking chair with the seat covered in nails sticking upward (figure 13.2). The artist's statement for *Bound in Yes* was mounted nearby and an interactive challenged the visitor to respond to the question, "What is your *Yes*?"

Wall signage: *Bound in Yes*

Artist Statement: There is no wrong way to feel however there can be an affirming way to respond. As we sit in the seat of historical perspective and cozy up to even the prickliest of privileges the passage of time enables, the question of what does one do with all this information, knowledge, and weight looms ominous. In the face of the human behavior that fueled/fuels the atrocities depicted in WITHOUT SANCTUARY, *Bound in Yes* asks you to share what this horrifying and resounding expression of "no" inspires you to affirm, do, construct, build, facilitate, and say yes to. *Bound in Yes* asks, "What is your *Yes*?"—John W. Love, Jr.

Instructions: What is your *Yes*?

Figure 13.2. *Without Sanctuary* **exhibit opening.**

Grab a marker and tag, gather up your thoughts, and express what *WITHOUT SANCTUARY* inspires you to say *yes* to. When you're done attach your tag to the "chair of yes."

The seat of nails quickly filled with tags.

By listening and using what was heard to influence exhibit design and messaging, the Levine Museum shaped its presentation of *Without Sanctuary* to align with community interests. The Sunday before opening, the *Charlotte Observer* ran a front-page story that not only told about the exhibit, but also explored a famous lynching case in a nearby town that almost no one had ever heard of. The exhibit attracted visitors of all backgrounds, including Bank of America's Global Diversity and Inclusion Council, with members from around the United States and the world. They, along with the bank's CEO and his executive team, visited the moving exhibit and conducted their own debrief as part of an annual convening. Visitors reported overwhelmingly that the exhibit opened them up to new perspectives and demonstrated that Charlotte had the courage to confront tough issues, past and present.

FACILITATED DIALOGUES

The Levine Museum has learned that exhibits have the potential to help people think and talk about difficult issues. Addressing a tough topic "on the slant" by having people react to a "third thing" such as an exhibit helps people open up. Dialogue participants describe their reactions to the exhibit, and in doing so often share stories and insights that would never be voiced in day-to-day conversation.[24] Such shared storytelling promotes receptive listening and often generates new questions. It fosters feelings of safety and connection that often did not exist beforehand. It moves people in unexpected ways and allows them to explore difficult issues that previously seemed too contentious to address head on.

Speaking of Change

Speaking of Change dialogues complemented the 2009–2010 exhibition *Changing Places: From Black and White to Technicolor.* Whether a native, a newcomer from elsewhere in the United States, or an immigrant from abroad, every Southerner during the first decade of the twenty-first century was coping with the challenges of blending old and new cultures. The *Changing Places* exhibit used first-person stories and a wide variety of interaction strategies to draw visitors in, helping them make this exhibition their own. It was designed to bring people of different backgrounds together and to spark conversation across cultural boundaries.[25]

Like *Conversations on Courage, Speaking of Change* was offered to "intact groups" such as a nonprofit board, a Sunday school class, or a corporate board. The aim was to create an experience that would continue to resonate and be referred to as the group goes about its activities long after the museum visit. Each session included a brief orientation by a facilitator, an exhibit visit, time for personal reflection, followed by sharing of personal reactions with one other person, and then facilitated dialogue among the whole group. Talk moved from the personal (what touched them in the exhibit) toward what their organization might do for the community in an era of cultural change (figure 13.3). People opened up emotionally, discussing fears and frustrations, concerns and ambivalence.[26] Participants self-reported that the "Getting Past Us and Them" section of the exhibit was the most impactful.[27] To enter this dimly lit area, visitors had to literally push past stereotypes: in the doorway hung long plastic strips with derogatory terms heard in the community. Inside they watched video clips of diverse teens describing how they had been stereotyped and bullied at school. Post-It boards asked: Who judges you without knowing you? Who do you judge?

More than 1,600 adults in 118 groups participated in the *Speaking of Change* dialogues. (The Levine Museum also offered for the first time facilitated dialogue for youth; *Turn the Tables* attracted more than 1,200 teens in 52 groups.) Interestingly, Mecklenburg County decided to make the museum's dialogues an integral component of its diversity training for employees. More than 400 county staff members in 14 groups participated,

Figure 13.3.   *Changing Places* **exhibit sparks conversation.**

representing all departments, from parks and recreation to tax collection, from sanitation to libraries. A follow-up survey of dialogue participants and two follow-up dialogue sessions, one of county employees and one of noncounty participants, indicated that participants were influenced by *Speaking of Change* dialogues to enact inclusive behaviors and actions at the individual, organizational, and community level; the overwhelming majority of actions cited were individual actions. The evaluation team of UNC Charlotte scholars published their findings in the journal *Museums and Social Issues*. In the article titled "Speaking of Change in Charlotte, North Carolina: How Museums Can Shape Immigrant Receptivity in a Community Navigating Rapid Cultural Change," they reported the following results:

> Specifically, we demonstrate how through its exhibit and dialogue programming, the museum deepened understanding of immigration in ways that led to a warmer welcome and proactive inclusion. This research illuminates the critical role of museums in guiding community receptivity towards immigrants in a way that provide a counterbalance to reactive or hostile responses.[28]

COURAGE in the City

In 2011, the Levine Museum piloted a new paired dialogue model for adults. Two complementary exhibits provided the catalyst for dialogue between African Americans and Latinos: the *COURAGE* exhibit, which had been reinstalled as part of the museum's twentieth-anniversary celebration, and *PARA TODOS LOS NIÑOS: Fighting Segregation Before Brown v. Board*, which traced the background of the 1946 Mendez case that ended school segregation for Mexicans and Mexican Americans in California. The series of six dialogues titled *COURAGE in the City: Educational Equity in the Multicultural South* paired six to twelve representatives of an African American group with six to twelve representatives of a similar Latino group. Paired groups included attorneys, journalists, women, business people, grassroots activists, and community development professionals. African American and Latino cofacilitators guided each two-and-a-half-hour experience that included exhibit viewing and discussion. Evaluation showed that the response of participants was overwhelmingly positive. Both African Americans and Latinos reported that awareness of one another's history had increased, that they had discovered previously unknown commonalities of experience, and that some attitudes about educational equity had shifted and would likely lead to changes in behavior.[29] One direct outcome was the start of a Teen Book Club by one of the participating organizations. During Black History Month, the Latin American Coalition invited Latino and African American teens to read *The Warmth of Other Suns* by Isabel Wilkerson and explore how the migration stories of the Great Migration paralleled those of today's immigrants. The teens shared their new insights at an (Im)Migration Community Forum hosted by the Levine Museum.

COMMUNITY BUILDING CONTINUES

In September 2015, the Levine Museum launched its most ambitious project to date: ¡NUEVOlution! *Latinos and the New South* (figure 13.4). It builds on the past decade of innovative work in community engagement and more than three years of listening and learning through the Latino New South Learning Network. Thanks to an Innovation Lab grant from the American Alliance of Museums' Center for the Future of Museums, in association with the MetLife Foundation, the Levine Museum, in partnership with the Atlanta History Center and the Birmingham Civil Rights Institute, used listening sessions in our three cities to learn and build trusting working relationships with dozens of Latino and Latino-serving organizations. What was heard was synthesized in a summative document titled "Working with Latino Partners: Seven Insights." The insights shaped the development of the 3,500 square foot bilingual exhibit and twelve months of planned complementary programming and dialogues. The Levine Museum also drew on lessons learned through its active involvement since

Figure 13.4. *¡NUEVOlution!* ignites cross-cultural interaction.

2008 with the International Coalition of Sites of Conscience, particularly its Immigration and Civil Rights Network and its National Immigration Dialogue Project.

¡NUEVOlution! explores a topic that many historians consider to be the biggest story in southern history since the Civil Rights Movement. Over the past twenty-five years, the southeastern United States has led the nation in Latino population growth. In Charlotte, Latinos have grown from 1 percent of the population in 1990 to 13 percent in 2015. This seismic demographic shift has brought dramatic change. The transformation has introduced new language, cultural, and religious traditions, food ways, music, and sports interests. This puts the South at the cutting edge of a nationwide trend that is seeing new Latino populations where none previously existed in nearly every US state.

How are Latinos reshaping the South and how is the South reshaping Latinos? What does it mean to be Latino in this newest "New South"? The Latino story in the Southeast is the lens through which visitors to the exhibit come to understand a broader set of forces impacting their region, their communities, and themselves as individuals. *Encuentros*—a Spanish word with multilayered meanings, "encountering, discovering, confronting, coming together, growing"—is the organizing principle of *¡NUEVOlution!* The exhibition showcases stories of real people, Latino and non-Latino, from across the South telling their own stories and looks back to explore parallels with earlier southern history. The exhibition asks numerous questions: How are people grappling with difficult issues such as identity, belonging, and exclusion? How do Latinos and non-Latinos relate to each other, their communities, and themselves? How are people drawing on the resources of tradition, both in the many home cultures of Latin America and also in the diverse history of the South to help navigate change? How are people resisting change? How are communities responding to those resistant to change? How are people working together and in isolation to construct an inclusive and welcoming South?

Interactive art pieces, Post-It boards, electronic touchscreens, and a story kiosk give visitors in the exhibit multiple ways to give their feedback and share their own stories. Pop-up activities take content to hard-to-reach audiences in community venues, accompanied by new media methods of capturing first-person stories and responses that can be harvested and incorporated into the main exhibit. Virtual programming, such as tweet chats, are giving voice to younger audiences as they explore history and stereotypes and how they are portrayed in the New South. *NUEVO Día* dialogues will be offered using three different models. With a major goal of sparking cross-cultural interaction and understanding, ¡NUEVOlution! builds on and expands the museum's longstanding dialogue-based strategies.

CONCLUSION

In an already complex and contested racial landscape, southern society is currently being remade. As old and new cultures mix and spawn an unprecedented multicultural, multiethnic future, the task of increasing the community's shared capacity for empathy is more important than ever. The Levine Museum of the New South plays an active role in strengthening the community's empathetic muscle. With intention and focus, it offers experiences that help museum visitors come to know and empathize with people different from themselves. Institutionally, the museum strives to conduct its work in ways that model dialogue and empathy.

What is the biggest lesson of the past decade? With shared empathy, individuals can move from isolation to belonging, from division to connection, from suspicion to trust, and come together to begin the hard work of creating a cohesive diverse community that values and gives opportunity to all its residents. Such a civic culture honors individual and group identities while encouraging shared participation and decision making. As the *Changing Places* promotional campaign stated, "We may walk in different shoes, but we tread on common ground."

NOTES

1. Jeff Hayward, Review of *Changing Places: From Black and White to Technicolor*, in *Curator*, October 2013.

2. Owen J. Furuseth, "The Restructuring of Our Community: The Changing Charlotte Region," presentation at the Arts and Science Council Executive Directors' Retreat, August 23, 2003.

3. Foundation for the Carolinas, *Social Capital Benchmark Survey Executive Summary for the Charlotte Region*, February 28, 2001.

4. Robert R. Archibald, "Introduction," in *Mastering Civic Engagement: A Challenge to Museums* (Washington, DC: American Association of Museums, 2002).

5. John Kuo Wei Tchen, "Creating a Dialogic Museum: The Chinatown History Museum Experiment," in *Museums and Communities: The Politics of Public Culture* (Washington, DC: Smithsonian Institution Press, 1992).

6. Danielle S. Allen, "Talking to Strangers," Foundation for the Carolinas Annual Meeting Keynote Address, February 18, 2003.

7. Stephanie Counts and Linda Ketner, *COURAGE Evaluation Report*, April 26, 2005.

8. Ibid.

9. Ibid.

10. Ibid.

11. Furuseth, "The Restructuring of Our Community."

12. Charles Leadbeater, "The London Recipe: How Systems and Empathy Make the City," *Centre for London*, 2014.

13. Tammy Bormann, "Planning, Designing and Facilitating Dialogue," presentation for Museum Professionals in the Civil Rights Network of the International Coalition of Sites of Conscience, June 14–16, 2011.

14. Andy Goodman, *Storytelling as Best Practice*, 7th edition, January 2015.

15. Ibid.

16. Robert McKee, "Storytelling that Moves People," in *Harvard Business Review*, June 2003.

17. Bormann, "Planning, Designing and Facilitating Dialogue."

18. Tom Hanchett, "An Idea-Based Exhibit: Platform for Participation," in *Museums of Ideas: Commitment and Conflict* (MuseumsEtc., 2011).

19. Goodman, *Storytelling*.

20. McKee, "Storytelling that Moves People."

21. Dina Bailey, Richard Cooper, Charles Davis, and Katie Johnson, *"Without Sanctuary" Project Research Brief*, National Underground Railroad Freedom Center, 2009.

22. Janeen Bryant, "Shhh! The Transformative Power of Listening," presentation at the National Innovation Summit for Arts and Culture, Denver, CO, October 20–23, 2013.

23. Janeen Bryant and Kamille Bostick, "What's the Big Idea? Using Listening Sessions to Build Relationships and Relevance," AASLH Technical Leaflet no. 263 in *History News*, Summer 2013.

24. Hanchett, "An Idea-Based Exhibit."

25. Ibid.

26. Ibid.

27. Susan B. Harden, Heather A. Smith, and Paul N. McDaniel, *Changing Places Dialogue: Speaking of Change Evaluation Report*, July 1, 2010.

28. Susan B. Harden, Paul N. McDaniel, Heather A. Smith, Emily Zimmern, and Katie E. Brown, "Speaking of Change in Charlotte, North Carolina: How Museums Can Shape Immigrant Receptivity in a Community Navigating Rapid Cultural Change," in *Museums and Social Issues* (October 2015).

29. Susan B. Harden, *COURAGE in the City Evaluation Report*, October 2011.

healing
collaboration
learning
empathy
perseverance

14

Learning from the Challenges of Our Times

The Families of September 11 and Liberty Science Center

Donna Gaffney and Emlyn Koster

> Empathy is the most mysterious transaction that the human soul can have, and it's accessible to all of us, but we have to give ourselves the opportunity to identify, to plunge ourselves in a story where we see the world from the bottom up or through another's eyes or heart.[1]
>
> —Sue Monk Kidd

By now the stories are all too familiar. Boston. Damascus. Ferguson. Katmandu. London. New Orleans. New York. Northeast Japan. Oklahoma. Oslo. Paris. Port au Prince. San Bernardino. Shenzhen. Western Sumatra. It seems that tragedy befalls communities in ever-increasing numbers and with ever-increasing regularity. Whether such catastrophes are caused by forces of nature, human conflict, or engineering failure, everyone is a potential witness to the social, physical, and emotional devastation wrought by such events. Technology and social media extend the reach of destruction, violence, injury, and loss, changing the social environment. Somehow people and communities, wounded and dazed, come together in a spirit of selfless collaboration to help, to heal, and to learn from tragedy and its aftermath. Empathy is the foundation of this human response.

Naming empathy and using it in a sentence is easy. Describing its presence is far more difficult. What does it look like? What does it feel like?

On a cool night in Rhode Island, barely one month after September 11, 2001, college students, parents, and other community members gathered on the banks of the Providence, Woonasquatucket, and Moshassuck Rivers in downtown Providence. They came together to experience *WaterFire*, a unique sculptural installation of one hundred water-borne bonfires glowing against the dark water. Amid soaring music, crackling embers, and the glow of braziers, small boats with volunteers clad in black silently tended the fires. Observers stood in silence in what Professor Jerry Blitefield describes as going beyond "the ideological and the individual . . . it unites us physically and intentionally as a congregation not in observance of any shared *then* but only of a shared *now*; it makes us present to each other in a way that changes not necessarily how we view ourselves as Americans, but how we view ourselves as human beings: not as a people, but just people."[2] The experience of *WaterFire* was profound. Standing silently shoulder to shoulder, strangers began to connect. They listened to each other in conversations that began with the almost sacred question, "Where were you on September 11?" They told their stories and listened carefully to the stories of others, sometimes dry-eyed and sometimes tearful. In many ways, this is the feeling of empathy, for both the one who expresses it and the one who receives it. Presence. Silence. Listening. Transformation. The glow of the fires, the soothing ebb of the river water, the music, and the almost invisible helpers tending to the fires all contributing to a place where empathy is practiced and felt.

TRAUMA, EMPATHY, AND COMPASSION

Reeling from the catastrophic events of September 11, the global community was in varying states of denial, shock, anger, and grief. The terrorist attacks traumatized countless people, especially those who were in harm's way and narrowly escaped death. People who witnessed the events firsthand or were related to those who died, worked, or lived near the attacks were not immune to their shattering effects. Still others, feeling some degree of security in their distance from the three epicenters of New York, Washington, and Shanksville, Pennsylvania, found themselves reacting with horror and fear as they watched graphic media reports. For the first time, citizens of the United States realized what other countries have long known; we are no longer safe on own shores.

The expression *fight or flight* has become so commonly used that many think it requires no further discussion in order to be understood. Yet this essential self-preservation reaction to threat is complex, involving a constellation of physiological, affective, and cognitive responses that are universally experienced in the face of danger.[3] The emotions evoked by a traumatic event last long after the event is over. The fear of death and helplessness experienced during the moments of terror persist even after one is out of harm's way.[4] The surreal memory of disintegrating buildings can intrude into daytime consciousness and nightmares, unbidden but present just the same. Horrifying images can intensify emotional and bodily reactions. Plagued by ongoing and encompassing hyper-alertness, people tried to get their lives back together but it was difficult and took time. Trauma encompasses every aspect of one's being. Even the physical reactions persist, and in some cases, as with posttraumatic stress disorder, individuals may never fully recover.

Nowhere were these tumultuous experiences felt more acutely than in Manhattan and the adjacent communities of New Jersey and Brooklyn. Liberty Science Center is located across the Hudson River from what is now known as Ground Zero. This museum's observation tower provided an eerie vantage point for the unfolding events. Staff members were witnesses to the tragedy. Many lived locally or had family or friends in downtown Manhattan. Trauma counselors helped personnel come to terms with what had happened and offered guidance on how to interact with visitors. Empathy was not only communicated to the community outside the institution, but also to colleagues who worked with each other every day. Some authors refer to this concept as internal empathy and emphasize its importance in "strengthen[ing] empathy within an organization, generating more meaning and satisfaction internally."[5] Furthermore, empathy is a key variable that creates "a culture that positions courage and nonjudgment as the fulcrum to an openly creative and innovative dynamic."[6]

How does empathy affect individual lives and communities? The concept of empathy is not new, but it has evolved since experimental psychologist E. B. Titchener coined the term in 1909.[7] Empathy was first translated from the German *Einfühlung*, "to feel one's way into," and then into the Greek *empatheia*, "in (en) suffering or passion (pathos)" (Eisenberg). Titchener described empathy in an interpersonal context as the "full sympathy" of the experimenter with his experimental subject; "he must think . . . as they think, understand as they understand, speak in their language."[8]

Empathy is the ability to share the emotions of another or anticipate how an individual is likely to feel in a particular situation.[9] It is not emotional mirroring, nor is it sympathy. Sympathy is feeling the emotion *for* the other person rather than feeling the emotion *as* the other feels it.[10] Empathy is being attuned and responsive to the affective states of others. Cognitive empathy is one's ability to *understand* the emotional experience of the other person, while affective empathy is *feeling* the other's emotional response.[11]

While empathetic individuals are often compassionate, compassion is not the same as empathy. The word *compassion* means to "suffer together." It is the feeling that surfaces when one witnesses another person's distress *and* has a strong desire to help relieve the other person's suffering.[12] The empathetic person can take the perspective of another person and feel his or her emotions, deeply and with understanding, but may not necessarily have the desire or actually take action to relieve the associated distress.

Author and psychologist Carl Rogers believed that empathy was the cornerstone of the human relationship. He described empathy as a dynamic process, not a state of being:

> To be with another in this [empathetic] way means that for the time being you lay aside the views and values you hold for yourself in order to enter another's world without prejudice. . . . In such situations deep understanding is, I believe, the most precious gift one can give to another.[13]

Rogers was clear that empathy had strong application to other settings or relationships: "If we think, however, that empathy is effective only in the one-to-one relationship we call psychotherapy, we are greatly mistaken. Even in the classroom it makes an important difference. When the teacher shows evidence that he/she understands the meaning of classroom experiences for the student, learning improves."[14] Perhaps the same argument could be made for the healing of beleaguered communities.

The September 11 attacks posed long-term crises, relocation of workplaces or homes, and loss of jobs and property. Stressors continued for months afterward, from changing traffic patterns and air quality concerns to a call to arms for a new war in the Middle East. Crises can be opportunities for learning and raising one's functioning to a higher level.[15] But traumatic events may have the opposite effect, leaving one in a position of instability and vulnerability. The recovery process after a traumatic event must begin with safety, and therein lies the significance of sanctuary.

TRAGEDY STRIKES AND A JOURNEY BEGINS

At 8:48 am on September 11, 2001, the staff of Liberty Science Center (the Center) in Jersey City, New Jersey, was among those who witnessed one of the most terrifying events of the new century. Although still reeling from their own trauma, they became key participants for the rescue and recovery efforts in New Jersey following the terrorist attacks on the World Trade Center in New York City.[16] Mandated to close their doors to the public for two weeks, staff nonetheless made their facility, time, and talents available to citizens of the metropolitan area. The lessons learned by the staff and their community partners extended far beyond the Center's spirit of selfless collaboration and commitment (textbox 14.1).

Working with the New Jersey Department of Mental Health, Disaster Services, the Center provided many forms of assistance. In those early hours following the terrorist attacks no one was sure exactly how or what could be done in the face of such enormous tragedy. The Center was in full support mode to set up the New Jersey Family Assistance Center located a mile away. Processing credentials, providing language translation

ORIENTATION AND GUIDELINES FOR LSC INTERPRETERS AT THE FAMILY ASSISTANCE CENTER

Dear Liberty Science Center Interpreters,

Thank you so much for offering your services to the friends and families of the World Trade Center disaster victims. These are difficult times and your help is invaluable. We also hope that you and your family are safe and coping with the tragedy as well as possible.

The process for working with the families and companions is described below. A trained mental health companion accompanies each family while they are at the Family Assistance Center. You will be interpreting for the companion and the family member who is answering questions that the companion has asked. We want to assure you that interpreters will not be alone with the families.

Securing Interpreters for Families:
1. A companion will meet the family of the victim when they first enter the FAC (Family Assistance Center). At that time language needs will be assessed.
2. LSC will be notified and an appropriate interpreter will be identified. It is our hope that you will be able to arrive at the FAC in about an hour's time.
3. Interpreters should report to the registration desk at the FAC entrance.
4. The companion will introduce him/herself to you and then introduce you to the family.
5. The companion will determine the family's needs by asking you to translate questions and statements regarding services at the FAC.
   a. Counseling
   b. Reposting a missing person
   c. DNA laboratory
   d. Social security benefits
   e. Unemployment benefits
   f. Victim's Compensation

In addition, there will be meals and refreshments, childcare, spiritual services, telephones and computers available. Note: You and the companion will stay with the family for as long as they wish. If an individual requires all services at the FAC, you may be at the Center for several hours.

Although there may be difficult moments (tearfulness, crying, anger, etc.), you will not be alone with the family nor will you be expected to

(continued)

know what to say to them in those situations. The companion will be responsible for support and comfort language. You may have some suggestions as well.

Words and phrases for comfort and support are generally simple and heartfelt:
   "I am so sorry that you are going through this difficult time."
   "It is good you came here today."
   "I can see how upsetting this is for you."
   "What you are feeling is commonly experienced by people in similar situations."
   "What do you need to do today?"
   "How can we help you?"
   "We will stay with you throughout your time here today."
   "Who do you have at home to help you (talk to)?"
   "Do you need to fill out a missing person's report?"
   "It is important to identify your loved one, for that reason we need to obtain some of his/her personal objects (toothbrush, hair brush). These items can help the lab people do the proper tests."
        Or
   "It is important to identify your loved one, for that reason we may need to ask your (relative's name) to have a swab rubbed on the inside of his/her cheek for the laboratory people."

© Donna A. Gaffney, 2001

Textbox 14.1. This one-page guide, Orientation and Guidelines for Liberty Science Center Interpreters, was used by staff to assist their work at both Liberty Science Center and at the nearby New Jersey Family Assistance Center. The Family Assistance Center offered personalized attention to family members and others affected by the 9/11 attacks, allowing them to effectively access the services available. *Source*: Donna A. Gaffney.

services, and partnering with the Red Cross were only a few of the many tasks needed to launch the New Jersey Family Assistance Center, located one mile nearer to Ground Zero in a historic train terminal at the Hudson River bank.

   Although people were bustling about the Center, there was a palpable sense of calm and comfort. Each exhibit—from the estuary overlooking the Hudson River with its fish tanks and marsh environments to a just-arrived traveling exhibit about building construction, to a gallery of live animals on predator-prey relationships the simplicity of suddenly core challenges was perceptible. There was no question that a space originally designed to promote the wonders of learning about science, then transformed into an emergency center, could also provide the essential components of trauma recovery: an empathetic milieu with compassionate people offering support, comfort, and a feeling of coming home (textbox 14.2).

After giving their diverse talents and support to establishing the Family Assistance Center, staff members were ready to resume their mission. As they did so, the Center took the unusual step of issuing a statement that was published in the *New York Times*, the *Star-Ledger*, and the *Jersey Journal* in 2001:

> The trustees, president, employees, and volunteers of Liberty Science Center express their heartfelt sympathy to the many families, friends and communities of those who have suffered losses, were injured, or are still missing as a result of the terrorist attacks at the World Trade Center, the Pentagon, and in Pennsylvania.
>
> In the aftermath of this tragedy, Liberty Science Center has assisted by providing a site for medical personnel, stranded commuters, the news media, police communications, and meetings of displaced corporations. Also, with New Jersey's Family Assistance Center now located nearby in Liberty State Park, we have issued security passes for all of this Center's staffing, provided all food service there through our contract caterer Volume Services America, and are open to the families of victims.
>
> Liberty Science Center joins the countless other voices that call upon us all to strive for greater global harmony. We also wish to express our desire for the peaceful use of science and technology in society.

PROVIDING SANCTUARY

A *sanctuary* is sacred space. During the Middle Ages, sanctuaries were asylums, places of safety and protection for those in danger. To harm a person who sought shelter in the sanctuary was sacrilege. The sanctuary provided a physical place of refuge and respite. However, by providing physical safety, it also provided emotional and social safety.

In *Creating Sanctuary*, Sandra Bloom states that in order for healing to begin, one must start with a place of safety.[17] This feeling of safety is achieved through four different elements: a physically safe environment, psychological safety and social safety, the ability to trust oneself and other people, and, finally, behavioral safety, knowing that one will be secure with the appropriate structures, limits, and expectations in place. Bloom is convinced that play, investigation, and learning are also parts of the healing process. Like schools, a museum setting can lend itself to the creation of sanctuary-like environments offering a sense of safety and an opportunity to develop attachments.[18] In addition, it offers a cooperative context for learning in groups while maintaining individual integrity.[19]

FAQ about the WTC Disaster

QUESTIONS CHILDREN AND FAMILIES MAY ASK
WHEN VISITING LIBERTY SCIENCE CENTER (LSC)

1. **"Can you see where the towers stood from LSC?"**
   Be honest and identify the areas in the Center from which the *skyline* can be seen. The fact is that unless you are very familiar with the area you will not know where the towers stood.

2. **"What does the site of the terrorist attacks look like?"**
   It looks like a skyline. You cannot see any of the damaged areas. In addition to the buildings of lower Manhattan you can also see the Verrazanno-Narrows Bridge and the Statue of Liberty.

3. **"Is this going to upset my child?"**
   If you and your child are very familiar with the location of the World Trade Center, you may be moved by its absence. If you are not familiar with the skyline of lower Manhattan, you will probably be curious as to where the towers stood.

4. **"Is Liberty Science Center safe?"**
   We have always provided safety for our guests. We have taken every measure to assure continued safety for our guests as well as our staff.

5. **"I am afraid I will see reminders of the disaster at Liberty Science Center."**
   There are no reminders of the disaster visible from the Liberty Science Center.

6. **"What can I do to prepare my child before I come to the center?"**
   Be honest with children. Younger children (under 6 or 7) may not realize that LSC is across the Hudson River from lower Manhattan. Honestly answer their questions. Older children who are aware of the event and followed media reports, may want to know where the buildings stood. Talk to them ahead of time and let them know that there will be an opportunity to see the skyline if they desire. You may want to point out that the LSC is across the river and two miles from lower Manhattan. Also put the site of the towers in context, the skyline includes many important points of interest: the Statue of Liberty, Ellis Island, the Verrazanno-Narrows Bridge, etc.

7. **What to do if a guest becomes emotional.**
   It is natural in the early weeks following a disaster to feel upset or even cry when one returns to a familiar place for the first time. If a guest

becomes tearful and is alone, you may want to approach him or her and ask, "Is there anything I can do?" If other people are with this person, allow them to support each other. You can also acknowledge that such emotional reactions are commonly experienced following the events of September 11th.

8. **What to say if guests ask what you saw or did on September 11, 2001.**
Simply state the truth. If you were on site that day, you may want to say something like this, "Yes, the staff was here that day." If they ask more questions or want details, simply state, "It was quite difficult to believe . . . but we are glad to be back and glad to have you back too!"

9. **What to do if someone becomes very upset.**
You may want to let your supervisor know. Sometimes people are overcome with emotions when they least expect it and just need some time to collect themselves.

© Donna A. Gaffney, 2001

Textbox 14.2.   Prior to the reopening of Liberty Science Center after the 9/11 attacks, staff and administrators prepared for visitor questions and concerns. This one-page guide provided suggested responses to children and families while visiting Liberty Science Center. *Source*: Donna A. Gaffney.

Science centers and interactive museums offer two critical elements necessary for healing: social support (peers, museum guides, teachers, and chaperones) and the ability to control outcomes (though experimentation and fine motor manipulation). In addition, these experiences are offered in a safe, structured setting. Experiential and interactive museums are bathed in colorful images that surprise and entertain, bringing a sense of joy to the entire learning environment. The trauma psychologists who worked with Liberty Science Center's staff following the terrorist attacks of 9/11 regarded its resources and stance as a sanctuary.[20] The setting of the Science Center not only provides opportunity for growth-promoting experiences, but also challenges its visitors to seek them out within the context of a vibrant, dynamic world. Bloom has said, "If we are to survive as a viable species on a viable earth, we must become grounded again in the values of the earth."[21]

After 9/11, museums and science centers recognized the contribution they could make to healing and recovery, and many opened their doors without charge. Tony Millica of the Children's Museum of Southeastern Connecticut stated, "This is a small thing, but if people put together a lot of small efforts maybe that can make a big impact."[22] Like others around the country, the Museum of Fine Arts in Boston was open free of charge to the public for two weeks in September 2001. Galleries and gardens offer visitors places of peaceful reflection during such difficult times. Anne d'Harnoncourt, the late director and CEO of the Philadelphia Museum of Art, stated, "Just as a museum can be a place for great excitement and discovery, it can also be a welcoming place for contemplation, solace, and inspiration during a troubled time."[23] Science centers and children's museums can provide similar experiences to those too young to understand how their world has changed. The Brooklyn Children's Museum offered children a safe place to play as well as the opportunity to share their thoughts and feelings on a Compassion mural.[24] This trend continues to the present day with the Boston Children's Museum offering free admission to the public the day after the Boston Marathon bombing.[25]

In 2001, Liberty Science Center's permanent exhibits offered children and adults countless opportunities to begin the healing process. The Health Floor housed the ever-popular *Touch Tunnel*, the educational point of which was to raise awareness of being blind. Children and adults entered the pitch-black, carpeted tunnel on hands and knees, while a smiling, helpful guide gave advice on navigating the tunnel: "Keep your hand on the left wall, we will watch you as you go through the tunnel. If you want to leave at any time, just let us know." As if by magic, the floating voice in the darkness asked at key twists and turns, "Are you okay? Do you want to come out now?" Young visitors discovered that even if something appears frightening, they could, with help, rely on their senses of touch, hearing, and even smell. Children learned to use their resources to meet the challenge of strange new environments.

Grounding is a crucial concept for those who have been exposed to traumatic experiences. Judith Herman, author of *Trauma and Recovery*, refers to the importance of reconnection.[26] Grounding is a way to reconnect. It is time for people to move beyond a trauma orientation and reconnect to life. Those who experience trauma often struggle with a number of responses: physical, psychological, and social. One of the most challenging is dissociation, the experience of splitting consciousness from the reality of the event. Simply put, trauma causes the person to feel numb and "go though the motions" without consciousness or emotional awareness. Grounding experiences help to bring a person back to the present tense, to reconnect with the world.

Nature and science museums provide a multitude of sensory experiences that serve to reconnect and reintroduce the visitor to nature. At Liberty Science Center, the top-floor *Estuary* exhibits were a particularly powerful place for reconnecting in 2001. Floor-to-ceiling windows showcased the panorama of the New York skyline. The Twin Towers of the World Trade Center were conspicuously absent, yet in the midst of such a painful reminder of loss the *Estuary* returned the visitor to the place where the river meets the sea. Black drum fish and American eels peacefully swam past each other in saltwater tanks, their fins moving with the grace of silken wings. They move in slow motion and mesmerize adults and children; one's breathing slows and it is impossible to turn away from them. Across the room, the stream table allowed the curious to determine the shape, direction, and structure of a stream. Make a dam, touch sediment, turn the faucet on full force, and watch what happens. It is a miracle and a mystery, all in one. The plants of the salt marsh and sandy beaches grow with resilience and vigor, all within the confines of a glass and steel environment. This multisensory experience allows people to see, smell, touch, and hear the surrounding environment.

Grounding experiences allow one to return to what is predictable and stable. When the world is not to be trusted, it feels safer to test out the laws of nature—and always come to the same conclusions. Experiments provide opportunities to validate. At the Center's energy exploration exhibits, visitors moved levers, pushed buttons, and pulled controls as they explore the Earth's energy. They waited for the consequences of their actions and learned that the creation of energy, although powerful and exciting, was predictable.

Grounding experiences and finding sanctuary assist in the healing process following traumatic events. But are these short-term solutions? Or is there a long-term benefit to such activities? Perhaps it is best to look to the concept of resilience to understand the complexities of recovery and growth after trauma.

Resilience has become a very popular concept in the educational and counseling fields. New programs integrate a resiliency focus as they plan for educational interventions that build growth-promoting behaviors in children. What is resilience and why focus on it, especially during times of community or crisis? Recovery from trauma requires strengths and strategies to stave off the long-term consequences of a catastrophic event. Rather than identify the risk factors or deficits that could result in future problems, a prevention paradigm is required, a shift to a resource-based resilience focus. Bonnie Benard's words succinctly state the obvious: "Solutions do not come from looking at what is missing; solutions will come by building on strengths."[27]

Resilience is apparent when one perseveres in the face of disaster. Resilient individuals thrive and succeed in spite of what appear to be insurmountable odds. Researchers find that resilience enables a person to bounce back or survive a disappointment, obstacle, or setback.[28] Yet it may be more than that; it may be one's capacity to *bounce forward* from adversity, strengthened and more resourceful.[29]

People are not born resilient; they build resilience over time. Experiences and the support of empathic people contribute to this dynamic building process. Anyone, no matter what age, can build resilience.

Resilience can protect people from the consequences of trauma, loss, stress, and crisis. The best way to build on one's strengths is within the safety of sanctuary. While family and school offer safety and comfort, other resources have been overlooked, and the science center and interactive museum are among them. The characteristics of resilience include resourcefulness and problem-solving ability, identification and mobilization of support systems, curiosity and intellectual mastery, empathy, compassion and caring for others, memories of helpful, sustaining people, awareness and a sharing of feelings, a desire and ability to help others, and, finally, a feeling of competence.[30] Resilient people do not manifest all these characteristics simultaneously. The characteristics are building blocks, each one providing support for the further development of the others. How can interactive museums and science centers strengthen and reinforce these qualities?

While the primary goal of science centers is to offer science education through interactive exploration, it is clear that its social value extends far beyond education. The exhibits, programs, and activities also promoted resilience in an environment that was supportive, comforting, and grounding. These are qualities of an empathetic museum. The interaction of strategy and empathetic environment not only promotes resilience in visitors and the surrounding communities, but was also instrumental in healing trauma after 9/11. People of all ages gravitate toward that which is safe and familiar. The Center offered a unique opportunity for families and children after the terrorist attacks of 2001; it provided a safe, familiar environment while promoting healing.

Phillip Auerswald emphasizes how "good works that go above and beyond what traditional entrepreneurs and businesses deliver—is a dearly held tenet of the social change movement."[31] Like many other institutions in 2001, the response of the Center after the 9/11 attacks was motivated and inspired by the empathetic concern of administration and staff. September 11, 2001, brought to light the importance and necessity of the social value of museums (figure 14.1). In fact, the Center embraced social value as a key goal of its mission statement. The lessons are many, particularly because the 9/11 terrorist attacks occurred at a time of increasing external consciousness on the part of museums.[32] By 2002, there was a profound sense of urgency to deliver good works at times of need.

Phills and colleagues define *social value* as "the creation of benefits or reductions of costs for society."[33] Organizations and institutions work to identify and address the needs and problems that face society in general and their communities in particular. The manner in which organizations address these needs is to "go beyond the private gains and general benefits of market activity."[34] These added and enhanced benefits surpass what is necessary or expected and can change the greater

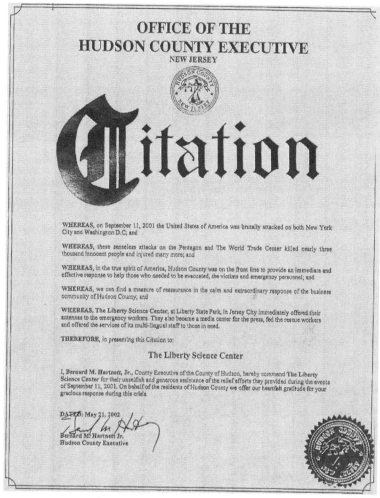

OFFICE OF THE
HUDSON COUNTY EXECUTIVE
NEW JERSEY

Citation

WHEREAS, on September 11, 2001 the United States of America was brutally attacked on both New York City and Washington D.C; and

WHEREAS, these senseless attacks on the Pentagon and The World Trade Center killed nearly three thousand innocent people and injured many more; and

WHEREAS, in the true spirit of America, Hudson County was on the front line to provide an immediate and effective response to help those who needed to be evacuated, the victims and emergency personnel; and

WHEREAS, we can find a measure of reassurance in the calm and extraordinary response of the business community of Hudson County; and

WHEREAS, The Liberty Science Center, at Liberty State Park, in Jersey City immediately offered their antennas to the emergency workers. They also became a media center for the press, fed the rescue workers and offered the services of its multi-lingual staff to those in need.

THEREFORE, in presenting this Citation to:

The Liberty Science Center

I, Bernard M. Hartnett, Jr., County Executive of the County of Hudson, hereby commend The Liberty Science Center for their unselfish and generous assistance of the relief efforts they provided during the events of September 11, 2001. On behalf of the residents of Hudson County we offer our heartfelt gratitude for your gracious response during this crisis.

DATED: May 21, 2002

Bernard M. Hartnett Jr.,
Hudson County Executive

Figure 14.1. In May of 2002, the Hudson County Office of the Executive awarded Liberty Science Center a citation expressing deep gratitude for the center's generous and unselfish relief efforts during the events of September 11, 2001, and in the weeks that followed. *Source:* Emlyn Koster.

society; however, they have the greatest impact for those who are disadvantaged, disenfranchised, or, as in the case of the 9/11 attacks, vulnerable in the aftermath of disaster.[35] Social value generates increased social justice, embedded social protection, and stronger community cohesiveness.[36] These are crucial elements as communities recover and heal after tragedy.

ONE YEAR LATER

At the one-year commemoration of 9/11, Liberty Science Center had forged new relationships. A great deal was learned in the early weeks and months after the terrorist attacks. Fear and confusion gave way to resolve and commitment (figure 14.2). There was an overwhelming need to do more, to be involved, and to reach out to each other and our communities. By early 2002, new nonprofit organizations were created to address the needs of those affected by the terrorist attacks. In October 2001, Families of September 11 (Families) was created by family members of those who died in the 9/11 terrorist attacks. The organization's goal was to support families and children by offering updated information on issues of interest, access to resources, relevant articles, and advocacy to raise awareness about the effects of terrorism and public trauma. In

Figure 14.2.   The "Tribute in Light" memorial was conceived in 2002 by artists and designers under the sponsorship of the Municipal Arts Society of New York City and Creative Time. Eighty-eight 7,000-watt xenon light bulbs are positioned into two forty-eight-foot squares in the shape and orientation of the World Trade Center Twin Towers. This memorial honors those who died, were injured, or profoundly affected by the terrorist attacks in New York City. In addition, the memorial pays homage to the thousands of first responders and volunteers who served on that day and in the months and years after. This photo was taken from Liberty State Park, New Jersey, on September 11, 2006, the five-year commemoration of 9/11. Annually, the twin beams continue to shine skyward from dusk on September 11 until dawn on September 12. *Source*: Department of Defense, US Air Force. Photograph by Denise Gould.

addition, they championed domestic and international policies that responded to the threat of terrorism, including support for the 9/11 Commission.

As a direct result of the authors' collaboration during the immediate response after 9/11, the Center and Families joined forces in early 2002: each was committed to making a difference in this new post-9/11 world. Families was particularly dedicated to educating teachers and children about 9/11. MaryEllen Salamone, cofounder of Families and a widow and mother of three small children, was the driving force behind the initiative. The groundwork began prior to the one-year commemoration of 9/11. The Center, Families, the New Jersey Department of Disaster Response, and the NJ Traumatic Loss Coalitions produced a thirty-minute video to prepare teachers for classroom discussions about 9/11. This guide was not a history lesson, but an empathy-based approach that recognized everyone's emotional struggles reliving 9/11. The Center once again met the public's needs by providing support, information, and education, as well as donated time, personnel, and space to film this important teacher guide. This video was mailed to over five hundred schools in New Jersey and provided the foundation for the Families of September 11 and Liberty Science Center curriculum project, the For Action Initiative (the Initiative).

OVER THE NEXT FIVE YEARS

Over the next five years, there were many education-focused conversations within the partnership. Increasingly joined by others, the coauthors of this chapter continued to meet regularly, offering support and commitment to Families for a new and innovative education project. Specifically, a 9/11-related curriculum had become a clear need. A number of groups were writing lessons that narrowly focused on "the day of" or a minute-by-minute timeline or political responses. Classroom discussions were limited and textbook entries were sparse or nonexistent. The question of how young people could understand this moment in history, in all of its complexity as well as its consequences, became our top priority.

There are events on the world stage that significantly change our lives. For most adults, and for children in particular, these events can be confusing or frightening. Fortunately, young people are not alone. Educators and families, in an effort to spare children the horrors of war, terrorism, or disaster, may edit out these life-altering moments of our collective history for fear of upsetting the younger generation or for fear that adults will not know how to present the material in age-appropriate ways.

Each year, the commemoration of the 9/11 terrorist attacks coincides with the start of the school year. Teachers as well as parents are faced with the difficult task of determining *how* to discuss and recognize those terrifying events. However, the lessons learned from that day extend *beyond* commemoration, an opportunity in fact for students to learn about the complexities of today's world: threats to the global community, causal factors and the consequences, and also how we can empathize, take action, and help others. September 11, 2001, became an especially poignant case study for students to explore these issues.

The first wave of social studies and history textbooks included brief discussions of the terrorist attacks. A number of authors, universities and educational groups had taken steps to identify relevant materials and lesson plans for students regarding 9/11. However, as David McCullough eloquently states, a historical event is about more than a date or statistic, it is about all facets of life.[37]

The Initiative curriculum project was founded on the belief that young people need to learn more than dates and facts about an important historical event. They must see the event in its social context and understand the perspectives and emotions of others. They need to know how to value, respect, and appreciate the views of other people, even when they don't agree with them. If ever there was a time for an empathy-based curriculum, it was in the aftermath of 9/11.

The Initiative placed the events of 9/11 in a larger and more meaningful educational context. In order for students to be able to think critically about the events of 9/11, they need to understand much more than the events of that day. Only after they understand violence, terrorism, and the human, political, and historical contributing factors will they fully understand 9/11 and other events like it. And only after they fully understand what happened on 9/11 can they become leaders who will make a difference in the world.

The goals of the Initiative are to provide educators and community representatives with the tools they need to help students understand these historic events and to inspire change by empowering students to contribute positive actions and live resiliently. Educators play a crucial role in helping children cope with the stresses and anxieties related to world events such as terrorism and disaster.

In 2007, the Initiative held an inaugural conference, *Learning from the Challenges of our Time: 9/11, Terrorism and the Classroom* on July 1, 2008, at the Jennifer A. Chalsty Center for Science Learning and Teaching at the recently expanded and renewed Liberty Science Center.[38] The purpose was to engage a panel of professionals and experts to determine the best way to create a guide on teaching the complexities of today's world, including but not limited to 9/11.

Former New Jersey governor Thomas Kean, the cochair of the National Commission on Terrorist Attacks on the United States and coauthor of its concluding report, gave the keynote presentation. He emphasized the importance of education and how teachers had the most difficult task when talking about 9/11 in the classroom. He also stressed that educators must look at the events of 9/11 from all perspectives and subject areas:

> September 11, 2001 was an event that changed our time and our world. We need to use care and sensitivity to teach our children so they will understand, now and in the future. . . . We must tell the story [of September 11, 2001], how people suffered loss—that was unimaginable—yet out of that tragedy came the most remarkable resilience.[39]

Conference panel presentations included national experts who addressed the value of curricular guidelines on terrorism and 9/11, the involvement of museums and science centers, the role of teaching and the teacher, and the impact of trauma and the importance of empathy. Author Joan Bauer urged students to learn about 9/11 through personal stories. The participants engaged in networking activities and toured the Center, specifically its *Skyscraper* exhibition and its latest traveling exhibition titled *Goose Bumps! The Science of Fear*. Educators were invited to join the initiative and participate in the process of curriculum development. Also central to this entire journey was the fact that the Center had, by then, become a benchmark in the museum field for its social responsibility. The Center had also chosen to reopen, following its 2005–2007 expansion and renewal, with the premiere of a new traveling exhibition about the Islamic world's contributions to scientific knowledge in premedieval times.[40]

A DECADE LATER

In the summer of 2011, after three years of development, the Initiative officially launched *Learning from the Challenges of Our Time: Global Security, Terrorism, and 9/11 in the Classroom* (figure 14.3). This age-appropriate, empathy-based K–12 curriculum is organized around seven themes and spans multiple subject areas: human behavior, violence, aggression and terrorism, historical context of terrorism, a contemporary case study in terrorism (9/11), challenges and consequences in a post-9/11 world, remembrance and the creation of memory, and building better futures: narrative, recovery, and responsibility. Each of its fifty-eight lessons includes opportunities for reflection and taking action. Educators are given tools to provide a safe space for classroom discussion as well as helping students understand the perspectives and emotional experiences of others in the classroom and

LEARNING FROM THE CHALLENGES OF OUR TIMES:

Global Security, Terrorism, and 9/11 in the Classroom

A New Curricular Initiative for Students in Grades K-12

Figure 14.3.   In preparation for the ten-year commemoration of 9/11, the For Action Initiative released *Learning from the Challenges of Our Times: Global Security, Terrorism, and 9/11 in the Classroom*. The curriculum guide included lessons for students from kindergarten to high school as well as teacher resources. *Source*: The For Action Initiative, Donna Gaffney, Chairperson.

the community. Storytelling, interviews, and personal narratives are essential teaching strategies for the curriculum. As a result, students foster their own sense of resilience *and* make the world a better place in which to live and coexist in a diverse global society.

A NEW PATH

After a decade of shared goals and successful accomplishments, person-nel and organizational structures at the Center and Families changed. The board members of Families believed that many of their goals had been achieved and considered sunsetting the organization. The Initia-tive planned to operate independently with volunteer support. How-ever, in 2012 an unexpected gift to Families prompted the board to reconsider their plans. The donation would make it possible to create a new website, further develop and refine the lesson plans, and actively promote the project among American educators (figure 14.4). With such ambitions in mind, the board of Families voted to transition the organization to a new identity with a continuity of mission, the previ-ously described Initiative. This reflected both the evolution of Families and the Initiative's goal to make the curriculum accessible across the nation. Meanwhile at the Center, leadership had changed and so had its mission. Formerly stated as, "We engage diverse audiences in rel-evant issues that connect nature, humanity and technology—Through innovative and meaningful experiences, we inspire action to strengthen communities and advance global stewardship," it had become, "to get learners of all ages excited about the power, promise, and pure fun of science and technology".[41]

Although the goals of the Initiative continued to be realized, its message had not reached the national community as envisioned. In

Figure 14.4.   In 2013, the For Action Initiative launched a new, easily navigable website Housing refined lessons and educator resources for teachers and students. *Source*: The For Action Initiative, Donna Gaffney, Chairperson.

A Lesson From Nature: Cold Penguins to the Middle

Helping children and families understand the importance of empathy and support in an unpredictable world is challenging. This illustration has proven to be a poignant reminder that allows us to reflect on the need for human connections following traumatic events and loss. We all have times of vulnerability and times of strength. Although this lesson from nature is primarily for children, its profound meaning is equally applicable to adults and it is just possible that these words will provide a self-care reminder for professionals and caregivers as well.

It is said that when the Antarctic weather becomes truly inclement, the Emperor penguins gather in densely packed huddles to keep each other warm and thriving. Not only do the huddles allow the birds to stay warm and conserve energy, they are in constant motion traveling across the frigid landscape. In fact, every minute or so, all penguins take very small steps creating a "wave" through the entire huddle. The tiny two to four inch steps keep the penguins packed together and allow new penguins to join the periphery, and the entire huddle moves forward. Their movements are coordinated so that no one gets stuck or jammed together like cars in rush hour traffic. The birds on the periphery of the huddle are buffeted by the frozen air and fierce winds. Those in the middle of the huddle stay warm. And when the Emperor chicks are old enough to stand on their own two feet, they join together in their own huddle. The Emperor penguins spend hours if not days in huddles depending on the length and severity of the storms they experience.

Like the penguins of Antarctica, human beings try desperately to keep safe and comforted in the midst of the "storms" of crisis or loss.

(continued)

At times we may feel very cold, needing to connect with those around us. However, at other times we are capable of offering warmth and protecting others. And lastly, if we all work together we can move forward for the good of everyone. The lesson of the Emperor penguins can serve us well.

Photo: J. Burnak, with permission by B. Wienecke
Zitterbart DP, Wienecke B., Butler JP, Fabry B. Coordinated movements prevent jamming in an Emperor penguin huddle. PLoS ONE 6(6)

Dr. Donna Gaffney, DNSC, FAAN and children's literature expert Mary Galbraith thank their colleagues at Liberty Science Center in New Jersey, in particular Dr. Emlyn Koster, for their research on the Emperor penguin's survival strategies. We are especially grateful to our penguin expert, Dr. Barbara Wienecke from the Australian Antarctic Division.

Textbox 14.3.   A Lesson From Nature: Cold Penguins to the Middle was written to provide an illustration to students and those needing support follolwing trauma and loss. Since 2002, the essay has been adapted and used in a wide range of settings. Source: Donna A. Gaffney and Mary Galbraith; photo by J. Burnack with permission by Barbara Wienecke.

order to grow and preserve the legacy of the Initiative and Families, the board considered donating the organization's assets to another nonprofit. Once again, the long-term collaboration of the authors served as a guide for the future. The Initiative had already distinguished itself from other 9/11 groups and educational programs at 9/11 museums. Continuing that trend, the board proposed that the resources and assets of the Initiative would be gifted to the Newseum in Washington, DC. This unique organization shares the mission, values, and goals of the Initiative and the dedicated work of the original collaboration. The Initiative's resources would become a part of the Newseum's innovative NewseumED website, which extends the reach of the Initiative's work into the national and international educational communities. It was only right that a curriculum that so valued the human narrative would continue on in an institution dedicated to telling the stories of our time:

The Newseum is dedicated to free expression and the five freedoms of the First Amendment: religion, speech, press, assembly and petition. Through exhibits, programs and education, the Newseum works to ensure that these fundamental freedoms remain strong and protected both today and for future generations.[42]

NOW IN THE NATION'S CAPITAL

The events of 9/11 provide a powerful educational opportunity for a deeper understanding of the First Amendment and the challenges posed to the five freedoms in a post-9/11 world. Many students today were born after the terrorist attacks, and their knowledge of that day comes from history books and television specials. A critical part of understanding the events of 9/11 involves examining how the attacks shaped today's society and the impact on government, the press, national security, and the public's views on the First Amendment.

The Newseum enthusiastically supports the mission of the Initiative. Educators and students will learn about 9/11 not as an isolated event covered in a single textbook chapter or class period, but as a frame through which connections can be made to other subjects and curriculum requirements. The content will be evaluated and tested to meet standards, including the Common Core and other state and district standards.

The new curriculum is offered at NewseumED.org free of charge in preparation for the fifteenth commemoration of 9/11. The work of the past fifteen years and the innovative future directions were celebrated at a symposium for policymakers, thought leaders, and educators at the Newseum in the spring of 2016. Many of those who committed to the ideals of the curriculum were present, including the authors of this chapter.

REFLECTIONS ON THE JOURNEY

We began as unlikely collaborators during one of the darkest days in American history. Our careers and backgrounds are so dissimilar that we could barely imagine how our professional lives could ever intersect: a mental health professional specializing in trauma and the president of a science center. We found sanctuary in words and spaces. We listened and learned from each other and those most directly impacted by the tragedy of 9/11. We committed to a vision for the future based on what we learned.

Long partnered with schools, we now know that museums can take their places as innovative contributing partners in their communities.[43] Mental health professionals, educators, and museum staff have unique opportunities for collaboration—to listen, to understand, and ultimately to respond to the needs of citizens as well as their own colleagues at times of crisis (textbox 14.3). Museums have the potential to not only open their doors as a sanctuary, but also to become vibrant and valued contributors for the betterment of their communities, as Daniel Goleman notes:

When we focus on ourselves, our world contracts as our problems and preoccupations loom large. But when we focus on others, our world expands. Our own problems drift to the periphery of the mind and so seem smaller, and we increase our capacity for connection—or compassionate action.[44]

NOTES

1. Felicia R. Lee, "Giving Voice, and Finding Her Own," *New York Times*, January 7, 2014, C1.

2. Jerry Blitefield, "WaterFire: Providence's Epideictic Sublime," *WaterFire. org*, http://waterfire.org/wp-content/uploads/2015/11/Jerry-Blitefield-Waterfires-Epideictic-Sublime.pdf (accessed January 8, 2016).

3. John Archer, "Behavioural Aspects of Fear," in *Fear in Animals and Man*, ed. Wladyslaw Sluckin (New York: Van Nostrand Reinhold, 1979), 56–85.

4. Donna Gaffney, "Psychobiology of Trauma: Impact on Memory and Response," in *Medical Response to Adult Sexual Assault*, ed. Linda Ledray, Ann Burgess, and Anthony Giardino (St. Louis: G. W. Medical Publishing, 2011).

5. Rachel K. Hellgren, "Designing for Museum Relevancy: Improving Innovation and Adaptability in Museum Management with Design Thinking" (PhD diss., Kent State University, 2015), https://etd.ohiolink.edu/!etd.send_file?accession=kent 1429521944&disposition=inline (accessed January 8, 2016).

6. Ibid., 50.

7. Edward Bradford Titchener, *Lectures on the Experimental Psychology of the Thought-Processes* (New York: Macmillan, 1909), 21.

8. Ibid., 89.

9. Nancy Eisenberg, "Empathy-Related Emotional Responses, Altruism, and Their Socialization," in *Visions of Compassion: Western Scientists and Tibetan Buddhists Examine Human Nature*, ed. Richard J. Davidson and Anne Harrington (New York: Oxford University Press, 2002), 131–64.

10. Nancy Eisenberg, Natalie D. Eggum, and Laura Di Giunta, "Empathy Related Responding: Associations with Prosocial Behavior, Aggression, and Intergroup Relations," *Social Issues and Policy Review* 4, no. 1 (2010): 143–80.

11. Arnaud Carré, Nicolas Stefaniak, Fanny D'Ambrosio, Leïla Bensalah, and Chrystel Besche-Richard, "The Basic Empathy Scale in Adults (BES-A): Factor Structure of a Revised Form," *Psychological Assessment* 25, no. 3 (2013): 679; Simone G. Shamay-Tsoory, "Empathic Processing: Its Cognitive and Affective Dimensions and Neuroanatomical Basis," in *The Social Neuroscience of Empathy*, ed. Jean Decety and William Ickes (Cambridge, MA: MIT Press, 2009), 215–32.

12. Jennifer Goetz, Dacher Keltner, and Emiliana Simon-Thomas, "Compassion: An Evolutionary Analysis and Empirical Review," *Psychological Bulletin* 136, no. 3 (2010): 351.

13. Carl R. Rogers, "Empathic: An Unappreciated Way of Being," *The Counseling Psychologist* 5, no. 2 (1975): 5.

14. Ibid., 9.

15. Donna A. Gaffney, "The Aftermath of Disaster: Children in Crisis," *Journal of Clinical Psychology* 62, no. 8 (2006): 1001–16.

16. Donna Gaffney, Karen Dunne-Maxim, and Mary Ann Cernak, "The Science Center as Sanctuary: A Place of Comfort During Traumatic Times," *The Journal of Museum Education* 27, no. 1 (2002): 22–27; Emlyn Koster, "A Tragedy Revisited," *Muse: Journal of the Canadian Museum Association* 20, no. 5 (2002): 26–27.

17. Sandra Bloom, *Creating Sanctuary* (New York: Routledge, 1997).

18. S. Bloom, "Creating Sanctuary in the School," *Journal for a Just and Caring Education* 1, no. 4 (1995): 403–33; Ervin Staub, "The Origins of Caring, Helping, and Nonaggression: Parental Socialization, the Family System, Schools and Cultural Influence," in *Embracing the Other: Philosophical, Psychological and Historical Perspectives on Altruism*, ed. P. M. Oliner, S. P. Oliner, Lawrence Baron, L. A. Blum, D. I. Krebs, and M. Z. Smolenska (New York: New York University Press, 1992), 390–412.

19. D. W. Johnson and R. T. Johnson, "Why Violence Prevention Programs Don't Work—and What Does?" *Educational Leadership* 52, no. 5 (1995): 63–69.

20. Gaffney, Dunne-Maxim, and Cernak, "The Science Center as Sanctuary," 23.

21. Bloom, *Creating Sanctuary*, 231.

22. Gaffney, Dunne-Maxim, and Cernak, "The Science Center as Sanctuary," 24.

23. Anne d'Harnoncourt, quoted in ibid.

24. Barbara Hoffman, "After Tragedy Families Come First: We Have Ideas on What You Can Do Together," *New York Post*, September 15, 2001, http://nypost.com/2001/09/15/after-tragedy-family-comes-first-we-have-ideas-on-things-you-can-do-together (accessed February 11, 2016).

25. Gretchen Jennings, "Museums and the Boston Marathon Bombings," *Museum Commons*, April 23, 2013, http://www.museumcommons.com/category/boston-childrens-museum (accessed January 10, 2016).

26. Judith Herman, *Trauma and Recovery* (New York: Basic Books, 1992).

27. Bonnie Benard, *Fostering Resiliency in Kids: Protective Factors in the Family, School, and Community* (Portland, OR: Far West Laboratory for Educational Research and Development and the Western Regional Center for Drug-Free Schools and Communities, 1991), 2, http://www.friendsofthechildrenboston.org/mentors/articles/Benard%20-%20%20Fostering%20Resiliency.pdf (accessed February 12, 2016).

28. Timothy Dugan and Robert Coles, ed., *The Child in Our Times: Studies in the Development of Resiliency* (New York: Brunner/Mazel, 1989).

29. Froma Walsh, "Bouncing Forward: Resilience in the Aftermath of September 11," *Family Process* 41, no. 1 (2002): 34.

30. David Fletcher and Mustafa Sarkar, "Psychological Resilience, A Review of Definitions, Concepts and Theory," *European Psychologist* 18, no. 1 (2013): 12–23, https://www.researchgate.net/publication/263651506_Psychological_Resilience_A_Review_and_Critique_of_Definitions_Concepts_and_Theory (accessed February 12, 2016).

31. Philip E. Auerswald, "Creating Social Value," *Stanford Social Innovation Review* (January 8, 2009), http://ssrn.com/abstract=1376425 (accessed February 11, 2016).

32. Emlyn Koster, "From Apollo to the Anthropocene, the Odyssey of Nature and Science Museums in Externally Responsible Contexts," in *Museums, Ethics and Cultural Heritage*, ed. Bernice Murphy (Paris: International Council of Museums, in press).

33. James A. Phills, Kriss Deiglmeier, and Dale T. Miller, "Rediscovering Social Innovation," *Stanford Social Innovation Review* 6, no. 4 (2008): 34–43, http://ssir.org/articles/entry/rediscovering_social_innovation#sthash.2w3g6DiK.dpuf (accessed January 9, 2016).

34. Ibid., 6.

35. Ibid.

36. Ibid.

37. David McCullough, "Historical Perspectives on Significant Past Presidencies," annual Thomas H. Kean Visiting Lectureship, Drew University, Madison, NJ, April 29, 2009.

38. Emlyn Koster, "The Reinvented Liberty Science Center," *LF Examiner—The Independent Journal of the Large Format Picture Industry* 10, no. 7 (2007): 1.

39. Thomas H. Kean, "Learning from the Challenges of Our Time" Keynote Address, For Action Initiative Inaugural Symposium, Liberty Science Center, Jersey City, NJ, July 7, 2008.

40. Edward Rothstein, "Touch Me, Feel Me Science," *New York Times*, July 20, 2007, E 27.

41. Mission Statement, Liberty Science Center, http://lsc.org/about-us/history-mission (accessed January 9, 2016).

42. Newseum.org, http://www.newseum.org/about (accessed January 9, 2016).

43. Koster, "From Apollo to the Anthropocene."

44. Daniel Goleman, *Social Intelligence: The New Science of Social Relationships* (New York: Bantam, 2006), 54.

empathy → emotion → understanding → vision → walking → emotion → understanding

15

Walk With Me

The Birmingham Civil Rights Institute

Laura Caldwell Anderson

In 1988, visionary leaders in Birmingham, Alabama, sought to design a place for experiencing the city's struggle for civil and human rights. Founding task force and board members focused on design of a living institution in which persons not engaged in events of the recent past would walk in the footsteps of persons who made sacrifices necessary to effect change. Today, the Birmingham Civil Rights Institute (BCRI) mission statement reflects founders' early interests: *To enlighten each generation about civil and human rights by exploring our common past and working together in the present to build a better future.* When this history-making place opened to the public in 1992, visitors found themselves slowly climbing, pounding pavement, and clapping their hands—in essence, invited to join a freedom movement that continues today.

Walk with me
Through tireless sacrifice
And terror-filled nights
Through segregated stations
and intolerant faces
the birth pains of a nation
Come and walk with me
Under the booming voice of the King
The endless courage of Shuttlesworth
The strength of Rosa Parks
And the days of dogs attacking children
As they danced in Kelley Ingram Park
This was Birmingham
And this was Birmingham

Talk to me about boycottin' buses and marching through Selma
About Bloody Sundays and sit-ins
Cold stares and painful tears
Talk to me about a movement for justice and a struggle for peace
A vision of human rights for every breathing life
A vision of human rights for every breathing life
Hold hands with me across oceans and seas
Through the wisdom of Ghandi's independence through peace
To the fight against apartheid and the will of Mandela
A world connected by the strength of its mothers
Hands bound together facing their oppressors
Defiantly free
Beautifully human
With bullet proof ideas
And mountains of bravery
Stand against racism, poverty, and human slavery
A song for human rights
A song for human rights
From the shanties of Soweto to the heartland of Mexico
From the deserts of Darfur to the projects of Detroit
From Sarajevo to Beijing
A melody rings like a song of endless hope
It is the blood in all our human veins
A truth that binds us all
A glory we must attain
Human rights
A vision of human rights for every breathing life
A vision of human rights for every breathing life
Come and walk with me
Come and walk with me

Lyrics to "Walk With Me" (2008) by Sharrif Simmons
for Birmingham Civil Rights Institute

"It is not always easy to be reminded about this part of our US History," wrote Cindy Ann, a visitor to the Birmingham Civil Rights Institute in a review of her experience there, "but it is very important to know. The visitor goes through stages and reads signs along the way."[1] We presume that this museum visitor and reviewer refers to literal locations within the BCRI galleries, but is it possible that she refers to stages of understanding or development of empathy toward those who brought about the changes that we now credit the Civil Rights Movement for having effected in the United States south and beyond? Founders of BCRI would like to believe it is possible. Development of empathy and understanding in visitors was a distinct goal of the group of community leaders, scholars, educators, and design professionals who led the effort to build an institute—not a museum of memories and established facts, but a living institution committed to social justice in the present through understanding of the past—in Birmingham, Alabama, in the 1980s (figure 15.1).

Documents prepared in 1987 for the Birmingham Civil Rights Institute Task Force of the City of Birmingham by the American History Workshop consulting firm reflect the founders' focus on creating a place—initially referred to as a Civil Rights Museum—that would encourage visitors to "walk through history."

Walking, purposeful walking, was a basic element of the activist strategy of the Civil Rights Movement. Simple walking, natural to people of all ages

Figure 15.1. The Birmingham Civil Rights Institute opened to the public in 1992. Founders laid the groundwork for a place that would afford visitors an opportunity to "walk through the history of our times and experience for themselves the drama" of the extraordinary and courageous story of the Birmingham Civil Rights Movement. *Source*: Copyright Birmingham Civil Rights Institute.

and levels of experience and knowledge, became a statement of the people's presence and their self-initiated progress toward freedom and equality. The markers of the movement did not proceed in lock-step. They did not mirror one another's outward movements but drew strength instead from their common nonviolent self-discipline in the face of antagonism and provocation. Walking left their minds and hearts free for the expression of community feeling and their voices free to join in song.

Moving through the Civil Rights Museum should afford visitors an opportunity to reenact such purposeful walking for themselves. They will walk through the history of our times and experience for themselves the drama of this extraordinary and courageous story.[2]

Other key recommendations made by the consulting firm expanded on the idea of capturing the "walking" theme. The firm underscored in its report to the task force that the success of the founders' vision would depend upon capturing the theme in the design of the building—in infusing every aspect of the visitor experience and making it a reenactment, to the extent possible, of the progress embodied in the Civil Rights Movement itself.

When BCRI's founding board members commissioned a capital campaign feasibility study in 1991, results included expression of several respondents' wishes to know "if the Board of Directors of the Birmingham Civil Rights Institute has considered the emotional impact of the museum's exhibits. Specifically, respondents ask how visitors to the museum will feel after viewing the exhibits." Without knowing it, members of the corporate community who served as respondents for the study alluded to that which BCRI board president emerita and founding board chair Odessa Woolfolk now refers to as the "DNA" of the institute:

> It was so important to [the founding task force and planning committee members] to have people understand what the Movement was all about. To accomplish understanding was the value of the entire project—to use history to make people respond emotionally to today's issues differently as a result of having visited the institute and heard first-hand accounts of what happened in Birmingham in the past. Fostering empathy is our DNA.[3]

Empathy, then, within the context of the Birmingham Civil Rights Institute would be defined as intentional and grounded in storytelling. It was the aim of Woolfolk and other creators of the BCRI permanent exhibition to craft an experience immersive enough in voices from Birmingham's recent past to provoke emotional responses in visitors. Founding task force members fully embraced the concept of using symbolic, physically expressed architecture designed to lead visitors in a literal climb—only gradually and not too steeply—through the unfolding story of the movement for civil and human rights in Birmingham, Alabama, in the twentieth century.

The story that was agreed upon for the permanent exhibition at BCRI begins around 1921, on the occasion of the fiftieth anniversary of the city's 1871, post–Civil War founding as an industrial center of the so-called New South. To help the people of Birmingham commemorate their founding, then president Warren Harding visited the city and gave a speech attended by both blacks and whites. At BCRI, an introductory film, "Going Up to Birmingham," sets the stage for visitors' gallery experience by explaining that migrants to the city's mines and mills from rural Alabama fields contributed the back-breaking labor that made a thriving economy possible. The film ends with an actor's voice reenacting Harding's Birmingham speech: "Let the black man vote when he is fit to vote; prohibit the white man voting when he is unfit to vote. Whether you like it or not, unless our democracy is a lie you must stand for that equality." At that, as the screen rises to reveal the permanent exhibition, a narrator's voice explains: "Blacks cheered. Whites were silent. They did not seem to hear."

No music follows. However, in the space that is slowly revealed, the Barriers Gallery, audio and video elements combine with fabricated recreations of public spaces associated with the early to mid-1900s—"white" and "colored" water fountains, a trolley car, a soda fountain, school classrooms—to put visitors in spaces of segregation. Posted nearby are segregation ordinances that spell out ways in which black and white persons were once forbidden from interacting. For example:

SECTION 597: NEGROES AND WHITE PERSONS NOT TO PLAY TOGETHER

It shall be unlawful for a Negro and a white person to play together or in company with each other in any game of cards, dice, dominoes, checkers, baseball, softball, football, basketball or similar games.[4]

Both the inequities and the joys of life in a state of separately developed cultures are depicted in the gallery. The strength of the African American church, the relative wealth of the historically, yet now struggling, black business district, the vibrance of jazz and blues music pouring out of theaters and dance halls; these sights and sounds are juxtaposed with images of lynched bodies, profiles of individuals martyred or challenged by the legal system to find equal justice, and a courthouse scene evocative of the struggles of an African American veteran who, after putting his life on the line for democracy in Europe or the Pacific, returned to postwar America to be spat upon during attempts to register to vote in Alabama or anywhere in the South.

Here wood flooring turns to concrete and pavement slants upward. Black images in the white mind are presented in a physically narrow space—corporate symbols like Aunt Jemima, as American as apple pie, plus images from the 1915 film *Birth of a Nation*, which was endorsed upon its release by then president Woodrow Wilson. The visitor's slight climb ends in a confrontation with ghostly images of children and adults, black and white, of varying ages, screen printed onto glass panels. Also exhibited is a Ku Klux Klan robe alongside an actual burned cross—evidence from a 1996 hate crime prosecuted by the federal government in Alabama.

Today in this space, one can read words projected onto a wall, a development that came along with BCRI's redesign to embrace the Americans with Disabilities Act. For its first sixteen years, however, and according to original design, visitors only heard disparate voices—opinions and ideas about African Americans in the South—delivered via a steady stream of audio commentary. The design of this Confrontations Gallery challenges visitors' perceptions and relationships with stereotypes while reflecting the reality of a society built on the perpetuation of dangerous stereotypes, particularly of African Americans in the US South. It is intended to be somewhat scary and children often express genuine fear in the space.

Determination of the effectiveness of the Confrontations Gallery at compelling emotion and empathy is gauged from visitor comments. Andrea B., upon visiting BCRI in 2014, posted on a travel website:

> I don't often think about the flow, layout, and staging of exhibits, but the Civil Rights Institute does such an outstanding job of using the space itself, the flow of visitors through the space and the design of the exhibits to really add to the story being told. This was less a museum than a full sensory experience. This layout was amazing as was the decision to let people of that time and place speak for themselves. As you move deeper into the museum, the exhibits start to give a sense of some of the prevailing attitudes in the south. It is one thing to read racially charged words; but it is quite a different thing to hear and see people saying these things.[5]

Use of audio tracks continues past this point, as does a gradual climb. Flooring takes the form of pavement, and the story of the civil rights movement develops from a struggle based primarily in the legal system to one incorporating nonviolent direct action protest. Barber shop and funeral parlor conversations are overheard. The path, though still narrow, widens a bit and a feeling of anticipation builds. The Montgomery Bus Boycott—not the first economic protest of its kind in the United States, but singular in its impact, duration, and incubation of future leaders, namely Rosa Parks and Martin Luther King Jr.—is about to leave its mark on the people of Alabama and the nation. The year the BCRI visitor is encouraged to experience is 1955.

From this point forward, events comprising the struggle for civil and human rights in the United States are presented in rapid-fire succession. Information about successful demonstrations and protests in the name of equal justice and access to economic, educational, and public accommodation opportunities is presented in a timeline style at this point. Stories of success are punctuated by accounts of terrorism and violence, tragic murders of engaged citizens by law enforcement and vigilantes. Evocative images and text about the period from 1955 through the present is provided—facts, figures, dates, and names. However, rich audio and video resources are also employed to convey the motivations of the thousands of persons who found the courage necessary to put their bodies on the line in order to bring about social change and more equitable conditions in the United States for African Americans (figure 15.2).

The final gallery of the permanent exhibition, the International Human Rights Gallery, was constructed and opened in 1994, two years after BCRI's initial opening. In early May 1993, BCRI staff and board members met with design consultants to craft a proposal and concept relative to the Human Rights Gallery. Weeks later, the BCRI board of directors received the following report on an agreed-upon concept for the "Beyond Birmingham: Human Rights Around the World" exhibit and its "cognitive and affective goals," among which were: "to encourage involvement with and responsibility for rights of people in all countries" and "to help visitors put themselves in the place of someone currently fighting for human rights."[6]

While developers of the galleries at BCRI intended for visitors to be moved emotionally by the exhibit's sights and sounds, they also took into account the crucial role to be played by human beings—volunteers, many of whom,

Figure 15.2. **A young visitor to BCRI uses a touchscreen monitor to select and view a videotaped interview with a foot soldier in the Birmingham movement.** *Source*: Copyright Birmingham Civil Rights Institute.

it was hoped, would be veterans of the movement for civil and human rights. Founding task force members foresaw a potential for fostering understanding and empathy in visitors by positioning these veteran volunteers, known locally as "foot soldiers" of the movement, throughout the galleries and particularly as greeters to welcome individuals, families, and groups to the institute. Over the years, some such veterans reached legendary popular status and became well known for their contributions to a unique visitor experience available only with, and through, them. The fact that the volunteers give of their time and personal experiences strengthens their impact.

Employees, too, affect the visitor experience. In today's BCRI, one might likely encounter Mrs. Yvonne Williams. Her technical title is resource gallery attendant. The way she describes her position, however, is as a living witness to what happened in Birmingham in the mid-1950s and 1960s and, therefore, a "visitor counselor and therapist." Many visitors to BCRI, according to Mrs. Williams, reach the end of the gallery experience displaying signs of physical and emotional exhaustion. "They express anger, frustration, and confusion. They cry," she says. "I'm not a statue, so they talk to me. One woman once tried to apologize to me for what white people did to African Americans. I said, 'Come on now, we've got to make this world a better place. You haven't done anything to me.' And she left feeling more hopeful. But I just have to listen to people." Ready with a box of tissues and a willingness to listen, she is also able to share her own stories—of growing up in Birmingham, hearing and feeling the bombing of the Sixteenth Street Baptist Church in September 1963, facing her own first real interaction with whites as a school teacher in an integrated classroom in 1971, and witnessing her husband's harassment at the hands of fellow firefighters who were not ready to welcome an African American to their unit in 1978. Reflecting on her vantage point as an employee of BCRI, she states:

> It's a place that impacts people. I love reading the comment cards, almost all of which are positive and indicate that people are moved and inspired by what they see and hear. I say to the younger visitors, "It's a blessing that you weren't here, but you've got to *try* to understand what happened here so that we do not repeat it."[7]

Building in opportunities for visitor interaction with movement veterans is one thing, but founders of BCRI could not have predicted the role that fellow visitors might play in one another's experiences. One instance of empathy-fostering value in a shared experience between strangers is reflected in an early review of BCRI written for the *Los Angeles Times* by poet and Birmingham native Anne Whitehouse:

> The steady stream of visitors in the museum included several families, black parents who had brought their children to learn about their past. Their remarks

deepened my experience of the museum. One woman pointed to a picture of Dr. Abraham Woods, the pastor of St. Joseph Baptist Church, at the time a local civil rights leader and now the second vice president of the Institute's Board of Directors. "He was my teacher," I heard her announce to her son in a tone of quiet pride. She smiled at me when she noticed I was listening, and I felt moved by her personal connection to the history here. "My grandparents marched with King," a thin little black girl with another family told me softly. She burst into tears before a picture of a beat-up white Freedom Rider, his teeth knocked out, the blood streaming down his face.[8]

Interaction with fellow visitors has both positive and negative potential in any museum, but in an institution like the Birmingham Civil Rights Institute, in a city like Birmingham, Alabama, and a mere thirty years—at the time of its opening—beyond the height of movement activity that resulted in change in laws and policies, the potential for meaningful personal encounters with the past was significant at its opening and remains considerable at the quarter-century mark (figure 15.3).

Development of empathy not only in visitors, but also in members of BCRI was another goal of the founders. A sustaining membership program

Figure 15.3. Plaster cast figures representing no particular individuals comprise a processional of figures leading humanity beyond events of the twentieth century in Birmingham and into the future. *Source*: Photo by Carol Highsmith for Library of Congress.

was designed to engage persons in the local community who wished to interact more deeply with the resources of the institute. For this audience, programming ideas were based on getting eyewitnesses to the historic Movement to express their thoughts and feelings to audiences in lectures, symposia, oral history interview recordings, and other program settings. Reaching programming audiences has long been considered a crucial means of moving them beyond the what-happened-here, informational format one might expect from a museum and into a frame of mind of questioning one's own courage and engagement with civil and human rights struggles in the present.

BCRI utilizes partnerships with a wide variety of organizations resulting in exhibits and programs that raise awareness of, and perhaps empathy with, a surprising number of human rights issues, causes and interest groups. And these organizational partnerships often work both ways, increasing others' understanding of the breadth and depth of BCRI's concerns—reflective of those who organized the Alabama Christian Movement for Human Rights, for example, in 1956 when the state of Alabama outlawed the NAACP from operating. Leaders of the local Movement elected to use the term "human rights" in their name purposefully, making the case for work that was aimed at improving life for all people, not only African Americans. High-profile partnerships of the last five years at BCRI include hosting the premiere and now the travelling version of *Living in Limbo*, a path-breaking exhibition of portraits of lesbian families in Alabama and Georgia; sponsorship of a travel and cultural exchange for youth from Birmingham and Soweto, South Africa to visit their respective communities and share with them public interpretations of the comparative similarities between the experiences of individuals and cultures engaged in the anti-Apartheid and US Civil Rights struggles; debut of *Family Matters*, a photography exhibition aimed at initiating a conversation about social change and the need for family acceptance for lesbian, gay, transgendered, and queer youth; and *Sickle Cell Disease on Canvas*, art created by individuals living with the often-misunderstood disease.

In principle and in fact, BCRI does very few programs or exhibitions in isolation. Partnerships are key to success, but particularly so when one outcome sought is increased understanding, awareness of, or action by visitors or participants in response to presentation of stories of struggle. BCRI often partners with organizations that assist persons belonging to groups that struggle for recognition, equitable access to resources, or redress of past wrongs. The institute itself, then, does not endorse particular paths to justice or equity. Rather, as a respected and neutral entity, BCRI "champions civil and human rights by facilitating an atmosphere of dialogue and understanding" as one of its core values.

Beyond exhibitions and programs, a third element of the BCRI project was renovation and redesign of historic Kelly Ingram Park, referred to by many as "sacred ground" for its place in history. The site, located across the street from BCRI, is well-known for its confrontations between young civil rights movement demonstrators and members of Birmingham's "public safety" officers who wielded attack dogs and fire hoses in 1963. Employing some of the same symbolic architecture used inside BCRI, landscape architects and urban planners designed a "sculpture garden and freedom walk" to serve as an extension of the BCRI experience. Following completion of its renovation, then-Mayor Richard Arrington dedicated the park formally as "A Place of Revolution and Reconciliation."[9] The park contains commissioned works of art depicting ordinary citizens' encounters with violent racism and oppression as well as their prayerful moments of inspiration and resolve. The sculptures are connected by a circular walkway. Named for Kelly Ingram, a white Alabamian and the first American serviceman killed in the First World War, the space is now dedicated to remembrance of the demonstrations that made headlines around the world in 1963. The park's older trees tower above the redesigned space bearing scars from the highly-pressurized water that tore at their bark.

As recently-appointed President and CEO of BCRI, Andrea Taylor lately finds herself looking upon those trees and the sacred ground—geography that holds meaning for persons near and far. Embarking on plans for commemorating BCRI's 25th anniversary, Taylor contributes a fresh perspective on the work of BCRI and what she believes sets the institute apart from other museums dedicated to interpreting movements for civil and human rights:

> The emotional experience for many a visitor to BCRI is comparatively raw. One is more likely here to bump into a person who lived through segregation and discrimination or lost a friend, acquaintance, or family member to hate-related violence. Many of those who were wounded by events in the past are still alive. Encountering the raw emotion associated with the recent past always fosters empathy in visitors. Our challenge during a visit is to help channel empathy and avoid frustration or despair. We aim to inspire hope in our members and visitors—as well as their mutual respect and understanding for others.[10]

BCRI's stated vision is to stand strong as the cornerstone of the civil rights story, a living memorial with an on-going mission. Whether or not the vision is met or shared is difficult to gauge. In a public post two years ago, Kamilah K. offered this reaction to BCRI:

> I had an awesome, emotional experience in this museum. . . . I will say I shed a tear or two as I walked through a time warp showing the struggles and achievements of the civil rights movement. I loved how in the end, the museum poses the question. "What are you fighting for?" Whether it's world peace, hunger,

death penalty, corrupt leaders, etc., I left with the message that we can all make a change no matter who we are and where we are from.[11]

As a case study, BCRI indicates that visitors are hungry for information about recent history, or answers about how and why injustice has occurred in the past and found redress over time. When presented with material designed to compel their feelings and an emotional reaction, however, they may go a step further—developing empathy that helps them discover their own paths forward in terms of how we might ultimately treat one another with equity and justice. Anecdotal, yet publically accessible, responses to experiences at BCRI suggests, above all, that many visitors are willing to explore their feelings and that they realize the potential that this exploration has for their consideration of persistent issues confronting human kind in the present.

NOTES

1. Cindy Ann, review of Birmingham Civil Rights Institute, December 2014, Trip Advisor, accessed November 25, 2014, http://www.tripadvisor.com/ShowUserReviews-g30375-d106398-r325995687-Birmingham_Civil_Rights_Institute-Birmingham_Alabama.html.

2. "Walking to Freedom: The Museum of America's Civil Rights Revolution," Program Statement prepared for the Birmingham Civil Rights Institute Task Force, City of Birmingham, Alabama by American History Workshop (June 1987). Robert C. Corley Papers, Birmingham Civil Rights Institute Archives, Box 4.

3. Interview by author with Odessa Woolfolk, November 27, 2015.

4. Posted in the galleries of the Birmingham Civil Rights Institute, a copy of the Birmingham Segregation Ordinances is also available in a digitized format through PBS Learning Media: http://d43fweuh3sg51.cloudfront.net/media/assets/wgbh/iml04_doc_bhamseg/iml04_doc_bhamseg.pdf.

5. Andrea B., review of Birmingham Civil Rights Institute, December 10, 2014, Yelp, accessed November 25, 2014, http://www.yelp.com/biz/birmingham-civil-rights-institute-birmingham.

6. "BCRI Board of Directors Meeting Agenda," May 20, 1993, document in possession of Odessa Woolfolk.

7. Author interview with Yvonne Williams, November 30, 2015.

8. Anne Whitehouse, "Memorial to an Uncivil Era: A Personal Journey to Alabama's new Birmingham Civil Rights Institute, dedicated to remembering what was once 'the most segregated city in America,'" *Los Angeles Times*, April 11, 1993.

9. Richard Arrington, Jr. *There's Hope for the World: The Memoir of Birmingham, Alabama's First African American Mayor* (Tuscaloosa: The University of Alabama Press, 2008), 177.

10. Author interview with Andrea Taylor, November 24, 2015.

11. Kamilah K., review of Birmingham Civil Rights Institute, November 8, 2013, Yelp, accessed November 25, 2014, http://www.yelp.com/biz/birmingham-civil-rights-institute-birmingham.

Index

277

About the Editor and Contributors

Laura Caldwell Anderson is archivist and director of special projects at the Birmingham Civil Rights Institute (BCRI) in Birmingham, Alabama. A native of Rome, Georgia, she has a BA from the University of Montevallo in intercultural studies, an MA from the University of Alabama in American studies, and an MA from the University of West Georgia in history. A graduate of the Seminar for Historical Administration, she is active in the American Association for State and Local History. She is a contributing author to *Museums in a Global Context: National Identity, International Understanding* (2013).

Mary Beth Ausman has served as a director of research and evaluation at Discovery Place, Inc., since 2013. A graduate of Davidson College and Harvard University Graduate School of Education, she holds a BA in art history and an EdM with a concentration in arts in education. With over twenty years' experience in the nonprofit education sector, she originally worked in museum education and subsequently spent ten years as an independent cultural education evaluation consultant. She joined the Discovery Place, Inc., team to provide institutional oversight of its evaluation program, as well as its longitudinally funded education projects.

Miriam Bader is education director at the Lower East Side Tenement Museum, where she oversees the administration of tours, school programs, and accessibility. She also serves as an educational consultant for the National Park Service, Singapore Tourism Board, and other organizations providing customized training on storytelling, staff recruitment and hiring, and teacher professional development. Her educational approach is based in constructivism and imaginative education, and includes inquiry, hands-on learning, and place-based experiences. She received her MA in museum education from Bank Street College.

Dina Bailey is former director of educational strategies for the National Center for Civil and Human Rights. Previously, Dina acted as the director of museum experiences for the National Underground Railroad Freedom Center. She began her career as a high school English teacher. Her degrees include a BA in middle/secondary education from Butler University, an MA in anthropology of development and social transformation from the University of Sussex, and a graduate certification in museum studies from the University of Cincinnati. She has been published in both the formal education and museum fields. She is currently on the board of the American Association for State and Local History and the board of the Association of African American Museums.

Kamille Bostick is vice president of education at the Levine Museum of the New South. She received a BA in print journalism from the University of South Carolina and an MA in English from the University of Georgia. A former reporter for the *Augusta (GA) Chronicle* covering youth, lifestyles, and race relations, she also taught American and British literature in Charlotte Mecklenburg Schools and English composition at area community colleges.

The Botín Foundation was created in 1964 by Marcelino Botín Sanz de Sautuola and his wife, Carmen Yllera, to promote social development in Cantabria, Spain. The foundation now operates across Spain and Latin America, contributing to the overall development of society by exploring new ways to uncover and support creative talent and create social wealth. The Botín Center, designed by architect Renzo Piano in the city of Santander, is the most important project in the foundation's history. The art center will contribute, through the arts, to the development of creativity as a way to stimulate cultural, economic, and social growth.

Janeen Bryant is former vice president of education at the Levine Museum of the New South. She now serves as southeastern regional director for leadership for educational equity. She holds a BA in anthropology from Davidson College, where she was Bonner Scholar for Community Service, Kemp Scholar for distinguished research, Lilly Theological Vocation Fellow, and founded the campus student group Alchemy. A former Teach for America teacher in Charlotte Mecklenburg Schools, she also received an MA in management and leadership from Montreat College.

Jon Carfagno is director of learning and audience engagement at the Grand Rapids Art Museum (GRAM). He joined the GRAM in June 2009. Since joining, Carfagno has led numerous initiatives that have brought local, statewide, and national recognition to the museum. For instance, his team's work in the area of school programs has been recognized by grants from the National Endowment of the Arts, as well as the Michigan Art Education Association's Distinguished Service Around. Jon currently serves as the vice president of the board for the Museum Education Roundtable, publishers of the *Journal of Museum Education*. A frequent speaker on the topics of human-centered design, methods of innovation, and organizational theory, he is most actively concerned about museum futures and sustainability. He holds an MA in art history with a distinction from the University of Massachusetts, a BA cum laude in art history and German from the College of the Holy Cross, and completed Kendall College of Art and Design's MBA certificate program in design and innovation management.

Orna Cohen is creator of many interactive exhibitions with international recognition. At Cité des Sciences, Paris, she created *La Cité des Enfants*, an interactive exhibition and workshop for children. In 2004, Orna was made Chevalier de l'Ordre des Arts et des Lettres by the French government to acknowledge her contribution to science and technology education. She cofounded Dialogue Social Enterprise to use exhibitions as catalysts for social change. Most recently, she has cocreated the exhibitions *Science of Sharing*, *Dialogue in Silence*, and *Dialogue with Time*.

Robert Corbin is a doctor of philosophy and National Board–certified science teacher serving as vice president of learning experiences at the Discovery Place Science Center in Charlotte, North Carolina. He is a North Carolina Science Leadership Fellow, associate professor at the University of North Carolina at Charlotte, and adjunct professor at Wingate University. He is an Arts and Science Council Lifetime Achievement Award recipient, Christa McAuliffe Fellow, North Carolina Science Leadership Fellow, Duke University Sawyer Fellow, Time Warner Cable All Star Teacher, Ben Craig Award recipient, Omnicron Psi Outstanding Science Teacher, Whitehead Educator of Distinction, and NAGT Outstanding Earth Science Teacher of the United States. He has written curriculum for Al Gore's film *An Inconvenient Truth*, Michael Pollan's *The Botany of Desire*, the Weather Channel, the Environmental Literacy Council, ASPCA, Duke TIP, and the North Carolina Department of Public Instruction. He serves on boards for the University of North Carolina at Charlotte, Appalachian State University, Wingate University, Mccoll Center for the Visual Arts, and Johnson C. Smith University.

Elizabeth Fleming has worked at the Museum of Life and Science in Durham, North Carolina, since 2007. With a BA in biology and an MA in teaching from the University of North Carolina at Chapel Hill, she worked in multiple formal and informal education settings before joining the exhibits team at the museum. In her current role as director for learning environments, she plays a key role in the research, design, installation, and evaluation of the museum's learning environments, in addition to collaborating on a variety of innovative projects with partnering institutions, such as *Science of Sharing*.

Seth Frankel is principal of Studio Tectonic in Boulder, Colorado. He brings more than twenty years of planning and design to museums, historical sites, zoos, arboreta, and parks. He provides master planning through full implementation for wide-ranging institutions. He is particularly focused on sites of conscience and peace museum, developing exhibitions around complex social history aimed at engaging the public toward social change. His work is found throughout the United States, as well as in Africa and Asia. Before establishing Studio Tectonic, Seth was an in-house designer at the Smithsonian Institution, as well as designer and managing director of other design firms. Seth holds a BA in design and humanities from the Evergreen State College.

Donna Gaffney, DNSc, FAAN, is chairperson of the For Action Initiative and advisory board member (2002–2012) for Families of September 11. She has long addressed trauma, loss, and violence in the lives of children and families. As a psychotherapist, she has counseled young people, schools, and communities in the aftermath of individual tragedies and national disasters such as Hurricane Katrina and the terrorist attacks of September 11, 2001. She is cofounder and chair of the For Action Initiative, an empathy-informed K–12 curriculum and website offering educational tools to help students understand the complexities of today's world. In addition to academic papers, she is author of *The Seasons of Grief: Helping Children Grow Through Loss* and has written teaching guides for the young adult books *911: The Book of Help* and *Breath to Breath*. She also coproduced the award-winning *Remembering September 11, A Guide for Schools*. She is advisor for research and content development at the National Alliance for Grieving Children.

Elif M. Gokcigdem, PhD, is a historian of Islamic art, a museums scholar, and the founder of *Empathy-building through Museums* initiative. She received her PhD in history of art from Istanbul Technical University and a graduate certification in museum studies from The George Washington University. Her academic studies focused on the symbolism of geometric patterns and figural imagery in medieval Islamic art. A native of Istanbul, she received the Turkish Education Foundation (TEV) scholarship in 1992 to conduct her graduate museum studies at GWU. Later she conducted her internship at the World Bank's Culture in

Sustainability Department and worked as a curatorial research assistant at the Islamic Arts Department of the Smithsonian Institution's Freer and Sackler Galleries. Gokcigdem held advisory roles as a member of the American Alliance of Museums (AAM) National Program Advisory Committee and The George Washington University Museum and the Textile Museum's Advisory Council. She is a contributor to the AAM's *Museums in a Global Context: National Identity, International Understanding.* For the past two decades, she has been working as a public affairs advisor at an international corporation. During the last decade, she was a member of the founding team and a senior advisor to the King Abdulaziz Center for World Culture, a major cultural institution with the goal of social transformation. She is a strong advocate for cross-disciplinary partnerships and dialogue toward designing and building sustainable cultural institutions, exhibitions, and experiences that empower their visitors with new knowledge, as well as tools to foster their innate knowledge and skills such as empathy, perspective taking, and contemplation. She can be reached through her blog at https://greatolivetree.wordpress.com.

Josh Gutwill, PhD, is director of visitor research and evaluation at the Exploratorium. His work includes research on learning in informal environments as well as evaluation of exhibits and programs to improve visitors' experiences. He is interested in fostering and studying learners' self-directed inquiry in science museum settings. His recent projects include investigating exhibit designs that promote metacognition about social interactions, studying STEM learning during making activities, and assessing the impact of science museum visitation on young adults' self-efficacy. He was a Co-PI on *Science of Sharing.*

Tom Hanchett served as staff historian at the Levine Museum of the New South from 1999 to 2015. He holds a BA from Cornell University, an MA from the University of Chicago, and a PhD from the University of North Carolina at Chapel Hill. He came to Charlotte in 1981 as historian for the Charlotte Historic Landmarks Commission, conducting studies of neighborhood architecture, 1930s music recording, and rural African American schools. His neighborhood research became the basis for his dissertation and subsequent book, *Sorting Out the New South City: Race, Class and Urban Development in Charlotte, 1875–1975.*

Susan Harris Mackay is director of the Department of Teaching and Learning at Portland Children's Museum, which includes Opal School and the Museum Center for Learning. She is a practicing teacher researcher who speaks to audiences at home and abroad on the rights of children within contexts for learning. She is a contributing author to *In the Spirit of the Studio: Learning from* *the Atelier in Reggio Emilia*, and *Language Development: A Reader for Teachers*, a member of the National Working Group for Make Education's *Makerspace Playbook*, and a 2015 TEDx West Vancouver speaker.

Andreas Heinecke, PhD, is best known as the creator of *Dialogue in the Dark* and founder of various social enterprises. He was the first Ashoka Fellow in Western Europe (2005) and became a Global Schwab Fellow of the World Economic Forum (2007). Andreas has received several awards, serves on multiple boards, publishes frequent articles, and teaches as professor of social business at universities in Germany and Hong Kong.

Zorana Ivcevic is associate research scientist at the Yale Center for Emotional Intelligence. She received her PhD from the University of New Hampshire and did postdoctoral work at Tufts University. Her research on emotions and creativity has been published in journals such as *Personality and Social Psychology Bulletin*, *Journal of Personality*, *Applied Cognitive Psychology*, and *Creativity Research Journal*, among others. She received the Award for Excellence in Research from the Mensa Education and Research Foundation and the early career award from the Society for the Psychology of Aesthetics, Creativity, and the Arts of the American Psychological Association.

Emlyn Koster, PhD, is director of the North Carolina Museum of Natural Sciences and was president and CEO of Liberty Science Center from 1996 to 2011. He was a field geologist, university professor, and research manager before being at the helm of the Royal Tyrrell Museum of Paleontology, Ontario Science Centre, Liberty Science Center, and at the North Carolina Museum of Natural Sciences since 2013. He is a member of the 2015–2016 global working group of the International Council of Museums to update the museum definition. Past president of the Geological Association of Canada, past chair of the Global Committee for the Association of Science-Technology Centers, he is currently also an adjunct professor of marine, earth, and atmospheric sciences at North Carolina State University. A long-time proponent for the external meaningfulness of museums, he advocates that the Anthropocene be embraced by nature and science museums as their holistic framework for content priorities. His educational, scientific, and humanitarian contributions have been recognized by awards and honors in Canada, France, and the United States.

Amy S. Landau is associate curator of Islamic and South Asian art at the Walters Art Museum. After receiving her PhD from the University of Oxford in 2007, she completed the exhibition *Pearls on a String: Artists, Patrons, and Poets at the Great Islamic Courts*, dedicated to stories about people and award grants by the NEH, NEA, and IMLS. Landau's research explores cultural exchange in the early modern period, with a special emphasis on Iran and the role of the twenty-first-century museum in presenting Islamic societies, past and present.

Troy Livingston is CEO of the Thinkery at Meredith Learning Lab in Austin, Texas. For ten years prior, he served as vice president for innovation and learning at the Museum of Life and Science in Durham, North Carolina, which afforded him the opportunity to work as a Co-PI on *Science of Sharing*. Troy is a passionate anti-racist and social justice advocate who looks forward to a day when museums are welcoming, inclusive, and essential in and to all communities—in short, museums that are empathetic to everyone. Troy is married to Kate Livingston of *ExposeYourMuseum* and has three teenage children.

Nadine Maliakkal is research assistant at the Yale Center for Emotional Intelligence. She received her BA in psychology at the University of New Hampshire and is currently working on training and supporting facilitators for the adolescent and family workshops teaching emotion and creativity skills at the Botín Center in Santander, Spain.

Hugh McDonald, PhD, is project director, researcher, and senior science writer at the Exploratorium in San Francisco. He was the principal investigator of the NSF-funded *Science of Sharing* project. Hugh has also served as content developer and writer/editor on numerous Exploratorium initiatives, including the *Mind and Seeing* exhibitions and the *Global Climate Change: Research Explorer* website. He was cocurator for the museum's Osher West Gallery, a large public space dedicated to exhibits and activities exploring cognition, social behavior, and the interplay between science, society, and culture. He obtained his PhD in social psychology from Indiana University.

Michele Miller Houck is associate executive director at Carolina Raptor Center, responsible for earned income programming. A graduate of Davidson College, she has a BA in history and a Non-Profit Management certificate from Wake Forest University. With over twenty years' experience in brand advertising and marketing with firms throughout the Southeast, she is a keen observer of the customer experience. She joined Carolina Raptor Center in 2010 as vice president of external relations and is currently responsible for public relations and marketing, the visitor experience, programs, volunteers, property management, and the retail operation.

Adam P. Nilsen is head of education and interpretation at the Phoebe A. Hearst Museum of Anthropology at the University of California, Berkeley.

He completed his PhD at Stanford University's Graduate School of Education with a concentration in learning sciences and technology design. His research focuses on the psychology of teaching and learning about people from other times and places. Previously, he was researcher at the Oakland Museum of California, where he curated exhibits on California history. He holds a BA from Stanford University and an MA from New York University, both in cultural anthropology.

Jordan S. Potash, PhD, ATR-BC, REAT, LPCAT (MD), LCAT (NY), is a registered, board-certified, and licensed art therapist and registered expressive arts therapist. As an art therapist for over fifteen years, he has worked with clients of all ages in many settings, including schools, clinics, and community studios. He is primarily interested in the applications of art and art therapy in the service of community development, social change, and cross-cultural understanding. He serves as assistant professor in the art therapy program at George Washington University in Washington, DC. More information is available at www.jordanpotash.com.

Adam Reed Rozan is director of audience engagement at the Worcester Art Museum in Massachusetts, helping lead this century-old institution into the future through innovative programming. An indefatigable advocate for visitors, he is part of a movement to revolutionize the museum visit. In his role at the Worcester Art Museum, he manages education, studio classes, marketing, design, and visitor services. He holds an MA in museum studies from Harvard University Extension School, where he is now an adjunct faculty member.

Thomas Wide is lead curator of *Turquoise Mountain: Artists Transforming Afghanistan*, an exhibition at the Smithsonian's Freer and Sackler Galleries. He received his DPhil in Oriental studies from Balliol College, Oxford. He lived and worked for several years in Afghanistan, most recently as the managing director of Turquoise Mountain, a cultural heritage organization based in Kabul.

Emily Zimmern served as executive director/president of the Levine Museum of the New South in Charlotte, North Carolina, from 1995 to 2015. Under her leadership, the museum received numerous honors, including the IMLS' National Award for Museum Service. She holds a BA and an MA in American history from Vanderbilt University and an MBA from Queens College. Active in civic affairs, she has held numerous leadership positions in local, state, and national nonprofit organizations. Most recently, she served as vice chair of the city of Charlotte's Immigrant Integration Task Force and board chair of the North Carolina Center for Nonprofits.